EMPLOYMENT, GROWTH AND DEVELOPMENT

This book examines the critical themes of employment, growth and development to focus on challenges and opportunities, both old and new, in the contemporary world economy. The essential theme that runs through the book is that there is a strong relationship not only between employment and growth, but also between employment and development, where the causation runs in both directions. The author shows how employment transforms economic growth into meaningful development by providing livelihoods and incomes to people. While the book is primarily concerned with developing countries, it considers industrialized countries as points of reference or comparison, since the latter are a large part of an interdependent world, in which problems faced by the two sets of countries are frequently connected and sometimes common. The ten essays in this volume also provide a macroeconomic analysis of development problems situated in the wider context of a changing world economy, exploring possible solutions, to understand the implications for countries and for people.

A timely collection by an eminent economist, this book will be useful to teachers, students and researchers in economics, especially those interested in macroeconomics, political economy and development studies.

Deepak Nayyar is Professor Emeritus at Jawaharlal Nehru University, New Delhi, where he taught Economics for 25 years, and was until recently Distinguished University Professor of Economics at the New School for Social Research, New York. Earlier, he taught at the University of Oxford, the University of Sussex and the Indian Institute of Management, Calcutta. He was Vice Chancellor of the University of Delhi (2000–2005). He also served as Chief Economic Adviser to the Government of India and Secretary in the Ministry of Finance (1989–1991). He was a Rhodes Scholar at Oxford, from where he has a D.Phil. in Economics, and is an Honorary Fellow of Balliol College, Oxford. He has published widely in academic journals. His books include *Catch Up: Developing Countries in the World Economy* (2013).

EMPLOYMENT, GROWTH AND DEVELOPMENT

Essays on a Changing World Economy

Deepak Nayyar

Routledge
Taylor & Francis Group
LONDON AND NEW YORK

First published 2017 by Routledge

2 Park Square, Milton Park, Abingdon, Oxfordshire OX14 4RN
52 Vanderbilt Avenue, New York, NY 10017

Routledge is an imprint of the Taylor & Francis Group, an informa business

First issued in paperback 2019

British Library Cataloguing in Publication Data
A catalogue record for this book is available from the British Library

Library of Congress Cataloging in Publication Data
A catalog record for this book has been requested

ISBN: 978-1-138-23134-4 (hbk)
ISBN: 978-0-367-27969-1 (pbk)

Typeset in Sabon
by Apex CoVantage, LLC

For
Dhiraj and Divya
Gaurav and Naira

CONTENTS

List of figures ix
List of tables x
Preface xii
Acknowledgements xv

Introduction 1

PART I
Employment and development **9**

1 The financial crisis, the Great Recession and the developing world 11

2 Why employment matters: reviving growth and reducing inequality 37

3 Macroeconomics and human development 53

4 The Millennium Development Goals beyond 2015: old frameworks and new constructs 81

PART II
Growth and development **107**

5 The West and the Rest in the world economy: the next transformation? 109

6 China, India, Brazil and South Africa in the world economy: engines of growth? 122

7 The emerging Asian giants and economic development in Africa 159

8 BRICS, developing countries and global governance 191

PART III
Development, polity and society **213**

9 Globalization and democracy 215

10 Discrimination and justice: beyond affirmative action 233

Index 253

FIGURES

6.1 GDP growth trajectories in China, India, Brazil and South Africa compared with Japan and Korea 129
6.2 Export growth in China, India, Brazil and South Africa compared with Japan and Korea 130
6.3 Current account balance in China, India, Brazil and South Africa, 1996–2006 146
6.4 Gross domestic savings (GDS) and gross capital formation (GCF) in China, India, Brazil and South Africa, 1996–2005 147

TABLES

6.1 China, India, Brazil and South Africa in the world economy: share in world population and world GDP, 1820–2001 123
6.2 GDP, population and GDP per capita: China, India, Brazil and South Africa, 2000 and 2005 125
6.3 Growth performance of China, India, Brazil and South Africa, 1951–1980 and 1981–2005 comparison with regions and country-groups (percentage per annum) 127
6.4 Trade flows: China, India, Brazil and South Africa, 2000 and 2005 (US$ billion) 143
6.5 Foreign direct investment: stocks and flows (US$ billion), 2000 and 2005 144
6.6 Foreign exchange reserves: China, India, Brazil and South Africa 1996–2005 (Special Drawing Rights [SDRs] billion) 148
7.1 China, India and Africa in the world economy (percentage share in population and income) 160
7.2 GDP, population and GDP per capita in China, India and Africa, 2000 and 2005 162
7.3 Growth performance of China, India and Africa, 1951–1980 and 1981–2005, comparison with country-groups (percentage per annum) 164
7.4 China and India: trade with Africa 168
7.5 Africa's trade with China and India 169
7.6 Composition of China's trade with Africa and the world (in percentage) 171
7.7 Composition of India's trade with Africa and the world (in percentage) 172
7.8 Composition of Africa's exports to China, India and the world (in percentage) 173

7.9 Composition of Africa's imports from China, India and the world (in percentage) 174
7.10 Foreign direct investment: China, India and Africa: stocks and flows, 2000–2005 176
8.1 BRICS and developing countries in the world economy, shares in world GDP and world population, 1820–1950 194
8.2 Shares of BRICS in PPP-GDP of developing countries and the world, 1980–2008 195
8.3 The shares of BRICS, the Next-14, developing countries and industrialized countries in world GDP and world population, 1980–2013 198
8.4 The shares of BRICS and the Next-14 in developing world GDP and developing world population, 1980–2013 199

PREFACE

This book brings together ten of my selected papers published earlier. The collection of essays analyses three critical themes that are closely related to one another, even if their interconnections do not receive sufficient recognition or adequate attention in the existing literature. The themes are employment, growth and development. The essays explore the nature of the relationships, to examine what this means for countries and for people, situated in the wider context of the world economy. The focus is mostly on developing countries. Yet, for the purpose of analysis, the discussion also considers industrialized countries, which constitute a large part of an interdependent world.

The essays in this volume have been published since 2010. This period has witnessed changes in the world economy that would have been difficult to imagine, let alone anticipate, at the turn of the century. For one, the financial crisis in the United States that surfaced in late 2008 spread through contagion across the world. Its transmission to the real sectors of economies was also rapid, as it led to a sharp contraction in output and employment. The Great Recession that followed in its aftermath persists even now. Recovery is slow, uneven and fragile. This is clearly the deepest crisis in capitalism since the Great Depression more than 80 years ago. For another, there has been a dramatic increase in the global economic significance of developing countries, which is reflected in their rising share of income, industrial production and trade in the world economy. This process began around 1980 and gathered momentum after 2000. It was reinforced by the resilience of many developing countries in the aftermath of the financial crisis, which have also experienced a slowdown in growth with a time lag, and by the more pronounced economic slowdown in industrialized countries that has persisted through the Great Recession.

It is worth highlighting three attributes of employment, growth and development in the world economy over the past three decades. Hence, these are not outcomes of the global financial crisis. But the persistent economic recession, as also the attempted solutions, have accentuated the consequential problems. First, employment creation has been too little and too slow. Output growth has been sustained by increases in labour productivity, rather increases in employment. Such jobless growth is the reality not only in industrialized countries, but also in developing countries. Second, economic growth has been more uneven across space and more volatile over time than it was 30 years earlier. And, since 2009, there has been a distinct slowdown in growth almost everywhere in the world. The slowdown is much greater in industrialized countries. But after an initial resilience and quick recovery, the slowdown has also spread to developing countries. Third, economic development has been uneven between countries in the world and unequal between people within countries. This is attributable in part to disparities in growth performance among countries and in part to rising economic inequality among people. Income distribution within countries has worsened almost everywhere in the world.

The book addresses these three issues, to focus on the challenges and opportunities, some old and some new, in a changing world economy. Employment is the connecting thread and the unifying theme. The discussion is, of course, related to the developments within countries, where the interaction of polity and society with the economy shapes outcomes.

In selecting and editing the essays, I have sought to drop those with a focus on the conjuncture or remove portions that are time specific. I have also tried to minimize overlap. Some overlap is inevitable and may even be necessary to develop nuances and build arguments from similar ideas in different contexts. The essays are presented here in three clusters rather than in chronological order of publication, which is conducive to thematic cohesion.

There were young scholars who helped me in the research process during the period in which these essays were written. I would like to thank Jonas Shaende in New York, as well as Ananya Ghosh-Dastidar and Atul Sanganeria in New Delhi, for valuable research assistance.

Some of these essays were the basis of public lectures or conference presentations at the New School for Social Research, New York; the World Institute for Development Economics Research, UNU-WIDER, Helsinki; Columbia University, New York; University of Witwatersrand, Johannesburg; University of Sao Paulo, Brazil; and the International Labour Organization, Geneva, where listeners came up with stimulating questions. Some of these essays, while work in progress, were presented at seminars in universities in many countries. In discussions that followed, I recall valuable comments from colleagues, researchers and students.

For critical comments and helpful suggestions on preliminary drafts of the papers, I would like to thank Yilmaz Akyuz, Andre Beteille, Duncan Foley, Sakiko Fukuda-Parr, Kevin Gray, Rolph van der Hoeven, Martin Khor, Jeff Madrick, William Milberg, Akbar Noman, Seeta Prabhu, Gustav Ranis, Sanjay Reddy, Willi Semmler, A.K. Shivakumar, Howard Stein, Frances Stewart, Jan Vandemoortele, Rob Vos, Guanghua Wan and Martin Wolf. For engaging conversations, incisive comments and constructive suggestions on my research during this period, including these essays, I am indebted to Amit Bhaduri, Ha-Joon Chang, Ron Findlay, Jose Antonio Ocampo, Joseph Stiglitz, Lance Taylor and Romila Thapar.

The enormous support from my family throughout has been invaluable. My wife, Rohini, provided the emotional and intellectual support. She has been a patient listener as a sounding board for ideas. She has been a perceptive reader of preliminary drafts. Her comments or questions often shaped rather than just improved my arguments. And she has been an incredible source of strength in my hours of frustration that are an integral part of the life of anyone who attempts to write. Above all, she has been wonderful in putting up with my obsessive preoccupations. My sons, Dhiraj and Gaurav, both economists, have contributed to my thinking in ways they might not even be conscious of. There have been questions that have persuaded me to think further about a subject. There have been conversations that have induced me to follow new leads. There have been discussions that have led me to clearer expositions or nuanced arguments. This book is dedicated to both of them and their spouses.

New Delhi
June 2016

ACKNOWLEDGEMENTS

The author would like to acknowledge the following academic journals and books where these essays were first published.

1 'The Financial Crisis, the Great Recession and the Developing World', *Global Policy*, Vol. 2, Issue 1, January 2011, pp. 20–32.
2 'Why Employment Matters: Reviving Growth and Reducing Inequality', *International Labour Review*, Vol. 153, Issue 3, September 2014, pp. 351–364.
3 'Macroeconomics and Human Development', *Journal of Human Development and Capabilities*, Vol. 12, Issue 1, February 2012, pp. 7–30. Copyright © United Nations Development Programme, reprinted by permission of Taylor & Francis Ltd, www.tandfonline.com on behalf of United Nations Development Programme.
4 'The Millennium Development Goals Beyond 2015: Old Frameworks and New Constructs', *Journal of Human Development and Capabilities*, Vol. 13, Issue 3, August 2013, pp. 371–392. © United Nations Development Programme, reprinted by permission of Taylor & Francis Ltd, www.tandfonline.com on behalf of United Nations Development Programme.
5 'The West and the Rest in the World Economy: The Next Transformation?' *Challenge*, Vol. 5, Issue 2, March–April 2014, pp. 26–41.
6 'China, India, Brazil and South Africa in the World Economy: Engines of Growth?' in Amelia Santos-Paulino and Guanghua Wan eds. *Southern Engines of Global Growth*, Oxford University Press, Oxford, 2010, pp. 9–43. Reproduced by permission of Oxford University Press.
7 'The Emerging Asian Giants and Economic Development in Africa', in Akbar Noman, Kwesi Botchwey, Howard Stein and Joseph Stiglitz eds. *Good Growth and Governance in Africa*, Oxford University Press, Oxford, 2011, pp. 536–564. Reproduced by permission of Oxford University Press.
8 'BRICS, Developing Countries and Global Governance', *Third World Quarterly*, Vol. 37, Issue 4, 2016, pp. 575–591.

9 'Globalization and Democracy', *Economic and Political Weekly*, Vol. L, Issue 19, 9 May 2015, pp. 47–54, and *Brazilian Journal of Political Economy*, Vol. 35, Issue 3, July–September 2015, pp. 388–402.

10 'Discrimination and Justice: Beyond Affirmative Action', *Economic and Political Weekly*, Vol. XLVI, Issue 42, 15 October 2011, pp. 52–59.

INTRODUCTION

This book brings together selected essays on employment, growth and development to focus on challenges and opportunities – old and new – in the contemporary world economy. The themes explored in this selection span a wide range of issues. Even so, there is an apparent unity in their diversity. The essays provide a macroeconomic analysis of development problems situated in the wider context of the world economy. The approach is in conformity with my instinctive preference to sketch the big picture with bold strokes on a wide canvas instead of attempting to join the little dots.

There are three other dimensions of coherence, which run through the essays that deserve emphasis. First, employment is the unifying theme. Indeed, the underlying argument is that there is a strong relationship not only between employment and growth, but also between employment and development, where the causation runs in both directions. And it is employment that transforms economic growth into meaningful development by providing livelihoods and incomes to people. Second, while the focus is often on developing countries, the discussion almost always considers industrialized countries as points of reference, comparison or analysis, since the latter are a large part of an interdependent world economy. It recognizes that problems in the two sets of countries are frequently connected and sometimes common. Third, in sharp contrast with mainstream economics, the approach is heterodox and unconventional in its analysis and diagnosis of development problems, as well as in thinking about possible solutions. It examines the implications not only for countries, so characteristic of the literature in this domain, but also for people.

It needs to be said that the essays in the volume cannot be divided into the usual categories or specialization areas in economics as a discipline, which is the norm in much of the literature. The reason is simple enough. The essays are in economics but explore many intersections:

macroeconomics and development economics, theory and policy, national economies and the global context or international economics and economic development. In some parts, these intersections stretch to economics and history, economics and politics or economics and sociology.

The rationale for this book is straightforward. It is not significantly different from that of other collections. Obviously, the whole cannot be greater than the sum total of the parts. But it is plausible to suggest that the whole is different from the parts by themselves. Taken together, the interconnections between essays are easier for readers to discern. What is more, articles in journals and papers in edited volumes, dispersed in space and time, are difficult to find, particularly for students. And I believe that this volume of collected essays will make access far easier for interested readers. I also hope that the book as a whole can reach out to a larger audience than each essay might have done. In a world of increasing specialization, it might also tempt readers who find something interesting, other than what they set out to read, between these covers.

The structure of the book, which provides a framework and a sequence, is simple. The essays are grouped into three thematic clusters, so that the book is divided into three parts: employment and development; growth and development; and development, polity and society.

Employment and development

The first set of essays provides a macroeconomic perspective on selected issues contextualized in the world economy. The critical importance of employment, in both developing countries and industrialized countries, is a theme that runs through these essays. The contrast with orthodox economics, which tends to neglect employment as an objective and unemployment as an outcome, is striking. The subjects might appear diverse, but employment is their common concern in the broad domain of macroeconomics. The Great Recession that followed in the aftermath of the financial crisis that surfaced in late 2008 persists. Recovery is uncertain and fragile. It is only increased employment that can provide a sustainable solution to the crisis, and in the process deliver growth with stability. Indeed, there is a strategic role for employment, for it is perhaps the only means of reviving growth and reducing inequality, thus addressing the two most serious problems that confront the world economy at the present conjuncture. In this context, it is important to recognize that there is a relationship between the state of economies at a macro level and the living conditions of people at a micro level. And the causation runs in both directions. But these interactions are seldom explored. Alas, the discourse on the Millennium Development Goals (MDGs) since the turn of the century, concerned with the well-being of people, did not quite address this problem, since it sought to focus on ends rather than means and aggregates rather than distributional outcomes. The recent debate on Sustainable Development Goals (SDGs) ended up with a longer and broader wish list. Yet, in thinking about the move from the old framework (MDGs) to the new construct (SDGs), it missed an opportunity to focus on employment as the link between the microcosm and the macrocosm.

Chapter 1 analyses the implications of the global economic crisis for developing countries, situated in the wider context of the world economy, to suggest that the crisis also provides an opportunity for rethinking policies at the national level and contemplating collective action at the international level, so that outcomes are more conducive to development. The world economy witnessed a collapse in international trade and a sharp contraction in both output and employment. But the developing world coped better than industrialized countries or transition economies, as the impact was less adverse and the recovery was somewhat quicker. China, India and Brazil stood out as exceptions. Initial conditions, policy responses and domestic demand shaped their resilience and recovery. However, it was always clear that these few countries, or some parts of the developing world, could not possibly drive recovery or turn into engines of growth for the world. The subsequent slowdown in emerging economies validates this hypothesis. Even so, their experience suggests important policy lessons. The prospects of recovery in the world economy remain uncertain. But the supposed trade-off between financial stability and economic growth is a false dilemma. Recovery is sustainable only if it is based on a rebalancing of the world economy that extends beyond current account deficits and surpluses to income-expenditure gaps and income distribution within countries. An increase in the share of wages in GDP, attributable to more employment or higher wages or both, would be conducive to growth everywhere. This is possible if full employment is the primary objective and wages keep pace with productivity growth. In the global context, international collective action is an imperative for crisis management and crisis prevention.

Chapter 2 addresses the fundamental question that does not receive the attention it deserves in orthodox macroeconomics: why employment matters. The global economic crisis has led to a sharp slowdown in growth and an even greater slowdown in employment creation. The resulting deterioration in the quality of employment has exacerbated the long-term trend of rising inequality. Jobless growth has dampened output growth through a worsening income distribution. Wages are costs on the supply side but also incomes on the demand side, so that profit-led growth and wage-led growth are complements, not substitutes. Thus, growth can create jobs while the jobs so created can drive growth. More employment and better jobs can also mitigate rising inequality. If macroeconomic policies focus on fostering employment creation and supporting economic growth rather than on price stability and balanced budgets, employment would revive growth and reduce inequality.

Chapter 3 analyses the interactions between macroeconomics, in terms of objectives and policies, and human development, which is about the well-being of people. Each can, and often does, exercise a significant influence on the other. Macroeconomics matters for human development because it determines the level of employment, the degree of social protection and the public provision of services such as healthcare or education. Human development has implications and consequences for macroeconomics since it can mobilize or claim resources to enlarge or diminish space for macroeconomic policies. The relationship exists and matters not only in poor countries, but also in rich countries. Employment, even if neglected, provides the critical link. The essay shows that the causation runs in both directions and could be either positive or negative. It also reveals similarities and differences in developing and industrialized countries. The political context is significant, everywhere, as interests, ideology and institutions influence economic policies in both sets of countries to shape outcomes.

Chapter 4 seeks to analyse the MDGs in prospect rather than retrospect. The idea is to learn from the past to consider correctives for the future. In doing so, it begins with a critical evaluation of their conception and design to focus on limitations that must be addressed. In contemplating the future, it suggests that such a framework is necessary but should not be more of the same. Thus, it explores possible options, such as structural flexibility at the national level and cognition of inequality in outcomes, which could provide the foundations of a modified framework or alternative construct. The essay argues that developing countries also need to formulate policies, redesign strategies and rethink development in their respective national contexts, learning from the experience of MDGs. In the international context, where the focus has been narrow and the progress has been slow during the lifespan of MDGs, there is need for cooperation among developing countries through better bargaining and collective action, which provides an opportunity to reshape unfair rules in the world economy that encroach upon policy space so essential for development. It would seem that the SDGs launched in September 2015, when the MDGs came to an end, are much larger in scope, based on much wider consultations, but do not quite incorporate lessons from the past that could have made them more effective or attainable.

Growth and development

The second set of essays is concerned with the broad contours of change in the world economy, starting around 1980, leading to some erosion in the economic dominance of industrialized countries and an increase in the economic significance of developing countries, both of which gathered momentum after 2000. This process was driven by differences in rates of economic growth between the two sets of countries. Hence, in analysing the ongoing transformation of the world economy, the crucial importance of growth is a theme that runs through these essays, which explore some intersections of economics and history. But it is also recognized that the benefits of growth are distributed in an unequal manner not only between countries, but also between regions and people within countries, so that the outcome is uneven development. It is essential to consider this evolution of developing countries in the world economy in retrospect and prospect. Comparisons with the past reveal that the 'rise of the West' and the 'fall of the Rest' were two sides of the same coin. Contemplating the future suggests that developing countries can sustain catching up only if their growth is inclusive, because it would enable them to mobilize their most abundant resource – people – for development. So far, growth and industrialization in the developing world is concentrated in a few countries, among which China, India, Brazil and South Africa are leaders. This has economic implications for other developing countries, industrialized countries and the world economy. China and India, both recipients of aid until not so long ago, now provide economic and technical assistance to Africa, and an evaluation of such a role reversal is instructive. The emergence of Brazil, Russia, India China and South Africa (BRICS) as a formation represents an intersection of economics and politics, which could influence the architecture of international institutions and of global governance, in a world where the beginnings of change in the balance of power are discernible. This might also shape trajectories of national development among countries that are latecomers.

Chapter 5 analyses the evolution of developing countries in the world economy in a long-term historical perspective, but with a focus on the period since 1950. Until the Industrial Revolution in Britain, Europe and Asia were largely similar in levels of economic development. Beginning around 1820, Western Europe followed by the United States shot ahead, while Asia experienced a rapid decline, which created an enormous divide between rich and poor countries by 1950. Divergence stopped thereafter. Convergence in incomes per capita was at best modest, but catch up in aggregate output, driven by economic growth, gathered momentum from 1980. Countries that led this process through industrialization did not rely merely on markets and openness. In fact, development is more about the visible hand of the State than the invisible hand of the market. But there is an exclusion of countries and people from this process, which is concentrated in a few countries, described as the Next-14. And growth has not always been transformed into meaningful development that improves the well-being of people. It is argued that the developing world can sustain its catching up only if economic growth, human development and social progress move in tandem.

Chapter 6 attempts to analyse the economic implications of the rise of China, India, Brazil and South Africa, for developing countries situated in the wider context of the world economy. It examines the possible impact of their rapid growth on the world economy, industrialized countries and developing countries. In doing so, it considers the main channels of transmission, to focus on international trade, investment, finance and migration. The essential question is whether, in times to come, these four countries could be the new engines of growth for the world economy. The answer is not quite. Rapid growth in China already supports growth elsewhere, so far primarily as a market for exports, while India and Brazil the potential to provide similar support, but South Africa does not even exhibit such a potential. However, in future, these countries could become engines of growth only if they could also provide resources for investment and technologies for productivity. Such a transformation is not yet on the horizon. Even so, rapid growth in these emerging markets, together with their large size, is beginning to change the balance of economic power in the world.

Chapter 7 highlights the increasing presence of China and India in Africa, to examine its implications for African economic development. It evaluates the main forms of economic engagement to focus on trade with some discussion on investment, aid and migration. It argues that the consequences could be positive if China and India provide markets for exports, resources for investment and finances for development, creating more choices and space for formulating policies that are conducive to national development objectives. The consequences could be negative if rapid growth in China and India competes with, but does not complement, the needs of development in Africa, perpetuating traditional patterns of specialization, which inhibit rather than foster industrialization in Africa. The actual impact will depend on how reality unfolds. It would depend even more, perhaps, on what African countries do in terms of initial conditions, better bargaining and appropriate policies, to maximize the benefits and minimize the costs associated with the process of growing economic interaction with China and India. The international arena will also matter in the spheres of bilateralism and multilateralism.

Chapter 8 analyses the implications and consequences of the rise of BRICS for the developing world and for global governance. In doing so, it examines their increasing importance among developing countries and their growing significance in the world economy, situated in historical perspective. It, then, considers the factors underlying the evolution of BRICS as an economic and political formation to explain not only the country-composition, but also the timing and the significance of their arrival on the global stage. This is followed by an analysis of the possible economic impact of rapid growth in BRICS in the future on other developing countries, which could be complementary or competitive and, on balance, positive or negative. The chapter goes on to discuss the potential influence of BRICS extending beyond economics to politics in the wider global context, with reference to how it could reshape international institutions or activate cooperation among developing countries.

Development, polity and society

The third set of essays stretches the canvas beyond the economy to polity and society. It is made up of just two essays, which are at best illustrative of some important intersections that are often neglected by economists in the belief that such subjects relate to other disciplines in the social sciences. These essays explore the intersection of economics with politics, and with sociology and law, respectively. In the process of development, some new problems surface while some old problems persist. The reconciliation of political democracy, which works on the principle of one person one vote, and market economy, which works on the principle of one dollar one vote, is difficult enough in the national context, but becomes more complex when global markets are juxtaposed with national governments in this era of globalization.

Discrimination associated with injustice in society should diminish with development, even if it cannot be eliminated, but often persists despite economic progress and affirmative action laws, because it is embedded in society through history. The essays suggest that such problems, whether rising economic inequalities or persistent social discrimination, can be addressed only if countries can provide social opportunities to their people, who are excluded, through access to education and to employment.

Chapter 9 is about globalization and democracy in a changing world. The gathering momentum of globalization in the world economy, since 1980, had coincided with the spread of political democracy across countries. Economies have become global. But politics remains national. This essay explores the relationship between globalization and democracy. It begins with a simple analytical construct derived from economics that suggests trade-offs between globalization, the nation state and democratic politics. In reality, of course, the relationship is neither linear nor characterized by structural rigidities. It goes on to analyse the relationship between market economy and political democracy in a national context to show that it is interactive, highlighting how such an approach is useful for an understanding of the international context. This leads into a discussion on how globalization might constrain degrees of freedom for nation states and space for democratic politics, and how political democracy within countries might exercise some checks and balances on markets and globalization. The essential argument is that the relationship between globalization and democracy is dialectical and does not conform to ideological caricatures.

Chapter 10 argues that affirmative action is necessary, but cannot be sufficient to resolve problems of discrimination and injustice in society. It begins with the origins of discrimination in historical perspective, explains how discrimination leads to exclusion, to show that embedded injustice is an outcome of the process. The conception of justice evolved over a long period of time that spanned centuries if not millenniums. Yet, it is clear that the quest for social justice, driven by political democracy, mostly through affirmative action, essentially surfaced during the second half of the 20th century. To consider why this might not have been sufficient to address the problems of embedded discrimination and continuing injustice, the essay discusses the logic, the necessity and the limitations of affirmative action. A dose of reality is imparted to the story with a tale of three countries – the United States, India and South Africa – even if the focus is on India. In conclusion, the chapter draws some lessons from experience to contemplate the future.

Part I

EMPLOYMENT AND DEVELOPMENT

1

THE FINANCIAL CRISIS, THE GREAT RECESSION AND THE DEVELOPING WORLD

The financial crisis in the United States, in late 2008, spread through contagion across the world. Its transmission to the real sectors of economies was also rapid, as it led to a sharp contraction in output and employment. The downturn moved quickly into a recession. Even if cycles are embedded in the nature of capitalism, it is clear that this Great Recession is the deepest crisis in capitalism since the Great Depression more than 75 years ago. There is, however, an important difference between then and now. Developing countries were not so connected with the world economy at that time. The focus then, it is no surprise, was on industrialized countries. Developing countries are much more significant and integrated into the world economy now. Hence, this time around, any meaningful analysis of crisis and recovery in the world economy must also focus on the developing world.

The object of this chapter is to analyse the implications of the financial crisis and the Great Recession for developing countries, situated in the wider context of the world economy, to suggest that the crisis also provides an opportunity for rethinking policies at the national level and contemplating collective action at the global level, so that outcomes are more conducive to development. First, it examines the impact of the crisis on the developing world. Second, it considers why the impact of the crisis and the recession on some emerging economies and on some parts of the developing world was less adverse and why their recovery was significantly faster than in the industrialized countries. Third, it explores how developing countries might address the problem in their respective national contexts, to mitigate the impact of the Great Recession at present and to reduce their vulnerability in the event of a future crisis. Fourth, it analyses the prospects of recovery in the world economy with a focus on the underlying macroeconomics, to suggest that a sustainable solution requires stability with growth. Fifth, it discusses the logic and the possibilities of international collective action, with particular reference to the opportunities for cooperation among developing countries, which is needed for crisis management and essential for crisis prevention.

It should be obvious that this chapter seeks to consider a wide range of issues in an endeavour to sketch the big picture. However, it needs to be said that there are some issues it does not consider. It does not attempt to outline the sequence of events or examine the underlying causes that led to this global economic crisis.[1] It does not attempt to survey the emerging literature on the impact of the financial crisis and the Great Recession on the developing world.[2] It does not attempt to examine the implications and consequences of the triple crisis, as the financial crisis has roughly coincided in time with the food crisis and the environmental crisis, for the developing world. Clearly, these aspects are also important, but such a discussion would require another essay.

Economic impact on the developing world

It is important to set the stage by highlighting the initial impact of the global crisis on development. The most obvious consequence was the slowdown in economic growth in much of the developing world. The channels of transmission for the slowdown in growth were: exports, remittances and capital flows. For exports from the developing world, primary commodities witnessed a collapse in prices, which was juxtaposed with sharply reduced levels of demand, while manufactured goods that are labour intensive in production witnessed a phenomenal contraction in demand across the world market. Indeed, in 2009, the sharp decline in world trade, almost unprecedented at 12.2 per cent, was far more pronounced than the reduction in world output at 2.3 per cent.[3] The rapid growth in remittances, particularly from migrants in industrialized countries, experienced a sharp slowdown.[4] And it is no surprise that foreign direct investment in the world economy was much reduced.[5] There was a complete collapse in flows of private capital and portfolio investment to the developing world.[6] But that might have been a blessing in disguise for most countries. It is clear that the slowdown in growth shaped outcomes in development through these channels of transmission. In the ultimate analysis, however, development is about the living conditions of people, ordinary people.

In a narrow sense, the poor are people who live below the poverty line of purchasing power parity (PPP) US$ 1.25 per day. This number is in the range of 1.35 billion people, which is a little more than 20 per cent of the world's population. These are estimates made by the World Bank which, some scholars argue, probably underestimate absolute poverty.[7] However, if the poverty line is drawn at PPP US$ 2 per day, the number of the poor is much larger at 2.55 billion people, which is almost 40 per cent of the world's population.[8] It is the population between the two poverty lines that, almost as large at 1.2 billion, is vulnerable in times of crisis because any shock, such as a bad harvest, high inflation or employment cuts, can push them further into poverty. Of course, those already below the poverty line of PPP US$ 1.25 per day are even more vulnerable, as such shocks erode their critical minimum levels of consumption.

The channels of transmission outlined above play a part in this process. In developing countries, exports are a very important source of employment and livelihoods. This is true not just in small countries that are export dependent, but is just as true in large economies such as China and India. It is widely recognized that China depends on the world economy, in particular the United States, as a market for its manufactured exports. India might appear less dependent. However, significant segments of its manufacturing sector, not only information technology but also clothing, leather, gems, jewellery, handicrafts and carpets, which export a very large proportion of their output, are an important source of employment. And it is people in these sectors, often the poor or the vulnerable employed in the production of leather, handicrafts and carpets, who have lost their livelihoods from the contraction in exports. Such vulnerability is obviously far greater in smaller countries of the developing world which have a much narrower range of specialization in exports. Remittances, research suggests, are much higher per capita for migrants at lower levels of income and skills than for migrants at higher levels of income and skills, because such remittances support either household consumption among the poor in the home country of the migrant or provide resources for assets that generate self-employment.[9] It is these that have come down significantly. And, last but not least, foreign aid inflows that have contracted in the least developed countries (LDCs) have had a serious impact on levels of social consumption, because they are often a primary source of finance which supports social consumption in countries where governments are strapped for cash or are in a perpetual fiscal crisis. The poor in the developing world are obviously the most vulnerable. Hence, the initial impact must have been adverse.

It is now two years since the crisis surfaced. Although it is not possible to come to definitive conclusions, available evidence on GDP growth rates suggests that outcomes are mixed. Growth performance was in conformity with longer term trends in 2007, but it was dampened by the financial crisis in 2008, while the full impact of the global economic crisis was felt in 2009. Annual GDP growth rates in these three years were: 3.8 per cent, 1.6 per cent and –2.2 per cent, respectively, for the world economy; 2.6 per cent, 0.5 per cent and –3.5 per cent for industrialized countries; 2.1 per cent, 0.4 per cent and –2.5 per cent for the United States; 2.9 per cent, 0.8 per cent and –4.1 per cent for the European Union; 8.4 per cent, 5.5 per cent and –6.5 per cent for the transition economies; 7.6 per cent, 5.4 per cent and 1.9 per cent for developing countries; 5.6 per cent, 4.1 per cent and –2.1 per cent for Latin America and the Caribbean; 6.0 per cent, 4.9 per cent and 1.6 per cent for Africa; 5.0 per cent, 4.6 per cent and –1.0 per cent for West Asia; 9.3 per cent, 6.3 per cent and 4.3 per cent for East Asia and South Asia.[10]

The impact of the crisis was not confined to a contraction in output. It also led to a sharp contraction in employment. It is estimated that, between 2007 and 2009, the number of unemployed people in the world rose from less than 180 million to 210 million, so that global unemployment increased by more than 30 million.[11] Of this increase, three-fourths was in the industrialized countries and one-fourth was in the emerging economies. The unemployment rate increased by 3 percentage points in the industrialized countries and by 0.25 percentage points in the emerging economies. And in the major industrialized countries, unemployment rates climbed to double-digit levels. The unemployment rate for youth, mostly new entrants into the labour market, which is historically more than twice that for higher age groups, jumped to unprecedented levels in some countries such as Spain where it rose from less than 20 per cent to almost 40 per cent. At the same time, the problem of long-term unemployment intensified in the industrialized world. The proportion of those unemployed for more than six months in the total number of the unemployed, which has been rising over time, also registered a sharp increase everywhere, and this proportion is now alarming at almost one-half in the United States.

Clearly, the adverse impact of the Great Recession on output and employment in the industrialized world and in the transition economies was substantial, while the developing world did not fare as badly as might have been expected. Some market economies in the European Union, in particular Portugal, Ireland, Greece and Spain, as also some transition economies in Eastern Europe, are in deep trouble. These countries have large external debts relative to foreign exchange reserves, or domestic financial vulnerabilities in the private sector some of which have been shifted to the government sector through bailouts. Many of the high-income emerging economies were, and remain, adversely affected. South Korea, Taiwan, Hong Kong and Singapore, as also Mexico and Turkey, which were highly dependent on the US and EU markets for their manufactured exports, are hard hit. Similarly, Chile, Malaysia and Thailand experienced a significant contraction in GDP, partly as a consequence of the sharp decline in exports. In contrast, some large developing countries, in particular China, Egypt, India, Indonesia and Nigeria, turned out good economic performances in the aftermath of the crisis, while Argentina and Brazil did not fare badly.[12] Apart from these large developing countries, surprisingly enough, some regions in the developing world, such as South Asia, North Africa and much of Sub-Saharan Africa, fared better than might have been expected.[13] But that is not all. The growth performance of the LDCs was surprisingly robust.[14] The good performance of South Asia and the reasonable performance of Sub-Saharan Africa, which are homes to most of the world's poor, implies that, at least so far, the impact of the Great Recession on world poverty might not have been as bad as expected. Obviously, growth, whether rapid or modest, is not sufficient to ensure the well-being of ordinary people, but a collapse in growth or a contraction in output would almost certainly have hurt the poor more. In fact, growth slowed down but remained positive in several parts of the developing world. It is clear that, in the absence of this growth, outcomes would have been much worse for people.

Resilience of three emerging economies

Given the diversity of countries in the developing world, it is difficult to provide a general explanation for the unexpected resilience of some economies following the global crisis. But it might be worthwhile to focus on three emerging economies – China, India and Brazil – that seem to have weathered the storm, in so far as the impact was less adverse and the recovery was faster. It is not as if the three were immune from the crisis in the world economy. The impact on some sectors of these economies, particularly those that were export dependent, was devastating in the short run. Yet, in retrospect, they turned out to be exceptions. Their experience might carry lessons for other developing countries, just as their performance might have implications for the world economy.

The impact of the global economic crisis was less adverse for four reasons. First, the initial conditions before the crisis were supportive.

Macroeconomic stability, reflected in fiscal situation, moderate inflation and large foreign exchange reserves combined with economic growth provided structural flexibility both at the macro and micro levels. Second, the financial liberalization was restrained. Integration into international financial markets was calibrated and deregulation of domestic financial sectors was paced. Third, safety nets for the poor and the vulnerable, even if limited, were in place. There was social protection in China, the National Rural Employment Guarantee programme in India and *Bolsa Familia* in Brazil. Fourth, the economic size of these countries, in terms of population if not income, meant that domestic consumption was a countervailing force, particularly as economic activity for significant proportions of the population was not quite connected with the world economy.

Their economic recovery was also significantly faster for three reasons. First, these countries adopted expansionary, countercyclical, macroeconomic policies, which were almost Keynesian and most unusual, until now, in the developing world. What is more, the response to the crisis was effective and fast. There was a massive fiscal stimulus in China. In contrast, the fiscal stimulus in India was modest. But there was a significant expansion in the National Rural Employment Guarantee programme and a large increase in salaries for government employees, both of which were put in place just before the crisis and became a de facto stimulus. Expansionary fiscal and monetary policies were introduced in Brazil. The existing macroeconomic situation and the presence of State financial institutions in the three economies made the task easier. Second, the size of the home market made a difference. The increase in aggregate demand came, in significant part, from segments of the population with a high propensity to consume, which was transmitted to the real sector of the economy. It meant that the Keynesian multiplier worked on output and incomes. Thus, domestic consumption drove recovery and sustained growth. Third, their financial sectors, which were less fragile and more regulated than elsewhere, did not absorb scarce resources from stimulus packages in recapitalization or bailouts, so that easier monetary policies meant lending for investment to the real sector in these economies rather than the creation of financial asset bubbles.

The reasons underlying the resilience of other emerging economies and developing countries that fared better were probably similar. The combination of factors could not have been the same because of differences in size and circumstances of countries. The relative importance of underlying factors would have been different. Even the underlying factors might have been different. Yet, there can be little doubt that initial conditions, policy responses and domestic demand shaped resilience and recovery, while prudence in deregulation and liberalization of financial sectors limited collateral damage. Fiscal space available to governments also made a difference. The significant increase in the share of developing countries in world income and world trade, which was clearly discernible by the mid-2000s,[15] also meant that there were some external markets and resources other than in the industrialized economies. It is almost certain that robust growth in Asia provided support to this resilience.

China, India and Brazil are large countries. Most small open economies in the developing world do not have similar space or flexibility. Yet, the experience of the giant economies does suggest some obvious lessons for smaller countries in the developing world. It would be wise to hasten slowly with capital account liberalization or retain to the option of introducing capital controls. It would be sensible to exercise restraint in the deregulation of domestic financial sectors. It would be necessary to stay prudent in macromanagement, so that there is some freedom to introduce countercyclical macroeconomic policies. It would be desirable to create social safety nets for the poor and the vulnerable. Of course, such lessons are more about prevention in future rather than cure at present. Even so, it is important to begin introducing correctives wherever possible.

In the wider global context, it is important to recognize the resilience of and the recovery in China, India and Brazil.[16] But it would be a mistake to conclude that these three countries can drive the process of recovery, or turn into engines of growth for the world economy.

Rapid economic growth in lead economies drives economic growth elsewhere in the world by providing markets for exports, resources for investment, finances for development and technologies for productivity. The classic examples – Britain in the 19th century and the United States in the 20th century – provide confirmation of the suggested economic causation and transmission mechanisms. Taken together, before the crisis, China, India and Brazil accounted for 10 per cent of world GDP at market exchange rates (and 25% of world PPP-GDP). Given this reality, economic growth in China, India and Brazil can provide only a limited stimulus to economic growth elsewhere, in large part, as markets for exports. But these countries cannot be characterized as engines of growth, at least not yet, in any of the other dimensions. Simply put, they are complements, not substitutes, which can provide some stimulus as the old engine of growth slows down.[17]

Even as markets for exports, there should be mechanisms through which these economies can transmit their growth dynamics to the rest of the world. India and Brazil do run current account and balance of trade deficits but, given their share in world trade, cannot contribute much to a recovery in world demand. China has a far larger economy and a much larger share of world trade. But it has a big current account surplus and a massive balance of trade surplus. In principle, China could stimulate growth elsewhere if it reduced its large trade surplus into at least a trade balance or turned it into a significant trade deficit. However, even this transformation would not suffice. The import content of Chinese exports is about 50 per cent, while the import content of its domestic consumption is only 10 per cent. Of its total imports, over 60 per cent are used directly or indirectly for exports, while less than 40 per cent are used for domestic investment or consumption. It would seem that China is a major importer but not a major market. Thus, *ceteris paribus*, a US$ 100 shift in the composition of aggregate demand from export markets to domestic consumption would reduce Chinese imports by US$ 40.[18] Obviously, China cannot turn into an engine of growth for the world economy even as a market for exports.

We know from experience that, during the second half of the 20th century, the United States economy has been, for better or for worse, the engine of economic growth in the world, insofar as it provides markets for exports, resources for investment and finances for development. There is reasonably strong evidence to suggest that growth in the United States leads the process of growth in the world economy.[19] This is attributable, in part, to the size of its economy in terms of income. But this is also attributable to its dominant role in the world economy, in terms of trade, investment, finance or technology, reinforced by its countercyclical stance in macroeconomic policies. Therefore, the prospects for recovery in the world economy, in the medium term, depend to a significant extent on the pace and the nature of recovery in the industrialized world, in particular the United States. These prospects are uncertain. And it is important to recognize the possibility that the Great Recession could persist. It would then become essential for developing countries to address the problem as best as they can in a national context.

The national context: constraints and choices

Ironically enough, there is an opportunity in this crisis for developing countries, in terms of rethinking policies and rethinking development. The dominant ideology of our times is beginning to lose its stranglehold on thinking, at least in political processes, if not in the ivory towers of academia. There is a growing recognition that markets are no magic wand, and that the invisible hand of the market is not visible because it is not there, and that markets are good servants but bad masters. And there are a number of ways in which this crisis could provide reasons to rethink policies and rethink development. The discussion that follows is illustrative, not exhaustive, because it seeks to focus on some selected issues, where orthodox prescriptions often accentuate rather than resolve problems of development.

First, there is both need and opportunity to reflect on macroeconomic objectives and macroeconomic policies. Such rethinking must begin by redefining policy objectives. In the short term or in crisis situations, the prime concern should not be the stability of prices alone. The stability of output and employment is just as important. In the medium term or in normal times, the essential objective of macroeconomic policies cannot simply be the management of inflation and the elimination of macroeconomic imbalances. It should be just as much, if not more, about fostering employment creation and supporting economic growth. The rethinking must also extend to reconsidering policy instruments. Fiscal policy cannot be reduced to a means of reducing government deficits or restoring macroeconomic balances. It is a powerful instrument in the quest for full employment and economic growth. Monetary policy cannot be reduced to a means of controlling inflation through interest rates. It is a versatile instrument where both the price and volume of credit can be most effective in the pursuit of development objectives. In sum, it is essential to return a developmental approach to macroeconomic policies, which is based on an integration of short-term countercyclical fiscal and monetary policies with long-term development objectives. This should shift the focus from the financial sector to the real economy, from the short term to the long term and from equilibrium to development. Economic growth with full employment should be the fundamental objective of macroeconomic policies, which must be an integral part of the mandate for central banks and finance ministries. It must be stressed that such a role for fiscal and monetary policies is critical not simply in crisis situations, but also in the pursuit of development.

Such rethinking is easier said than done, because it requires dispensing with two shibboleths that have shaped orthodox macroeconomic policies, particularly in difficult times or crisis situations: that government deficits must be reduced and that economies must accept the pain of adjustment. This belief system was dented in response to the global economic crisis but is beginning to resurface.

The obsessive concern about deficits in government finances borders on fetishism. It is essential to recognize the fallacies of such deficit fetishism.[20] Orthodoxy believes that reducing gross fiscal deficits is both necessary and sufficient for the macroeconomic adjustment. This is a myth. The size of the fiscal deficit, or the amount of government borrowing, is the symptom and not the disease. And there is nothing in macroeconomics which stipulates an optimum level to which the fiscal deficit must be reduced as a proportion of GDP. Indeed, it is possible that a fiscal deficit at 6 per cent of GDP is sustainable in one situation while a fiscal deficit at 4 per cent of GDP is not sustainable in another situation. The real issue is the allocation and end use of government expenditure in relation to the cost of borrowing by the government. Thus, government borrowing is always sustainable if it is used to finance investment and if the rate of such investment is greater than the interest rate payable. There is a similar fetishism about monetized deficits. It serves little purpose to eliminate the monetized deficits for fear of inflation, if the government continues to borrow as much from elsewhere instead of the central bank, but at a much higher cost. There are other important macroeconomic consequences of such monetarism. For one, it makes public debt much less manageable and reduces fiscal flexibility for governments as interest payments pre-empt a much larger proportion of government expenditure. For another, high interest rates, which may not dampen government borrowing in the short run if not in the medium term, crowd out private investment, as rates of return on borrowed capital used to finance investment need to be much higher.

The other shibboleth also dies hard. For economies in crisis, orthodoxy believes that governments should not attempt to attain full employment. Instead, governments are urged to accept the pain of adjustment in the form of lower output today for a higher output tomorrow. This recommendation conforms to the strong spring analogy: the harder you push the spring down, the greater the force with which it bounces back. But a weak spring might be a more appropriate analogy for the economy, for when it is pushed too hard, it may simply remain there if its restorative forces are destroyed. These are mere analogies but there is evidence in support of the latter. In developing countries, under normal circumstances, there already exists a procyclical pattern to macroeconomic policies, which are always the softer option for governments. Indeed, there are strong, embedded incentives or disincentives for governments to adopt procyclical fiscal policies.[21] The probability of such outcomes increases with orthodox stabilization and adjustment programmes, which advocate a restrictive fiscal policy and a tight monetary policy. In downturns, the social costs of procyclical fiscal policies are high, while growth is dampened, if not stifled. The correct response would be countercyclical macroeconomic policies, which are adopted as a rule by governments in industrialized countries.[22]

In the aftermath of the global economic crisis, the response of most developing countries, contrary to the orthodox belief system, was to adopt countercyclical policies in the form of a fiscal stimulus or monetary easing or both. There were three factors that made this possible. First, the response of the industrialized countries was clear in the form of expansionary macro policies. Second, there was an international effort, through the G20, to coordinate macroeconomic policies across countries. Third, much of the developing world, particularly the emerging economies, witnessed rapid economic growth combined with macroeconomic balances in the period before the crisis. In the process, obsessive concerns about governments' deficits were also given up for some time. However, even as the Great Recession persists, the shibboleths have surfaced once again. There are some exceptions, but the stimulus is coming to an end almost everywhere and the process of reversing the stimulus has begun in several countries. The message from the G20 is growth-friendly fiscal consolidation, which represents a return to orthodoxy through the back door. Following such advice would almost certainly be counterproductive at this juncture. It is essential for developing countries to resist this temptation and use the window of opportunity provided by the crisis to reinvent macroeconomic policies for development.

Second, there are important lessons to be learnt from the experience of financial deregulation and capital account liberalization, in both industrialized countries and developing countries, about what should not be done. It is clearly essential to learn that financial deregulation, such as doing away with the distinction between banking and non-banking financial intermediaries, is fraught with risk. At the same time, in thinking of integrating with international financial markets, it is clear that it would be wise to hasten slowly with capital account liberalization. For the same reason, it would be unwise to rely on portfolio investment inflows to finance current account deficits, because portfolio investment represents the intersection of two somewhat thin, very unstable markets in developing countries: namely stock exchange markets and foreign exchange markets. Indeed, wherever countries have moved to capital account liberalization, the option of introducing capital account controls must be retained.[23]

Third, it is essential to rethink the relative importance of the external and the internal in the process of development, in terms of markets and in terms of resources. It is necessary to recognize that the domestic market is critical in the process of development and that external markets are at best complements, but cannot be substitutes for the domestic market even in smaller countries. Of course, the validity of this argument depends in part on the size of a country. Even so, domestic markets are, at one level, constitutive of development because it means that ordinary people have purchasing power and are, at another level, instrumental in the process of development because they can drive processes of growth. Similarly, it is desirable to rely more on domestic resources for investment and think of external resources as complements rather than substitutes.

Fourth, in the national context, the time has come to recognize that there is a complex relationship between the State and the market. In the 1950s, most believed that the State could do no wrong, but four decades later dominant orthodoxy persuaded most that the State could do nothing right. The answer lies somewhere in between. The State and the market are complements and not substitutes. What is more, the relationship between the State and the market cannot be defined once and for all as ideologues attempt to do. In fact, the State and the market must adapt to each other as circumstances and times change.[24] If we look at the difference between success and failure in development during the 20th century, we find that successes have come in countries that have found this right blend of State and markets. It is time to give up the belief in the magic of the market to consider a more proactive role for the State, not just in education and health as the World Bank advocates, but also in terms of trade policy, industrial policy and technology policy. If development is to be people-friendly, it does mean that the State has to play a critical role in terms of providing investment in infrastructure, which is not forthcoming from the private sector, whether domestic or foreign players. The State also has to focus on expenditure in social sectors because, if development is about improving the living conditions of people, allocating resources to support social consumption is both constitutive of and instrumental in development. Most important, perhaps, it is vital to redress the balance in the respective roles of the market and the State, for the pendulum had swung to one end, because the exclusion of large proportions of the population from well-being cannot even sustain growth, let alone lead to development. And there is a developmental role for the State. So much of what needs to be done can only be done by the State. The reason is simple. Governments are accountable to people. Markets are not.

Recovery prospects in the world economy

On the surface, it would seem that the process of recovery has begun. Projections suggest that GDP growth in 2010 would be positive everywhere: in industrialized economies, in transition economies, in developing countries and in regions across the world, as also in major industrialized countries and emerging economies. It is expected that growth rates would be significantly higher than in 2009, possibly close to the 2008 levels.[25] The recovery in growth is expected to be the strongest in developing countries and the weakest in transition economies. There can be little doubt that this outcome is attributable, in large part, to countercyclical macroeconomic policies that were an integral part of strong national action and some international coordination. The fiscal stimulus and the monetary easing across countries were reinforced by massive bailouts for the financial sector in industrialized countries. This policy response pre-empted a protectionist reaction to the sharp contraction in world trade. But the prospects of recovery in the world economy remain uncertain. It is not clear whether recovery would be in the shape of a V (an upturn that would reverse the losses in output and employment), a U (output and employment would remain sluggish for some time despite positive growth) or a W (with a double dip that might follow a premature exit from stimulus packages).[26] The stimulus has come to an end almost everywhere, as there are no further cuts in interest rates or easing of credit, just as there are no more cuts in tax rates or increases in government expenditure. In fact, a reversal of the stimulus is on the cards, as monetary tightening has begun, while fiscal retrenchment is a distinct possibility. The message from the G20 is growth-friendly fiscal consolidation, while in the European Union (not only economies in crisis, but also Germany and the United Kingdom) decisions to sharply reduce fiscal deficits are in the process of implementation. This change in policy stance, somewhat premature, is bound to inflict social costs on the countries and dent the prospects of recovery in the world economy. For that reason, the mounting pressure in some industrialized countries to return to business as usual in macroeconomic policies must be resisted.

In a sense, the sequence of events that began in the lead up to the crisis continues on its course.[27] To begin with, the financial sector players sought to pass on bad loans to each other and spread toxic assets through the financial system. The next stage was that the financial sector sought to pass on assets to the rest of the private sector, which in turn was motivated by greed but ended up with a debt overhang that led to deleveraging. And when the crisis surfaced, the State provided the private sector, mostly in finance, with bailouts. This damaged government finances in deficit countries but rescued surplus countries from a demand contraction, as private deleveraging was partly compensated for by public leveraging. Ultimately, this process eroded the confidence of financial markets in government finances of deficit countries. Fiscal retrenchment is now on the cards as the next step. It is not clear how the system will adjust to what follows when government deficits are reduced. But it is clear that the fallacies of deficit fetishism in the national context could turn out to be even more dangerous in the international context.

The world economy is confronted with a serious dilemma. Restoration of growth based on debt-driven consumption and asset-price inflation in the United States and the EU deficit countries will only postpone adjustment, or the day of reckoning, and accentuate financial fragility. Fiscal consolidation and retrenchment by deficit countries and indebted consumers, even if it reduces financial fragility, will lead to global deflation and stagnation. But this supposed trade-off between financial stability and economic growth is a false dilemma, because neither growth nor stability would be sustainable for long. What we need is both. Stability *and* growth, together, can provide a sustainable solution.

Recovery would be sustainable if, and only if, there is a progressive reduction in and ultimate elimination of global macroeconomic imbalances. In this context, there is a natural focus on the United States, which is the largest importer and the reserve currency country, and China, which is the largest exporter and biggest lender to the United States. But such a characterization of the imbalances is incomplete and insufficient. For one, the current account deficits and surpluses of economies reflect gaps between income and expenditure at a macro level. For another, apart from the United States, some EU countries run large current account deficits, just as, apart from China, Germany and Japan, run large current account surpluses. The United States and the EU deficit countries have lived beyond their means for quite some time, while China, Germany and Japan have lived below their means for quite some time. This provides a more complete picture of imbalances in the world economy. The rebalancing that is needed, however, is easier said than done.

In the current account surplus countries, there is serious problem of underconsumption.[28] In China, for example, since the late 1990s, there has been a continuous decline in private consumption as a proportion of GDP which is attributable to the steady decline in the share of wages in GDP.[29] Similarly, in Germany and Japan, during the 2000s, there has been a discernible decline in the share of wages in GDP which has led to a decline in private consumption as a proportion of GDP since 2005 that was significant in Germany and modest in Japan. In the United States and the EU deficit countries, the share of wages in GDP has witnessed a similar decline, but private consumption has been sustained by debt financing and asset inflation, both of which have now come to an end. The global imbalances, then, are a matter of economics rather than geography. It is income distribution that lies at the heart of the problem. In these industrialized countries, and even more so in China, real wages lagged behind productivity growth, so that the share of wages in GDP fell while the share of profits in GDP rose. It is no surprise that markets and globalization strengthened capital and weakened labour. The mobility of capital and the immobility of labour, combined with flexible labour markets, reinforced the process.[30]

The rebalancing in the world economy, therefore, needs some redistribution of incomes within these countries. China needs to shift from export-led growth to consumption-led growth. Germany and Japan need to shift from external markets to domestic markets as a source of growth.[31] This is possible only if there is an increase in the share of wages in GDP and real wages keep pace with productivity growth. It requires the pursuit of full employment and an acceptance of higher wages. The United States, as also the EU deficit countries, need to shift from consumption-led growth to export-led growth. It might be difficult for exports to lead growth in the short run, as competitiveness is not simply a matter of exchange rates. And it might be difficult to squeeze consumption levels for people who have seen almost no increase in their real wages over a long period of time. Consumption based on household debt is obviously not sustainable. But consumption that is based on more employment and higher wages would be sustainable and could provide domestic demand to drive growth. Therefore, even in the deficit countries, an increase in the share of wages in GDP should be conducive to growth. The moral of the story is simple. It is time to place full employment centre stage once again as the primary objective of macroeconomic policies. For, what is good for employment is good for economic growth. The connection is causal. It is only increased employment that can provide a sustainable solution to the crisis and in the process deliver growth with equity. Such a rebalancing would also provide stability with growth.

International collective action: logic and possibilities

The logic of international collective action was recognized more than six decades ago. It was an integral part of the conception of the Bretton Woods institutions that were created at the end of the Second World War and in the aftermath of the Great Depression. The recognition of its significance diminished with the passage of time. In fact, with the advent of markets and globalization, by 1980 it was almost forgotten. There is an irony in the situation. In the mid-1940s, our understanding of collective action, the circumstances under which public, as opposed to private, action is necessary and desirable, was somewhat underdeveloped in terms of economic theory even if it was shaped by actual experience in the Great Depression. In the late 2000s, in terms of economic theory, our understanding of collective action is far more complete. Markets, by themselves, may not lead to efficient or otherwise desirable outcomes. And such market failure may occur when there are public goods (or bads), externalities and incomplete or imperfect markets. More than six decades later, actual experience of market failure that straddles geographical borders is also much greater. There are several examples: recurring financial crises, impending climate change, trafficking of people, trading in human organs, growing narcotics trade and so on. Clearly, the logic of international collective action is far stronger. Indeed, given the interdependence in the contemporary world economy, the need for international pubic action to address problems arising from market failure is greater than ever before. Yet, the effort is much less.

The recent global economic crisis is at least a prompt if not a wake-up call. It has, perhaps, led to a much-needed recognition of the logic of international collective action, which had been almost forgotten. Its significance is now widely accepted. But it would seem that the willingness and the ability of governments to coordinate, in terms of implementing such collective action, are not quite there. Both have to be created. The former needs economic persuasion and political acceptance. The latter needs creating institutional mechanisms and rethinking national sovereignty. The domains where this is necessary and desirable are many: global macroeconomic management, international financial markets and climate change are the obvious examples, but there are several others such as international migration or international crime. But the institutional mechanisms that exist are neither adequate nor appropriate.

The global economic crisis has highlighted the clear need for international collective action in coordinating global macroeconomic management, regulating international financial markets and reforming the international financial architecture. It would mean too much of a digression to enter into a discussion of these issues here.[32] Consider, for example, the attempt to coordinate macroeconomic policies after the financial crisis in late 2008. The G8 may provide a forum for consultation, but it cannot provide an institutional framework for the coordination of macroeconomic policies. The reason is simple enough. It cannot suffice, in part because it is driven largely by G8 (if not G1) interests and in part because it needs much wider representation. The G20 is wider in its membership but narrower in its jurisdiction, for its concerns are limited, despite recent attempts to make it larger than life at Washington DC, London and Pittsburgh. Similarly, the conference on Climate Change at Copenhagen in December 2009 floundered, in part, because of the absence of an institutional mechanism for consultations and negotiations. The outcome, such as it was, which was shaped by informal consultations between the United States on the one hand and Brazil, China, India and South Africa on the other, was not endorsed because most countries were not part of the process. The LDCs are almost always marginalized or ignored. This time around, even the EU was left watching on the sidelines.

The much-needed institutional mechanisms would materialize only when the costs and benefits of unilateral self-insurance within countries are compared with the costs and benefits of international collective action across countries.[33] In principle, it is possible to contemplate cooperation among nation states to create rules and norms for the market that transcend national boundaries, just as the nation state created rules and norms for the market within national boundaries. In practice, however, recognition of the benefits of such cooperation might not be motivation enough. Cooperation among nation states is far more likely to materialize, much like stable coalitions, if and when the costs of non-cooperation cross the threshold of tolerance. In either case, the nation state is the most important player in the game. Therefore, it is not possible to imagine good governance in the world without nation states, just as it is not possible to have good governance in countries without governments.

There is another window of opportunity at this juncture in time. And that window of opportunity is about the possibilities of cooperation among developing countries, which has so far been in the world of rhetoric rather than reality, words rather than substance. But this subset is an integral part of the logic of international collective action. What is more, the world has changed. In 2005, developing countries accounted for 81 per cent of world population and 22 per cent of world income (almost 45% of world GDP in PPP terms). But that is not all. In the same year, 2005, developing countries accounted for 34 per cent of world exports, 33 per cent of world manufactured exports, 25 per cent of world manufacturing value added and 30 per cent of the stock of inward foreign direct investment in the world economy. It would seem that developing countries are much more integrated with and far more significant in the world economy than they were 25 years ago.[34] It needs to be said that much of this significance is concentrated in a few developing countries: China, Hong Kong, India, Indonesia, Korea, Malaysia, Singapore and Thailand in Asia; Argentina, Brazil and Mexico in Latin America; and South Africa in Africa. In 2005, these 12 countries accounted for 60 per cent of the population and 68 per cent of the income in the developing world. These 12 countries also dominated the engagement of developing countries with the world economy in international trade, international investment and international finance.[35] Even so, it is plausible to argue that, though impossible to prove, this changed situation represents the beginnings of a shift in the balance of economic and political power in the world.[36] This, in turn, opens up possibilities.

In the international context, where the distribution of economic and political power is so unequal, the increased economic significance and political influence of developing countries provides an opportunity to reshape rules and institutions, even in a world of unequal partners. Developing countries as a group with mutual interests are more likely to be heard than single countries by themselves. There will always be some conflict of interest, but there will always be areas where it is possible to find common cause and accept trade-offs. This is already visible in the WTO, where solidarity among developing countries has enabled them to voice their concerns even if they have not yet been able to shape outcomes in negotiations.

At the same time, the large emerging economies – say Brazil, China, India and South Africa – taken together may be able to exercise significant influence through multilateralism, whether institutions or rules, in the global context. The United Nations, the World Bank, the International Monetary Fund (IMF) and the World Trade Organization (WTO) are among the most important multilateral institutions. In the United Nations, China alone is a permanent member of the Security Council with a right to veto. And it is also a member of the P-5. But India, Brazil and South Africa are engaged in knocking at the door, seeking permanent membership of the Security Council, with or without a right to veto. There can be little doubt that, if and when there is an increase in the number of permanent members of the Security Council in the United Nations, these three countries would have the strongest claim to permanent membership. In the World Bank and the IMF, China, India, Brazil and South Africa are permanent members of the Executive Boards. Given the democratic deficit in these institutions, which is embedded in unequal voting rights, China, India, Brazil and South Africa together could influence decisions or even reshape rules. So far, however, there is limited, if any, coordination among them for this purpose.[37] They have neither articulated collective voice nor exercised collective influence. The situation in the WTO is different. India and Brazil have been long-standing advocates of developing countries in the WTO. China has a low profile, possibly because of its recent accession. South Africa is not quite part of the strategic alliance among developing countries. But India and Brazil, along with the United States and the European Union, are now members of the *Quad*, which is the principal institutional mechanism for resolving differences and finding solutions. In sum, it would seem that China, India, Brazil and South Africa have a considerable potential for articulating a collective voice in the world of multilateralism. Coordination and cooperation among them carries a significant potential for exercising influence on multilateral institutions, which could reshape rules and create policy space for countries that are latecomers to development. Such coordination and cooperation, which is in the realm of the possible, has not yet surfaced in a substantive sense.[38] Even so, it is possible to discern beginnings. Brazil, China, India and South Africa together with Mexico constitute the Outreach-5, who have been invited to the G8 Summit in recent years. There is a hint of discontent about their status as observers, peripheral to deliberations and decisions. And the Outreach-5, acting together, are now seeking a place at the high table with the G8. The Climate Change Conference in Copenhagen saw an attempt at coordination among the four countries, who have now chosen to describe themselves as BASIC. Even so, it is important to recognize that once these countries become major players, there is a danger that they might opt for the pursuit of national interest rather than the spirit of solidarity among developing countries or the logic of collective action.

Conclusions

It is clear that the financial crisis of late 2008, which turned into the Great Recession, is the deepest crisis in capitalism since the Great

Depression more than 75 years ago. The difference worth noting is that developing countries, which were marginal then, are much more significant and integrated with the world economy now. This time around, however, the decline in the value and volume of world trade was almost unprecedented. There was also a sharp contraction in output and employment, which was far more pronounced in the industrialized countries. But developing countries also experienced a significant slowdown in growth, some more than others, which was transmitted through exports, remittances and capital flows.

It is two years since the crisis surfaced. On the whole, it would seem that the developing world coped better than the industrialized countries and the transition economies. For one, the impact was less adverse. For another, the recovery was somewhat quicker. But this was not so everywhere. Many of the high-income emerging economies were as adversely affected as the industrialized world. Yet, three emerging economies – China, India and Brazil – weathered the storm. Initial conditions, policy responses and domestic demand shaped resilience and recovery. Prudence in deregulation and liberalization of financial sectors limited collateral damage. Fiscal space available to governments also made a difference. The reasons underlying the resilience of other developing countries that fared better were probably similar, even if the relative importance of underlying factors differed across countries.

There are some obvious lessons for developing countries that emerge from this experience. It is essential to redefine macroeconomic objectives, so that the emphasis is on fostering employment creation and supporting economic growth instead of the focus on price stability alone. It is just as important to rethink macroeconomic policies, which cannot simply be used for the management of inflation and the elimination of macroeconomic imbalances, since fiscal and monetary policies are powerful and versatile instruments in the pursuit of development objectives. It is sensible to exercise restraint in the deregulation of domestic financial sectors. It is prudent to hasten slowly with capital account liberalization or retain the option of introducing capital controls. It is necessary to stay prudent in macromanagement, so that there is some freedom to introduce countercyclical macroeconomic policies. It is desirable to create social safety nets for the poor and the vulnerable. It is time to reconsider the relative importance of the internal and the external in the process of development, in terms of markets and resources, because complements cannot be substitutes. It is vital to redress the balance in the respective roles of the market and the State, so that the developmental role of the State is recognized rather than forgotten.

On the surface, it would seem that the process of recovery in the world economy has begun. The recovery is expected to be the strongest in developing countries, uneven in industrialized countries and the weakest in transition economies. Even so, it is clear that a few emerging economies, or some parts of the developing world, cannot drive recovery or turn into engines of growth for the world. What is more, it is not clear that the fragile recovery is sustainable and the prospects remain uncertain. The observed outcome is largely attributable to countercyclical macroeconomic policies that were an integral part of strong national action and some international coordination. There is, however, a change in the policy stance. The stimulus has come to an end. And fiscal retrenchment has begun in the leading industrialized economies of Europe. This is premature and is bound to dent the prospects of recovery in the world economy. The supposed trade-off between financial stability and economic growth is a false dilemma. Recovery would be sustainable if, and only if, there is a progressive reduction in global macroeconomic imbalances, which might be manifest in current account surpluses or deficits but reflect gaps between income and expenditure at a macro level. These imbalances are a matter of economics rather than geography. It is income distribution that lies at the heart of the problem. The rebalancing of the world economy, therefore, needs some redistribution of incomes within countries. In fact, an increase in the share of wages in GDP would be conducive to growth not only in the surplus countries, but also in the deficit countries. This is possible if wages keep pace with productivity growth and full employment is the primary objective. It is only increased employment that can provide a sustainable solution to the crisis, and in the process deliver growth with equity. Such a rebalancing would also provide stability with growth.

The recent global economic crisis has led to a much-needed recognition of the logic of international collective action, which had been almost forgotten. Its significance is now widely accepted. But the willingness and the ability of governments to coordinate, in terms of implementing such collective action, are not quite there. The much-needed institutional mechanisms would materialize only when the costs and benefits of self-insurance are compared with the costs and benefits of international collective action across countries. This comparison has been brought home with clarity by the global economic crisis. There is another window of opportunity at this juncture in time, which is provided by the possibilities of cooperation among developing countries in a world where there is a discernible shift in the balance of economic and political power. Even in a world of unequal partners, now more than earlier, developing countries as a group could exercise influence to reshape the rules and institutions that govern the world economy. The large emerging economies could play a leading role in this process.

Notes

1 For a discussion of the underlying causes that led to the financial crisis and turned it into the Great Recession, see Stiglitz (2010), Rajan (2010) and Taylor (2011). See also, United Nations (2009a).
2 The literature on the subject is limited but growing. See, for example, Akyuz (2010) and Naude (2010). There are also some studies that examine the impact of the global economic crisis on the developing world with reference to the MDGs. See United Nations (2009b) and UNDP (2010).
3 In fact, the value of world trade in 2009, in terms of US dollars, was 23 per cent lower than it was in 2008, which was in part attributable to the sharp decline in prices of oil and primary commodities. In comparison with the recent past, the contraction was perhaps even sharper than these figures suggest, because the financial crisis and the economic downturn beginning in September 2008 had already dampened growth in world trade and output during that year. In 2008, the volume of world trade increased by a modest 2.1 per cent, much less than the substantial 6.4 per cent in 2007. Similarly, growth in world GDP was only 1.6 per cent in 2008, which was much lower than 3.8 per cent in 2007. For details, see WTO (2010).
4 Data on remittances in 2009 are not yet available. World Bank (2010) estimates suggest that total remittances in the world fell by about 7 per cent from US$ 443 billion in 2008 to US$ 414 billion in 2009, whereas remittances to developing countries declined by 6 per cent from US$ 336 billion in 2008 to US$ 316 billion in 2009. The decline was significantly greater in Latin America and the Caribbean at 12 per cent, in Eastern Europe and Central Asia at 21 per cent and in the Middle East and North Africa at 8 per cent. South Asia was the exception, where remittances increased by 5 per cent in 2009, but at a much slower pace than in preceding years.
5 For example, in 2009 as compared with 2008, world foreign direct investment inflows dropped by 37 per cent to US$ 1,114 billion, while outflows dropped by 43 per cent to US$ 1,101 billion. This followed a significant contraction in 2008 when inflows fell by 16 per cent and outflows fell by 15 per cent as compared with 2007. Foreign direct investment inflows to developing countries dropped by 24 per cent from US$ 630 billion in 2008 to US$ 478 billion in 2009. See UNCTAD (2010).
6 It is estimated by the World Bank that flows of private debt and portfolio equity to developing countries collapsed from a level more than US$ 300 billion in 2007 to about US$ 50 billion in 2008 and –US$ 25 billion in 2009. See World Bank, Global Development Finance database online.
7 See, for example, Kaplinsky (2005) and Pogge and Reddy (2002).
8 The data on the number of the poor relate to 2005 and are obtained from the World Bank, *World Development Indicators*, online database. In 2005, the United Nations Population Division, UNDATA, reports world population as 6.5 billion.
9 For a discussion on this issue, see Nayyar (2002b).

10 See United Nations (2010).
11 For evidence on unemployment cited in this paragraph, see ILO-IMF (2010).
12 For evidence on GDP growth rates in the selected developing countries, see United Nations (2010).
13 In 2007, 2008 and 2009, respectively, GDP growth was 8.3 per cent, 6.5 per cent and 4.7 per cent in South Asia; 4.8 per cent, 4.4 per cent and 3.5 per cent in North Africa; and 7.9 per cent, 6.6 per cent and 2.3 per cent in Sub-Saharan Africa (excluding Nigeria and South Africa). See United Nations (2010).
14 In the least developed countries, GDP growth was 8.5 per cent in 2007, 7.2 per cent in 2008 and 3.3 per cent in 2009 (United Nations, 2010).
15 Between 1970 and 2005, the share of developing countries increased from 15.4 per cent to 21.5 per cent of world GDP, from 15.2 per cent to 33.8 per cent of world exports, from 8.8 per cent to 25.4 per cent of world manufacturing value added. See Nayyar (2009).
16 Available projections suggest that, in 2010, GDP growth in China, India and Brazil would almost return to its 2008 levels (United Nations, 2010).
17 The argument set out briefly in this paragraph is developed at length elsewhere by the author. See Nayyar (2010).
18 This convincing hypothesis is developed, with supporting evidence and arguments, by Akyuz (2010).
19 For a more detailed discussion, see United Nations (2006) and Nayyar (2010).
20 For a detailed discussion on the problems with such deficit fetishism, whether fiscal deficits or monetized deficits, see Nayyar (2008).
21 See Ocampo (2003).
22 For a discussion on the wisdom and necessity of countercyclical macroeconomic policies in developing countries, see Stiglitz et al. (2006).
23 The propositions about capital account liberalization and integration into international financial markets, set out briefly in this paragraph, are discussed in Nayyar (2002c).
24 This argument about the relationship between the State and the market is developed in Bhaduri and Nayyar (1996).
25 See United Nations (2010) and IMF (2010).
26 For a lucid analysis of the recession and the prospects of recovery, see Akyuz (2010).
27 This sequence is set out in a perceptive article by Wolf (2010) in what he describes as a game of 'pass the parcel', which cannot end well. It could also be described as a game of 'musical chairs'. In both games, when the music stops, a person is left holding the parcel or some persons are left standing. Even so, there is one winner at the end. But in this sequence, there are no winners.
28 This argument is developed, at some length, with supporting evidence by Akyuz (2010).
29 In China, private consumption as a proportion of GDP dropped from around 48 per cent in the late 1990s to about 36 per cent in the late 2000s. Over the same period, the share of wages in GDP fell from 53 per cent to 40 per cent, while the share of profits in GDP rose from less than 20 per cent to more than 30 per cent (Akyuz, 2010).

30 There was a redistribution of incomes from wages to profits associated with an increase in economic inequality almost everywhere that was attributable in large part to the advent of markets and the spread of globalization beginning *circa* 1980. See Nayyar (2003) and World Commission on the Social Dimension of Globalization (2004).
31 See Akyuz (2010).
32 For a detailed discussion, see Nayyar (2002a), Ocampo (2002) and Taylor (2002). For an analysis of the implications and consequences of financial contagion, see Reinhart et al. (2003). The experience of the recent financial crisis calls for further reforms in the international financial architecture to reduce the vulnerability of the world economy to recurrent crises and to remove the deflationary bias of policies embedded in the existing architecture. For a discussion, see Akyuz (2010).
33 For a more detailed discussion, see Nayyar (2002a).
34 The evidence on the significance of developing countries in the world economy, cited in this paragraph, is from Nayyar (2009).
35 For more detailed evidence on this concentration, see Nayyar (2009).
36 This hypothesis is developed elsewhere by the author. See Nayyar (2009).
37 There is, perhaps, a modest beginning in the G20, where India, Brazil and South Africa, with some participation from China, have made an attempt to coordinate their stance on reform and change in the IMF. But this is no more than a beginning. It has not influenced, let alone shaped, outcomes.
38 The implications and consequences of the emerging significance of Brazil, China, India and South Africa in the wider context of the world economy are analysed, at some length, in a recent paper by the author. For a detailed discussion, see Nayyar (2010).

References

Akyuz, Yilmaz (2010). 'Global Economic Prospects: The Recession May Be Over but Where Next?' *Research Paper 26*, South Centre, Geneva.

Bhaduri, Amit and Deepak Nayyar (1996). *The Intelligent Person's Guide to Liberalization*, Penguin Books, New Delhi.

ILO-IMF (2010). *The Challenges of Growth, Employment and Social Cohesion*, Oslo, 13 September 2010.

IMF (2010). *World Economic Outlook 2010*, International Monetary Fund, Washington, DC, available from http://www.imf.org/external/pubs/ft/weo/update/02/index

Kaplinsky, Raphael (2005). *Globalization, Poverty and Inequality*, Polity Press, Cambridge.

Naude, W. A. (2010). 'The Global Economic Crisis and Developing Countries: Impacts, Responses and Options for Sustained Recovery', *Poverty and Public Policy*, Vol. 2, No. 2, pp. 211–235.

Nayyar, Deepak (2002a). 'The Existing System and the Missing Institutions', in Deepak Nayyar (ed.), *Governing Globalization: Issues and Institutions*, Oxford University Press, Oxford.

Nayyar, Deepak (2002b). 'Cross-Border Movements of People', in Deepak Nayyar (ed.), *Governing Globalization: Issues and Institutions*, Oxford University Press, Oxford.

Nayyar, Deepak (2002c). 'Capital Controls and the World Financial Authority: What Can We Learn from the Indian Experience?', in John Eatwell and Lance Taylor (eds.), *International Capital Markets: Systems in Transition*, Oxford University Press, New York.

Nayyar, Deepak (2003). 'Globalization and Development Strategies', in John Toye (ed.), *Trade and Development*, Edward Elgar, Cheltenham.

Nayyar, Deepak (2008). 'Macroeconomics of Structural Adjustment and Public Finances in Developing Countries: A Heterodox Perspective', *International Journal of Development Issues*, Vol. 7, No. 1, June, pp. 4–28.

Nayyar, Deepak (2009). 'Developing Countries in the World Economy: The Future in the Past?', *WIDER Annual Lecture 12*, UNU-WIDER, Helsinki, February 2009.

Nayyar, Deepak (2010). 'China, India, Brazil and South Africa in the World Economy: Engines of Growth?', in Amelia Santos-Paulino and Guanghua Wan (eds.), *Southern Engines of Global Growth*, Oxford University Press, Oxford.

Ocampo, Jose Antonio (2002). 'Reforming the International Financial Architecture: Consensus and Divergence', in Deepak Nayyar (ed.), *Governing Globalization: Issues and Institutions*, Oxford University Press, Oxford.

Ocampo, Jose Antonio (2003). 'Developing Countries' Anti-Cyclical Policies in a Globalized World', in Amitava Dutt and Jamie Ros (eds.), *Development Economics and Structuralist Macroeconomics*, Edward Elgar, Cheltenham.

Pogge, T. W. and Sanjay Reddy (2002). *How Not to Count the Poor*, available from http://www.socialanalysis.org

Rajan, Raghuram G. (2010). *Fault Lines*, Princeton University Press, Princeton.

Reinhart, Carmen M., Graciela L. Kaminsky and Carlos A. Vegh (2003). 'The Unholy Trinity of Financial Contagion', *Journal of Economic Perspectives*, Vol. 17, No. 4, pp. 51–74.

Stiglitz, Joseph E. (2010). *Freefall*, W. W. Norton, New York.

Stiglitz, Joseph E., Jose Antonio Ocampo, Shari Spiegel, Ricardo Ffrench-Davis and Deepak Nayyar (2006). *Stability with Growth: Macroeconomics, Liberalization and Development*, Oxford University Press, Oxford.

Taylor, Lance (2002). 'Global Macroeconomic Management', in Deepak Nayyar (ed.), *Governing Globalization: Issues and Institutions*, Oxford University Press, Oxford.

Taylor, Lance (2011). *Maynard's Revenge*, Harvard University Press, Cambridge, MA.

UNCTAD (2010). *World Investment Report 2010*, United Nations, Geneva.

UNDP (2010). *What Will It Take to Achieve the Millennium Development Goals?* United Nations, New York.

United Nations (2006). *Diverging Growth and Development*, World Economic and Social Survey 2006, United Nations, New York.

United Nations (2009a). Report of the Commission of Experts of the President of the United Nations General Assembly on Reforms of the International Monetary and Financial Systems, available from http://www.un.org/ga/econcrisissummit/docs/FinalReport-CoE.pdf

United Nations (2009b). *The Millennium Development Goals Report 2009*, United Nations, New York.

United Nations (2010). *World Economic Situation and Prospects 2010*, update as of mid-2010, 7 July 2010, available from http://www.un.org/esa/policy/wess/wesp.html

Wolf, Martin (2010). 'This Global Game of 'Pass the Parcel' Cannot End Well', *Financial Times*, London, 29 June 2010.

World Bank (2010). *Migration and Development Brief 12*, 23 April 2010, available from http://www.worldbank.org/prospects/migrationandremittances

World Commission on the Social Dimension of Globalization (2004). *A Fair Globalization: Creating Opportunities for All*, ILO, Geneva.

WTO (2010). *International Trade Statistics*, World Trade Organization Press Release, Geneva, 26 March 2010, available from http://www.wto.org/english/news-e/pres10-e/pr598-e.htm

2

WHY EMPLOYMENT MATTERS

Reviving growth and reducing inequality

The object of this chapter is to analyse the critical importance of employment in the wider context of the world economy. It might be somewhat different from the conventional discourse and the usual debate on the subject. For one, it seeks to focus on the macroeconomic aspects of employment rather than the microeconomic concerns about the world of work. For another, it considers employment not only in developing countries, but also in industrialized countries.

In the second decade of the 21st century, the world economy is confronted with two serious problems. First, the financial crisis that surfaced in late 2008 led to a sharp contraction in trade, output and employment. It is more than five years since then. But the Great Recession that followed in its aftermath persists. Recovery is slow, uneven and fragile. In a few countries, where output has recovered, employment has not. In many countries, the crisis runs deep. And the prospects are uncertain (Nayyar, 2011a). The manifestations and the consequences are visible and tangible. Second, beginning around 1980, there has been a rapid increase in economic inequality among people almost everywhere in the world. The distribution of income between people within countries and people in the world as a whole has worsened (Nayyar, 2013). The share of the poorest 50 per cent of the population in national income has contracted almost everywhere (Palma, 2011), while the share of the richest 1 per cent or even 0.1 per cent, the super-rich or the ultra-rich, has risen rapidly almost everywhere (Atkinson, Piketty and Saez, 2012). This change is less visible and almost silent. Yet, it is politically unsustainable and ethically unacceptable (World Commission on the Social Dimension of Globalization, 2004; Piketty, 2014).

I shall argue that employment can provide a sustainable solution to both problems. It is the way forward for reviving growth and reducing inequality. The essential argument, developed in the macroeconomic sphere, is simple. The slowdown in economic growth and employment creation are both associated with a worsening income distribution. At the same time, deterioration in the quality of employment has accentuated economic inequalities. But there are no trade-offs between output growth and job creation. Growth can create jobs, and jobs can drive growth, reinforcing each other. More employment and better jobs would also mitigate problems arising from rising inequality. In this process, every dimension of employment matters, not only its quantum, but also its quality and terms.

The structure of the discussion is as follows. First, I will sketch a global picture to suggest that employment expansion is the path to growth with stability in the world economy. Second, I will consider the national context, to explain the phenomenon of jobless growth, in terms of underlying changes in income distribution which have not only squeezed employment, but also dampened growth. Third, I will discuss how to resolve this problem, which must begin with a rethinking of macroeconomic policies, to revive wage-led growth and stimulate profit-led growth, which shows that there are complementarities rather than trade-offs between employment creation and economic growth. Fourth, I will explain why employment matters as a solution rather than the problem, at every stage of development, not only in industrialized countries and emerging economies, but also in poor countries. At the end, I will draw together some simple yet striking conclusions that emerge.

Global perspective

The world economy is confronted with a serious dilemma. Restoration of growth based on debt-driven consumption and asset-price inflation in the United States and the EU deficit countries will only postpone adjustment, or the day of reckoning, and accentuate financial fragility. Fiscal consolidation and retrenchment by deficit countries and indebted consumers, even if it reduces financial fragility, will lead to global deflation and stagnation. But this supposed trade-off between financial stability and economic growth is a false dilemma, because neither growth nor stability would be sustainable for long. What we need is both. Stability *and* growth, together, can provide a sustainable solution (Nayyar, 2011a).

Recovery would be sustainable if, and only if, there is a progressive reduction in global macroeconomic imbalances. In this context, there is a natural focus on the United States, which is the largest importer and the reserve currency country, and China, which is the largest exporter and biggest lender to the United States. But such a characterization of the imbalances is incomplete and insufficient. For one, the current account deficits and surpluses of economies reflect gaps between income and expenditure at a macro level. For another, apart from the United States, some EU countries and some emerging economies run large current account deficits, just as, apart from China, Germany and Japan run large current account surpluses. The United States, the EU deficit countries and a few emerging economies have lived beyond their means for quite some time, while China, Germany and Japan have lived below their means for quite some time. This provides a more complete picture of imbalances in the world economy. The rebalancing that is needed, however, is easier said than done.

In the current account surplus countries, there is a serious problem of underconsumption. In China, for example, since the late 1990s, there has been a continuous decline in private consumption as a proportion of GDP, which is attributable to the steady decline in the share of wages in GDP (Akyuz, 2011). Similarly, in Germany and Japan, during the 2000s, there has been a discernible decline in the share of wages in GDP, which has led to a decline in private consumption as a proportion of GDP since 2005 that was significant in Germany and modest in Japan.

In the United States and the EU deficit countries, the share of wages in GDP witnessed a similar decline, but private consumption was sustained by debt financing and asset inflation, both of which have now come to an end. The story is similar but not quite the same in the emerging economies which have large current account deficits. The share of wages in GDP declined. This led to a decline in private consumption, as a proportion of GDP, which was not supported by debt financing. Yet, current account deficits persisted or surfaced because governments or private sectors (with increasingly unequal income distributions), or both, lived beyond their means.

The global imbalances, then, are a matter of economics rather than geography. It is income distribution that lies at the heart of the problem (Nayyar, 2011a). In Germany and Japan, but even more so in China, real wages lagged behind productivity growth, so that the share of wages in GDP fell while the share of profits in GDP rose. The story about changes in the share of wages and profits in GDP was roughly the same in industrialized countries and emerging economies that ran current account deficits. It is no surprise that markets and globalization strengthened capital and weakened labour. The mobility of capital and the immobility of labour, combined with flexible labour markets, reinforced the process (Nayyar, 2003a).

The rebalancing in the world economy, therefore, needs some redistribution of incomes within these countries. China needs to shift from export-led growth to consumption-led growth (Akyuz, 2011). Germany and Japan need to shift from external markets to domestic markets as a source of growth. This is possible only if there is an increase in the share of wages in GDP and real wages keep pace with productivity growth. It requires the pursuit of full employment and an acceptance of higher wages. The United States, as also the EU deficit countries, need to shift from consumption-led growth to export-led growth. It might be difficult for exports to lead growth in the short run, as competitiveness is not simply a matter of exchange rates. And it might be difficult to squeeze consumption levels for people who have seen almost no increase in their real wages over a long period of time. Consumption based on household debt is obviously not sustainable. But consumption that is based on more employment and higher wages would be sustainable and could provide domestic demand to drive growth. For emerging economies with current account deficits, export-led growth is a limited option for a few. However, if all of them adopt that strategy, it would only exacerbate global imbalances. But the domestic market could provide a more sustainable source of demand to drive economic growth. Therefore, even in the deficit countries, an increase in the share of wages in GDP should be conducive to growth.

The logic of the argument is simple. It is time to place full employment centre stage once again as the primary objective of macroeconomic policies, in both industrialized countries and emerging economies. For what is good for employment is good for economic growth. The connection is causal. It is only increased employment that can provide a sustainable solution to the crisis and in the process deliver growth with equity (Nayyar, 2011a). Such a rebalancing would also provide stability with growth.

National context

There is obviously some need for international collective action in the quest for better global macroeconomic management, at least through a coordination of national policies. The logic of this proposition is impeccable. Yet, it would seem that the willingness and the ability of governments to coordinate, in terms of implementing such collective action, is not quite there (Nayyar, 2002). Both have to be created. Until then, the problem has to be resolved essentially within countries. But there are constraints implicit in the phenomenon of 'jobless growth'. In this respect, the age of markets and globalization, beginning *circa*

1980, provides a sharp contrast with the golden age of capitalism from the late 1940s to the early 1970s. For one, rates of growth have been slower and more volatile. For another, levels of unemployment have been far higher while employment creation has been much slower.

It is plausible to suggest that economic growth over the past three decades has been sustained by increases in labour productivity rather than increases in employment. Technological progress has made it possible to use a small number of highly skilled workers at much higher levels of productivity, the benefits of which accrue in the form of higher profits and, to a limited extent, higher wages for a few so that much of the workforce is not part of these increments in output. The experience since 1980 suggests that this chain of causation describes the reality in most industrialized economies. It is just as true in many developing countries, in particular the emerging economies, where rapid economic growth has not been associated with commensurate employment creation, as the employment elasticity of output growth has declined almost everywhere in the age of markets and globalization.

This jobless growth is neither accident nor coincidence. It is the outcome of changes in policies that have stressed more openness in terms of trade, investment and finance. Such a worldview, of which orthodox macroeconomics and financial liberalization are an integral part, has meant an increase in the relative importance of foreign markets as compared to the domestic market, so that countries have sought to stimulate demand through an export surplus rather than demand management at home by governments through fiscal and monetary policies. There is, of course, a fallacy of composition here. It is not possible for all countries to achieve an export surplus at the same time. The export surplus of some must be matched by the import surplus of others. Even for some of the countries that run an export surplus, such policies may turn out to be counterproductive if the contraction in the domestic market turns out to be more than the expansion in external markets (Bhaduri, 2005a).

Yet, industrialized countries and emerging economies alike have attempted to be more price competitive than their rivals by reducing unit costs of production. This has been achieved by wage restraint and labour market flexibility on the one hand and raising labour productivity on the other. It is no surprise that integration into world markets has created a strong pressure to reduce costs through the labour market not simply to attain price competitiveness, but also to attract foreign investment. Such policies have carried the danger of a contraction in domestic demand, since wage restraint depresses consumption by workers at a macro level. At the same time, increases in labour productivity, brought about by a downsizing of the workforce through restructuring of firms at a micro level, reinforce this depressive effect.

The rate of employment growth in an economy reflects the difference between output growth and labour productivity growth. It is worth noting that there is a frequently observed positive association between output growth and productivity growth which reflects linkages between the supply side and the demand side (Nayyar, 2012). The essential idea is that more rapid output expansion may lead to the introduction of more productive technologies and the realization of dynamic scale economies, which are a function of cumulative past output or cumulative production experience and an increase in labour productivity. The cost reduction, insofar as it is passed on to consumers in the form of lower prices, would stimulate demand expansion in domestic and foreign markets. This increase in market size could once again facilitate the realization of scale economies, thus bringing about a cost reduction, just as a reduction in costs, if it lowers prices, could induce a demand expansion. However, for any technical change, if the rate of growth of labour productivity is faster than the rate of growth of output, the rate of employment growth declines and could after a point approximate to jobless growth. The cumulative causation then ceases to be virtuous, largely because there is little or no feedback on the demand side which turns out to be the weak link in the chain. In industrialized countries, this has been the case for the past three decades.

In the enthusiasm for supply-side economics, it is often forgotten that demand also matters. On the demand side, expansion can be wage-led when driven by consumption demand or profit-led when driven by investment demand, or a mix of both. During the golden age of capitalism, associated with rapid growth and full employment in the industrialized world, it was both wage-led and profit-led. In the age of markets and globalization, characterized by slower growth and much higher unemployment, it has clearly not been wage-led and has been only weakly profit-led. If aggregate demand is weakly profit-led, where a big change in productivity growth does not stimulate much growth in demand, the outcome would be little employment expansion. It is only if aggregate demand is strongly profit-led, where a big change in productivity growth does stimulate a significant demand expansion, the outcome would be more employment expansion which can at least maintain the rate of growth of employment (Taylor, 2010).

The story does not end with a recognition or explanation of the unfolding reality of jobless growth. It is also necessary to understand how and why this phenomenon might be responsible for lower rates of growth not only of employment, but also of output. The causation runs through income distribution. In industrialized countries, there is a redistribution of incomes from wages to profits and a redistribution of profits from the real sector, whether manufacturing or services, to the financial sector. The possibilities of wage-led growth are obviously constrained. But even profit-led growth is not quite feasible. The financial sector creates a demand for financial assets rather than goods and services, so that there is little or no employment creation. In fact, the shift in income and wealth to the super-rich creates a large demand drag. In developing countries, particularly emerging economies but elsewhere too, there is a similar redistribution of income from wages to profits that limits the possibilities of wage-led growth. There is, at the same time, a redistribution of profits, partly to the financial sector in emerging economies that are integrated into international financial markets, but in larger part to profits in the form of quasi-rents derived from property rights in land or in natural resources, acquired through patronage of governments, which also weakens profit-led growth.

The problem has been compounded by orthodox macroeconomic thinking, which is now deeply embedded in finance ministries and central banks across the world. Over the past three decades, the focus of macroeconomic policies, everywhere, has become narrower with the passage of time (Nayyar, 2007). In industrialized countries, with the decline of Keynesianism and the rise of monetarism, the objective shifted from full employment to price stability, premised on the belief that if the government achieves price stability, then the market will automatically achieve full employment. In the developing world, after many countries ran into debt crises or other forms of macroeconomic disequilibrium, macroeconomic policies sought to focus on stability defined largely in terms of prices rather than output or employment, so that controlling inflation and eliminating macroeconomic imbalances became the essential objectives. Again, the reason put forward was that if the government succeeded in achieving price stability in the short run all else, including growth, would follow. The presumption that full employment and economic growth would materialize as corollaries was belied by experience in both industrialized and developing countries (Stiglitz et al., 2006).

Resolving the problem

It would be exceedingly difficult to resolve these problems confronting the world economy without rethinking the macroeconomic policies that have accentuated the problems. The dominant ideology of our times has been dented, if not discredited, by the global economic crisis. And it is beginning to lose its stranglehold on thinking, at least in political processes, if not in the ivory towers of academia. There is a growing recognition that markets are no magic wand, and that the invisible hand of the market is not visible because it is not there and that markets are good servants but bad masters. It is clear that the financial crisis and the persistent recession provide an opportunity to rethink macroeconomic policies (2011b).

Such a rethinking must begin by redefining policy objectives. In the short term or in crisis situations, the prime concern should not be the stability of prices alone. The stability of output and employment is just as important. In the medium term or in normal times, the essential objective of macroeconomic policies cannot simply be the management of inflation and the elimination of macroeconomic imbalances. It should be just as much, if not more, about fostering employment creation and supporting economic growth. The rethinking must also extend to reconsidering policy instruments. Fiscal policy cannot be reduced to a means of reducing government deficits or restoring macroeconomic balances. It is a powerful instrument in the quest for full employment and economic growth. Monetary policy cannot be reduced to a means of controlling inflation through interest rates. It is a versatile instrument where both the price and volume of credit can be most effective in the pursuit of development objectives.

In sum, it is essential to return a developmental approach to macroeconomic policies, which is based on an integration of short-term countercyclical fiscal and monetary policies with long-term development objectives. This should shift the focus from the financial sector to the real economy, from the short term to the long term and from equilibrium to development. Economic growth with full employment should be the fundamental objective of macroeconomic policies (Nayyar, 2011b). Given the differences in the quality and maturity of institutions, the framework for macroeconomic policies in developing countries, in terms of objectives, instruments or stance, would have to be different from that in industrialized economies.

Such rethinking is easier said than done, because it requires doing away with some beliefs that have acquired sanctity in orthodoxy which exercises enormous influence. Orthodox macroeconomic policies are often shaped by a simple analogy between governments and households, which propagates the belief that, just as it is not possible for households to live beyond their means for it can only end in financial ruin, it is not possible for governments to live beyond their means for deficits and debt can both become unsustainable. The prescription is downsizing of government to balance income and expenditure. Of course, this reasoning is based on a false analogy. There is a fundamental distinction between good management of household finances by an individual and sensible management of the economy as a whole by the government. This distinction cannot and should not be blurred (Nayyar, 2012). The obsessive concern about deficits in government finances that borders on fetishism is misplaced. There is nothing in macroeconomics which stipulates an optimum level to which the fiscal deficit must be reduced as a proportion of GDP. The real issue is the end use, in relation to the cost, of borrowing. Thus, government borrowing is always sustainable, if it is used to finance investment and if the rate of return on such investment is higher than the interest rate payable. And it may sometimes be necessary for a government to borrow to finance non-investment expenditure, although that must be within limits (Nayyar, 2008). The essential point is that what is efficient for a household at a micro level is not necessarily efficient for the government at a macro level, because the whole is different from the sum total of the parts. Yet, orthodoxy about balanced budgets holds sway. However, this orthodoxy has somewhat different manifestations in industrialized economies and in developing countries (Nayyar, 2012).

In the industrialized world, the message of orthodox macroeconomics is clear. First, governments should focus on price stability and not on employment levels. Second, beyond balanced budgets, there is a need to downsize the government. The quest for price stability in a situation where rates of inflation are already so low leads to a slowdown in growth and an increase in unemployment combined with a downward pressure on real wages. It is no surprise that the stress on the supply side turns a blind eye to the demand side. Wages not only are costs on the supply side, but wages also determine market size on the demand side. And aggregate demand, which remains a determinant of growth, reinforces the slowdown. The belief in the necessity and virtue of downsizing governments leads, in one way or another, to a dilution and erosion of social protection. Unemployment benefits are streamlined. Pension plans are moved from defined benefit to defined contribution systems. Public provision of healthcare is reduced or significant user charges are introduced. Government support for education is lowered and fees paid by students are raised. In other words, there is a privatization of risk as forms of social insurance are progressively undermined. The increase in unemployment and the decrease in social protection, taken together, have the greatest impact on the living conditions of people who are most vulnerable. The economic downturn in industrialized countries, which followed the recent global financial crisis, did evoke a countercyclical policy response from governments, but given the bailouts for the financial sector it was inevitably associated with an increase in debts and deficits of governments. Orthodox macroeconomics seized the opportunity to argue that such deficits are unsustainable and cuts in government spending are essential. Fiscal retrenchment has begun, even if this solution turns out to be worse than the problem (Nayyar, 2011a).

In the developing world, orthodox macroeconomics prescribes two essentials. First, in situations of disequilibrium or crisis, governments should not attempt to attain full employment. Instead, governments are urged to accept the pain of adjustment, in the form of lower output today for a higher output tomorrow. This recommendation conforms to the strong spring analogy: the harder you push the spring down, the greater the force with which it bounces back. But a weak spring is a more appropriate analogy for the economy, for when it is pushed too hard, it may simply remain there if its restorative forces are destroyed. Second, as a rule, governments should just focus on price stability. This is simply not appropriate. In countries where inflation is already moderate or low, concerted policy efforts to reduce it further at the margin may yield only small benefits but impose large costs, for it squeezes employment in the short term and dampens growth in the medium term. The problem is that, in developing countries, even under normal circumstances, there is a procyclical pattern to macroeconomic policies. This problem is accentuated by orthodoxy in macroeconomics, which advocates a restrictive fiscal policy and a tight monetary policy (Nayyar, 2008). Fiscal contraction is associated with cuts in public expenditure on social sectors which hurt the poor, and cuts in public investment on infrastructure which constrain growth. Similarly, a tight monetary policy constrains growth, as higher interest rates dampen private investment and lead to more failures in firms.

The time has come to dispense with these shibboleths, not only to resolve the problem of jobless growth, but also to revive economic growth.

In industrialized countries, it is necessary to revive wage-led growth and strengthen profit-led growth. For the former, there are two essentials: the restoration of full employment as an objective and an increase in real wages. This would ensure that a part of the benefits from growth in output and productivity accrue to workers, which would mean some redistribution of income from profits to wages. That would stimulate consumption demand. For the latter, there has to be some redistribution of profits from the financial sector to the real sector, to stimulate investment demand. That would require closer regulation of innovative instruments, such as over-the-counter derivative swaps, in financial markets, which allow profits of the super-rich to be invested in financial assets rather than real products.

In developing countries, wage-led growth is possible only through employment creation, even if full employment is not an attainable objective, as it would drive growth through expanding consumption demand in the domestic market. It is just as important to stimulate investment demand not simply for profit-led growth on the demand side, but also for creating production capacities on the supply side. There are complementarities between public investment in infrastructure and private investment in manufacturing that could be exploited. At the same time, it would be wise to hasten slowly in financial deregulation and liberalization, which could redistribute profits from the real sector to the financial sector that could, in turn, dampen investment in manufacturing or services and curb the potential for employment expansion.

The moral of the story is clear enough. There are no trade-offs between job creation and output growth, so that it is misleading to present it as an either-or choice. In fact, there are strong complementarities between employment creation and economic growth. Growth can create jobs, and jobs can drive growth. Indeed, the two can reinforce each other through an interaction between the supply side and the demand side, to create a virtuous circle of cumulative causation. It is just as important to recognize that more employment generation or faster job creation in the process of economic growth would simultaneously address the problem of increasing economic inequality between people, by reducing inequality or preventing it from rising as much as it otherwise would. Similarly, an improvement in the quality of employment, which provides decent work (ILO, 1999), would also contribute to a reduction in economic inequalities. This is particularly important in developing countries where average income levels are low, but it is just as significant in industrialized countries where average income levels are much higher.

Employment as a solution

It is not surprising that my analysis of why employment matters, in the wider macroeconomic context of the world economy, has sought to focus on industrialized countries and emerging economies. But, it must be stressed that employment is of utmost importance at every stage of development.

In most countries at low levels of income and in earlier stages of development, which are capital scarce, there is surplus labour that is underemployed irrespective of the endowment of land or natural resources. Hence, their most abundant resource, labour, is underutilized. Macroeconomics in developing countries is, at least in part, about mobilizing and creating resources, not only financial resources, but also real resources, for development. Employment creation can both mobilize and create resources (Nayyar, 2012). It constitutes resource mobilization beyond financial resources, which are the usual concern of macroeconomics, in as much as it mobilizes the most abundant yet underutilized resource, people, for development. The absorption of surplus labour in employment, then, is an important source of economic growth. It constitutes resource creation in so far as it increases the productivity of labour, for any given level of technological development, introducing another source of economic growth. The same people, who constitute resources on the supply side, provide markets on the demand side in the process of development. This interactive causation, which is a potential source of economic growth, is possible but not automatic or assured. It may not materialize if employment opportunities are not created or are not sufficient.

Thus, employment matters as a driver of economic growth. And if economic growth is to be transformed into meaningful development, which improves the well-being of people, employment creation is essential insofar as it provides income opportunities. In countries where absolute poverty is widespread, social safety nets that require transfer payments in perpetuity might mitigate the situation, but employment that provides livelihoods is the only sustainable means of reducing and, ultimately, eradicating poverty. Given this reality, many governments in developing countries have discovered the idea of inclusive growth. Some of it is just populist rhetoric. In a few countries, governments in search of political legitimacy set aside resources for the poor, often in terms of allocations to social sectors or public services. But the bottom line cannot change. Any process of economic growth is pro-poor if, and only if, it creates employment opportunities that provide sufficient incomes to lift people out of poverty.

The conclusion that follows is simple. Employment is the solution, which must not be seen as a problem. For people who do not have the income to meet their basic needs, such as food, clothing and shelter, let alone healthcare and education, employment opportunities are the only sustainable means of reducing and eradicating their poverty. But that is not all. In poor countries, employment can drive economic growth both from the supply side and the demand side. The pursuit of full employment in industrialized countries and employment expansion in emerging economies could revive economic growth and drive recovery in the world economy. At the same time, employment, in the form of decent work that yields sufficient incomes, could also do much to address the problems associated with rising economic inequalities between people everywhere in the world.

In this context, it is necessary to recognize that, while the number of jobs created makes an enormous difference, the quality of employment also matters. This is so because the world of work is diverse (Sen, 2000; Nayyar, 2003b). Every person works in one way or another. But not everyone in employed. A significant proportion of this work, however, is not sufficiently recognized or adequately rewarded. There are many who work hard for a living. There are a few who hardly work and yet lead a comfortable life. There are some who work very hard but do not earn enough for a living. There are others who work but are not paid for their labour. The reality is complex and is changing. The developing world is full of overworked and underemployed or unemployed people. Many of them do not earn enough to meet their basic human needs. Working conditions are poor even in the formal sector and often worse in the informal sector. For a large proportion of the workforce, there is little, if any, security of employment. In industrialized countries, unemployment rates are much higher than in the past. Social protection is being diluted. Risk is being privatized. Hence, the unemployed are more vulnerable. There is also a casualization of the workforce, as permanent employees in the workplace are being turned into contract workers at home who are engaged for limited durations or specified purposes, so that work no longer means what it did. For such people, there is no security of employment. Superannuation benefits and healthcare benefits provided by the employer also cease. It would seem that, for a large number of people, the quality of employment is poor in developing countries and worsening in industrialized countries. In this situation, if employment created also provides decent work, it would be more effective in mitigating the rising inequality between people. Higher job quality would lower economic inequalities.

The moral of the story, then, is that a focus on employment, as the primary objective rather than as a residual outcome, is absolutely essential. Conventional thinking seeks to focus on the objectives of GDP growth at a macro level and productivity growth at the micro level. There is, perhaps, a more useful way of thinking about GDP growth directly in terms of employment growth. The growth of employment and the growth in labour productivity, measured as output per worker, together add up to the growth in GDP. If the employment growth rate is increased by 1 per cent, the GDP growth rate would also increase, provided labour productivity does not fall by 1 per cent or more. In other words, if it is possible to raise the employment growth rate, without inducing an equivalent or greater reduction in labour productivity growth, the growth rate of the economy can only be higher (Bhaduri, 2005b). It should thus be possible to focus on employment growth as the objective.

This should also lead to some rethinking about the meaning of efficiency beyond the usual conceptions of economic efficiency or technical efficiency. Indeed, employment expansion is at least as important as productivity increase. In a sense, both represent the utilization of labour as a resource. Why, then, is thinking about efficiency focus on one and neglect the other? It is time, perhaps, to reflect on the meaning of efficiency, which must extend beyond output per worker or productivity increase to expansion of employment and labour use. Such an idea could make a real difference.

Conclusions

In conclusion, it is worth reiterating the essential messages that emerge from this chapter. Governments should rethink macroeconomic policies by redefining policy objectives and reconsidering policy instruments, so that the focus is on fostering employment creation and supporting economic growth rather than on price stability and balanced budgets. Employers should recognize that wages are not only costs on the supply side, but are also incomes on the demand side, which means that profit-led growth and wage-led growth are complements not substitutes, and that what is good for employment is good for economic growth, where the connection is causal. Trade Unions represent their members who are employed, but they should also attempt to speak for, even if they do not represent, the unemployed and the underemployed, so that in situations of unemployment they should use their voice in the political process and influence on economic policies to maximize employment levels and, if possible, return to full employment, as the pursuit of this objective would be in the collective interest of workers. It is time, perhaps, for all three constituencies to strive for a social contract. This needs change in both economics and politics. In the sphere of economics, the meaning of efficiency must extend beyond output per worker and productivity increase to employment expansion and labour use. In the realm of politics, employment must once again become an integral part of the discourse and the process, as a primary objective rather than a residual outcome.

Acknowledgement

The author would like to thank Amit Bhaduri, Rolph van der Hoeven and Lance Taylor for helpful comments on a preliminary draft.

References

Akyuz, Yilmaz (2011). 'Export Dependence and the Sustainability of Growth in China', *China and World Economy*, Vol. 19, No. 1, pp. 1–23.

Atkinson, Anthony B., Thomas Piketty and Edward Saez (2012). 'Top Incomes in the Long Run of History', in A. B. Atkinson and T. Piketty (eds.), *Top Incomes: A Global Perspective*, Oxford: Oxford University Press.

Bhaduri, Amit (2005a). 'Joblessness', in E. Hershberg and C. Thornton (eds.), *The Development Alternative: Toward a People-Centred Approach*, New York: Social Science Research Council.

Bhaduri, Amit (2005b). *Development with Dignity: A Case for Full Employment*, New Delhi: National Book Trust.

ILO (1999). *Decent Work*, Report of the Director-General, International Labour Conference, Geneva: International Labour Office.

Nayyar, Deepak (ed.) (2002). *Governing Globalization: Issues and Institutions*, Oxford: Oxford University Press.

Nayyar, Deepak (2003a). 'Globalization and Development Strategies', in John Toye (ed.), *Trade and Development: Directions for the Twenty-First Century*, Cheltenham: Edward Elgar.

Nayyar, Deepak (2003b). 'Work, Livelihoods and Rights', *Indian Journal of Labour Economics*, Vol. 46, No. 1, pp. 3–13.

Nayyar, Deepak (2007). 'Macroeconomics in Developing Countries', *Banca Nazionale del Lavoro Quarterly Review*, Vol. LIX, No. 242, pp. 249–269.

Nayyar, Deepak (2008). 'Macroeconomics of Structural Adjustment and Public Finance in Developing Countries', *International Journal of Development Issues*, Vol. 7, No. 1, pp. 4–28.

Nayyar, Deepak (2011a). 'The Financial Crisis, the Great Recession and the Developing World', *Global Policy*, Vol. 2, No. 1, pp. 20–32.

Nayyar, Deepak (2011b). 'Rethinking Macroeconomic Policies for Development', *Brazilian Journal of Political Economy*, Vol. 31, No. 3, pp. 339–351.

Nayyar, Deepak (2012). 'Macroeconomics and Human Development', *Journal of Human Development and Capabilities*, Vol. 13, No. 1, pp. 7–30.

Nayyar, Deepak (2013). *Catch Up: Developing Countries in the World Economy*, Oxford: Oxford University Press.

Palma, J. Gabriel (2011). 'Homogeneous Middles vs. Heterogeneous Tails, and the End of the Inverted-U: It's All about the Share of the Rich', *Development and Change*, Vol. 42, pp. 87–153.

Piketty, Thomas (2014). *Capital in the Twenty-First Century*, Cambridge, MA: Harvard University Press.

Sen, Amartya (2000). 'Work and Rights', *International Labour Review*, Vol. 139, No. 2, pp. 119–128.

Stiglitz, Joseph E., Jose Antonio Ocampo, Shari Spiegel, Ricardo Ffrench-Davis and Deepak Nayyar (2006). *Stability with Growth: Macroeconomics, Liberalization and Development*, Oxford: Oxford University Press.

Taylor, Lance (2010). *Maynard's Revenge: The Collapse of Free Market Macroeconomics*, Cambridge, MA: Harvard University Press.

World Commission on the Social Dimension of Globalization (2004). *A Fair Globalization: Creating Opportunities for All*, Geneva.

3

MACROECONOMICS AND HUMAN DEVELOPMENT

Introduction

The object of this chapter is to analyse the relationship between macroeconomics and human development. The interdependence and the interconnections between them are seldom explored in the literature in either domain. There is, of course, some literature on economic growth and human development. And economic growth is an important dimension of macroeconomics. There is, also, an extensive literature on income distribution and economic growth. And income distribution matters for human development. But this paper is about neither of those intersections. It seeks to examine the interactions between macroeconomics, in terms of objectives or policies, and human development, which is about the well-being of people. Each can, and often does, exercise a significant influence on the other. Hence, it is necessary to understand the nature and the direction of causation. At the same time, even if the focus of the literature on human development is almost entirely on the developing world, it is necessary to recognize that this relationship also exists and could matter in industrial societies. The similarities and differences between poor countries and rich countries, in this sphere, deserve more attention.

The structure of the discussion is as follows. First, it explains why the intersection between macroeconomics and human development has diminished over time, although there was some cognition about it in the past and there is an obvious interdependence in the present. Second, it analyses the implications and consequences of macroeconomics for human development, which could be positive or negative, in both developing countries and industrialized countries. Third, it examines the implications and consequences of the quest for or attainment of human development for macroeconomics, which could be positive or negative, and may differ across countries depending on the level of income or stage of development. Fourth, it considers the significance of the political context, where ideology, institutions and interests exercise a strong influence on economic policies in both spheres to shape outcomes. The final section draws together some conclusions that emerge.

Diminishing intersections

The intersection between macroeconomics and human development has diminished significantly with the passage of time. The concerns of macroeconomics have become narrower, while the conception of development, in particular human development, has become wider.

Over the past three decades, the focus of macroeconomic policies, everywhere, has become narrower. In industrialized countries, the traditional objectives were internal balance and external balance.[1] Internal balance was defined as full employment and price stability, which would be conducive to economic growth. External balance was defined as equilibrium in the balance of payments, primarily with reference to the current account. The decline of Keynesianism and the rise of monetarism in the mid-1970s led to a profound change. The conception of internal balance came to be confined to price stability, so that full employment was no longer an integral part of the objective.[2] This was partly attributable to the belief that if the government achieves price stability, then the market will automatically achieve full employment. Since then, the notion of external balance has been progressively diluted in a world of capital account liberalization. In developing countries, the traditional concern was economic growth in the long term, subject to the constraints that inflation remained within limits of tolerance and that the current account deficit in the balance of payments remained within manageable proportions. The focus of policies shifted to macromanagement in the short term after many developing countries, to begin with in Latin America during the early 1980s and soon thereafter in sub-Saharan Africa, ran into debt crises or other forms of macroeconomic disequilibrium. Again, the reason put forward was that if the government succeeded in achieving price stability in the short run, all else, including growth, would follow. The presumption that full employment and economic growth would materialize as corollaries was belied by experience in both industrialized and developing countries.[3]

Macroeconomics was developed in and for industrialized economies. Theory and policy were both concerned with how monetary and fiscal policies should be used to attain stipulated objectives. The narrow focus led to an apparent convergence of objectives. Hence, this corpus of knowledge was sought to be used in developing economies without any significant modification. Such transplantation was simply not appropriate for two reasons.[4] First, the nature of relationships (between variables) and the direction of causation (what determines what) in macroeconomics are both a function of the setting or the context. The starting point for any macroeconomic analysis is the distinction between exogenous and endogenous variables or that between autonomous and induced changes. Such a distinction is essential in macroeconomic theorizing, which seeks to analyse implications and prescribe policies. It is important to recognize that this distinction is derived not from the analytical structure but from the institutional setting of models.[5] Second, there are systematic differences in the structural characteristics of developing economies as compared with industrialized economies. These span a wide range from differences in the constraints on output expansion, the degree of wage price flexibility, the sources of growth, the development of financial markets, institutions and instruments or the capacity of governments to finance their deficits to the ability to cope with shocks and crises.[6] There are also significant differences among developing countries. And even if some laws of economics are universal, the functioning of economies can be markedly different. Therefore, good economic theory and sensible policy analysis should recognize rather than ignore such myriad differences. But orthodox thinking, which became dominant, simply ignored these differences.

Until the early 1980s, macroeconomic policies in developing countries were embedded in broader growth-oriented development strategies. These policies recognized the differences in structural characteristics of economies and incorporated a longer term perspective. But this approach changed for two reasons. First, macroeconomic instabilities and crises in developing countries surfaced and spread. Second, there was a shift from the Keynesian consensus on countercyclical demand management for full employment to the more conservative monetarist view that sought to control inflation. The control of inflation and the elimination of (internal and external) macroeconomic imbalances became the essential objectives. Orthodoxy stressed the importance of a stable macroeconomic environment. Macroeconomic policies sought to focus on stability, defined largely in terms of prices. Short-term stabilization, in a narrow sense, came to be seen as the path to long-term growth. This new orthodoxy prevailed, as it was imposed on economies in crisis by the IMF and the World Bank and was reinforced by international financial markets. Inflation was reduced and fiscal balances were restored. But this did not contribute to higher or faster growth. Indeed, stabilization often induced procyclical macro policies that squeezed or stifled public and private investment, and thereby hurt economic growth.[7]

In sharp contrast, the conception of development, with its present focus on the well-being of people, has become much wider over the past 50 years. In the early 1950s, conventional thinking identified development with growth in GDP or GDP per capita. The earlier literature emphasized economic growth and capital accumulation at a macro level. The contemporary literature emphasizes economic efficiency and productivity increases at a micro level. Industrialization has always been seen as an essential attribute of development. The emphasis has simply shifted from the pace of industrialization to the efficiency of industrialization. The underlying presumption is that economic growth and economic efficiency are not only necessary, but also sufficient for bringing about an improvement in the living conditions of people. From time to time, dissenting voices questioned conventional wisdom to suggest other indicators of development, but these were largely ignored by mainstream economics. And, even 50 years later, orthodoxy, economic growth or increases in per capita remain the most important measure of development.

The early 1970s witnessed the emergence of a heterodox literature that suggested other indicators of development, such as a reduction in poverty, inequality and unemployment, which would capture changes in the quality of life.[8] This thinking moved further. Development, it was argued, must bring about an improvement in the living conditions of people. It should, therefore, ensure the provision of basic human needs for all: not just food and clothing, but also shelter, health care and education.[9] It was stressed that this simple but powerful proposition is often forgotten in the conventional concerns of economics. Such thinking culminated in writings on and an index of human development.[10]

In the late 1990s, Amartya Sen provided the broadest possible conception of development as freedom: a process of expanding real freedoms that people enjoy for their economic well-being, social opportunities and political rights.[11] Such freedoms are not just constitutive as the primary ends of development. Such freedoms are also instrumental as the principal means of attaining development. What is more, there are strong interconnections that link different freedoms with one another. Political freedoms help promote economic security. Social opportunities facilitate economic participation. Economic well-being supports social facilities and reinforces political rights. In this manner, freedoms of different kinds strengthen one another. The purpose of development, in this worldview, is to create a milieu that enables people – ordinary people – to lead a good life. Development must, therefore, provide all men and women the rights, the opportunities and the capabilities they need to exercise their own choices for a decent life.

It is essential, then, to make a distinction between means and ends. Economic growth and economic efficiency, or for that matter industrialization, are means. It is development which is an end. Much of the focus in the literature on development is on economies. But aggregates often conceal more than they reveal. Per capita income is only an arithmetic mean. Social indicators are also statistical averages. And neither captures the well-being of the poor. Even the human development index is not quite an exception. Thus, it is important to shift the focus from countries to people. However, in this conceptualization of development, people are not just beneficiaries. It is only if people are centre stage in the process of development as the main actors that development can empower people to participate in the decisions that shape their lives. The significance of this proposition is highlighted by the medieval distinction between agents and patients, which is invoked by Amartya Sen. He argues that the freedom-centred understanding of economics and of the process of development is very much an agent-oriented view. This is because individuals with adequate social opportunities can effectively shape their own destiny and help each other. They must not be seen primarily as patients or passive recipients of the benefits of cunning development programmes.[12]

The outcome of changing concerns and shifting emphasis is not surprising. In the conventional discourse on macroeconomics, human development is at best marginal and at worst irrelevant. In the unconventional discourse on human development, macroeconomics or its constraints are seldom recognized, even if its consequences are often highlighted. There is an irony in the situation that is striking, when compared with ideas from the past or juxtaposed with experience from the present.

The ideas that economic growth at the macro level is ultimately about the well-being of people at the micro level, or that investment in people, say in the form of education, supports productivity increase and wealth creation in the economy have a distinguished lineage in economics. For Adam Smith, the wealth created by labour in every nation provided necessities and conveniences of life to people, while the education of people was clearly an important source of the wealth of nations. In other words, even if not stated in an explicit manner, there is some implied connection between the wealth of nations and the well-being of their people.

The present situation in the world economy, as well as experience from the recent past, also highlights the intersection between macroeconomics and human development. The financial crisis that surfaced in late 2008, which turned into the Great Recession that persists in the world economy, led to a slowdown in growth and a contraction in employment not only in the industrialized countries, but also in the developing world, thus affecting the well-being of people everywhere.[13] The financial crisis in Asia during the late 1990s led to similar consequences albeit on a smaller scale. The story was not very different with the financial crises that ravaged many Latin American economies somewhat earlier in the 1990s. The change in macroeconomic objectives and the reorientation of macroeconomic policies, combined with financial liberalization, were almost certainly responsible for these outcomes. More of the same in terms of macroeconomic policies can only compound the problem. Yet, macroeconomic policies, even if very different, would have to be an integral part of any solution. Of course, this is just one dimension of the interdependence. It is, perhaps, more persuasive because the outcome is real and the connection is obvious.

However, it must be recognized that the relationship between macroeconomics and human development is complex. It has multiple dimensions. And the causation runs in both directions. The world of macroeconomics has important implications and consequences for human development. These could be positive or negative. But that is not all. There may also be discernible differences between developing countries and industrialized countries. The quest for, or level of, human development has significant implications and consequences for macroeconomics, which could be positive or negative, with plausible differences between developing countries and industrialized countries.

From macroeconomics to human development

Macroeconomic objectives and policies, everywhere, have distributional implications and social consequences. Such implications and consequences are often not among the core concerns of macroeconomics. Yet, macroeconomics has profound implications for the well-being of people. The living standards of people depend upon their private income and public entitlements. Thus, if we abstract from savings, private income which supports private consumption, in turn, depends on employment levels for those in the world of work and social protection for those who are unemployed. The level of employment and the degree of social protection are both determined in the sphere of macroeconomics. Public entitlements, which support social consumption, depend upon the magnitude of resources made available by governments for the public provision of services, such as health care and education, once again determined in the sphere of macroeconomics. Therefore, macroeconomic objectives and policies could improve or worsen the well-being of people. Of course, observed outcomes may also be shaped or influenced by a wide range of other factors.

The consequences may be positive where macroeconomic policies pursue full employment as an objective, strengthen social protection and set aside resources for social consumption. This also requires countercyclical fiscal and monetary policies in the short run which stabilize the level of economic activity, hence output and employment. At the same time, macro policies need to be conducive to economic growth in the medium term or long run.

It is worth noting that such macroeconomic policies were, in fact, adopted by the industrialized countries during the period from the late 1940s to the early 1970s. This era, described as the *golden age of capitalism*, was associated with full employment, price stability and rapid growth. It also witnessed a continuous increase in the real incomes of industrial workers who constituted a large proportion of the population in the industrialized world. Full employment was critical in the process, as it meant real wages could rise. Clearly, macroeconomic objectives and policies did contribute to an improvement in the well-being of people.[14]

During the same period, in developing countries, macroeconomic policies were shaped by growth-oriented development strategies with a long-term perspective. In these surplus labour economies, full employment was not an attainable objective. And even if there was no significant reduction in the incidence of poverty or improvement in the well-being of ordinary people, there was a substantial step up in growth rates that represented a radical departure from the past when compared with stagnation or decline in the colonial era. The problem was that economic growth was not associated with sufficient employment creation.[15] But this growth might have helped create the initial conditions and lay the essential foundations of subsequent development in some of these countries. In doing so, it might have created some space for progress in terms of human development.

It is plausible to argue that, though impossible to prove, the positive causation which runs from macroeconomics to human development is stronger in developing countries at low levels of income and low levels of human development, while it is weaker in industrialized countries at high levels of income and high levels of human development. The intuitive reasons are simple enough. For one, in developing countries, macroeconomic policies need to be conducive to employment creation, which provides livelihoods and must set aside resources for social protection as well as public entitlements to support consumption, health-care and education that are so essential for the poor who constitute a large proportion of the population. Starting from low levels of nutrition, health and literacy, at the margin, increases in private income, social protection and public entitlements can and do lead substantial progress in terms of the human development index.[16] For another, in industrialized countries that are at full employment, or close to it, and most people are already at high levels of nutrition, health and literacy, at the margin, increases in social protection or public entitlements cannot lead to much progress in terms of measures such as the human development index. However, even if levels of unemployment are high, which is a fact in industrialized countries, following the global economic crisis, levels of human development remain high in terms of nutrition, literacy and health.

The consequences may be negative where macroeconomic policies focus on price stability (at the expense of full employment), dilute social protection and cut public expenditure on social sectors. The problem may be accentuated if this is juxtaposed with procyclical fiscal and monetary policies in the short run, which tend to dampen, if not stifle growth in the medium term. Such causation from macroeconomics to human development, which is negative and can be cumulative, characterizes both developing countries and industrialized economies at the present conjuncture. It is driven in part by orthodox macroeconomics and in part by financial liberalization.

Orthodox macroeconomic policies are often shaped by a simple analogy between governments and households, which propagates the belief that, just as it is not possible for households to live beyond their means for it can only end in financial ruin, it is not possible for governments to live beyond their means for deficits and debt can both become unsustainable. The moral of the story is downsizing of government to balance income and expenditure. Given the dominant ideology of our times in both economics and politics, increasing income through taxation is ruled out. Indeed, tax cuts are often on the agenda. Expenditure cuts, then, provide the answer. Of course, this reasoning is based on a false analogy. There is a fundamental distinction between good management of household finances by an individual and sensible management of the economy as a whole by the government. This distinction cannot and should not be blurred. It is not possible for a household to live beyond its means because borrowing to meet consumption expenditure is unsustainable. It is possible for a government to borrow for financing investment expenditure, provided the rate of return on such investment is higher than the interest rate on borrowing. And, it may sometimes be necessary for a government to borrow to finance non-investment expenditure, although that must be within limits. The essential point is that what is efficient for a household at a micro level is not necessarily efficient for the government at a macro level, because the whole is different from the sum total of the parts. Yet, orthodoxy about balanced budgets holds sway. However, this orthodoxy has somewhat different manifestations in developing countries and in industrialized economies.

In the developing world, orthodox macroeconomics prescribes two essentials. First, in situations of disequilibrium or crisis, governments should not attempt to attain full employment. Instead, governments are urged to accept the pain of adjustment, in the form of lower output today for a higher output tomorrow. This recommendation conforms to the strong spring analogy: the harder you push the spring down, the greater the force with which it bounces back. But a weak spring is a more appropriate analogy for the economy, for when it is pushed too hard, it may simply remain there if its restorative forces are destroyed. Second, as a rule, governments should just focus on price stability.[17] This is simply not appropriate. Since the early 1990s, most developing countries and transition economies have experienced moderate or low inflation. In countries where inflation is already moderate or low, concerted policy efforts to reduce it further, at the margin, may yield only small benefits but impose large costs for it squeezes employment in the short term and dampens growth in the medium term.[18] The problem is that, in developing countries, even under normal circumstances, there is a procyclical pattern to macroeconomic policies.[19] This problem is accentuated by orthodoxy in macroeconomics which advocates a restrictive fiscal policy and a tight monetary policy. Fiscal contraction is associated with cuts in public expenditure on social sectors, which hurt the poor, and cuts in public investment on infrastructure, which constrain growth. Similarly, a tight monetary policy constrains growth, as higher interest rates dampen private investment and lead to more failures in firms.[20] The consequences for human development are obviously negative, as the resources available for social protection and public entitlements contract while dampened growth reduces employment possibilities.[21]

In the industrialized world, the message of orthodox macroeconomics is similar. First, governments should focus on price stability and not on employment levels. Second, beyond balanced budgets, there is a need to downsize the government. The quest for price stability in a situation, where rates of inflation are already so low, leads to a slowdown in growth and an increase in unemployment combined with a downward pressure on real wages. It is no surprise that the stress on the supply side turns a blind eye to the demand side. Wages are costs on the supply side, but wages also determine market size on the demand side. And aggregate demand, which remains a determinant of growth, reinforces the slowdown. The belief in the necessity and virtue of downsizing governments leads, in one way or another, to a dilution and erosion of social protection. Unemployment benefits are streamlined. Pension plans are moved from defined benefit to defined contribution systems. Public provision of healthcare is reduced or significant user charges are introduced. Government support for education is lowered and fees paid by students are raised. In other words, there is a privatization of risk as forms of social insurance are progressively undermined. The increase in unemployment and the decrease in social protection, taken together, have the greatest impact on the living conditions of people who are most vulnerable. The economic downturn in industrialized countries, which followed the recent global financial crisis, did evoke a countercyclical policy response from governments, but given the bailouts for the financial sector it was inevitably associated with an increase in debts and deficits of governments. Orthodox macroeconomics seized the opportunity to argue that such deficits are unsustainable and cuts in government spending are essential. Fiscal retrenchment has begun, even if this solution turns out to be worse than the problem. The problem of unemployment and the erosion of social protection can only persist, if not intensify. Clearly, such macroeconomic policies will adversely affect the well-being of vulnerable or poor people in industrial societies, even if it does not reflect in a measure like the human development index.

There are two dimensions of financial liberalization: deregulation of domestic financial sectors and capital account liberalization. It began life around 1980. This coincided with the changed thinking in macroeconomics. And it was not long before the internationalization of finance spread to developing countries and across the world economy. Such financialization of economies led to significant changes in the nature of and space for macro policies not only in industrialized countries, but also in the developing world.[22] Most important, perhaps, it reduced degrees of freedom in the use of macroeconomic policies. Integration into the world financial system constrained countries in using an autonomous management of demand to maintain levels of output and employment. Expansionary fiscal and monetary policies – large government deficits to stimulate aggregate demand or low interest rates to encourage domestic investment – could no longer be used because of an overwhelming fear that such measures could lead to speculative capital flight and a run on the national currency.[23] In fact, the oversensitivity of international financial markets to inflation meant that macroeconomic policies, everywhere, came to target inflation instead of employment levels or output stability. The outcome was economic volatility and increasing fragility reflected in boom-bust cycles, as capital flows tended to be procyclical. Financialization exposed emerging economies and developing countries to exogenous shocks and industrialized countries to endogenous shocks.[24] The mobility of capital in a world with almost no mobility of labour repressed wages and reduced taxes. Developing countries needed high interest rates and strong exchange rates to sustain portfolio investment, or other similar capital flows, in terms of profitability and confidence. Thus, exchange rates could no longer be used as a strategic device to provide an entry into the world market for manufactured goods, just as interest rates could no longer be used as a strategic instrument for guiding the allocation of scarce investible resources in a market economy. It would seem that the liberalization and internationalization of finance reinforced orthodox macroeconomics in coaxing or pushing governments to adopt policies that were not conducive to economic growth or employment creation, while the costs of the associated volatility, fragility and crises had to be borne by the poor in developing countries and the vulnerable in industrial societies.

It is reasonable to infer that the negative causation that runs from macroeconomics to human development exists not only in developing countries, but also in industrialized countries. After all, restrictive fiscal policies and tight monetary policies contract employment and dampen growth everywhere. However, the manifestations and the consequences are somewhat different. In developing countries, macroeconomic crises or orthodox policies cut public expenditure on social sectors, thus reducing public entitlements or social consumption. What is more, at low levels of income and low levels of human development, it hurts poor people whose private income is not large enough to support expenditure on healthcare or education, which public provision provides.[25] In industrialized countries, orthodox macroeconomic policies dilute, erode or undermine social protection, thus privatizing risk. Even at higher levels of income and higher levels of human development, which are just statistical averages, this has an adverse effect on the well-being of the people who are vulnerable or live in relative poverty. Financial liberalization, with the shocks or crises it unleashes, tends to reinforce such outcomes in both sets of countries.

From human development to macroeconomics

Given the strong causation that runs from macroeconomics to human development, it should be no surprise if human development has implications and consequences for macroeconomics. But this is not among the core concerns of the literature on human development. Indeed, this literature is conspicuously silent on the concerns and dilemmas of macroeconomics.[26] There is, however, some attempt to explore the dynamics of the relationship between economic growth and human development.[27] Of course, if human development does have an impact on growth or stability in economies at a macro level, it is bound to have implications for macroeconomic management and macroeconomic policies. The consequences may be positive, if human development makes macroeconomic management simpler and enlarges the space for macroeconomic policies. The consequences may be negative, if human development makes macroeconomic management more difficult and diminishes the space for macroeconomic policies. Clearly, it may be difficult to attribute cause and effect, since observed outcomes may also be shaped by a wide range of other factors.

There is a basic proposition in the existing literature that is widely accepted, which states that education contributes to economic growth through increased productivity. In agriculture, evidence suggests that education raises productivity by enabling farmers to use modern technologies.[28] This proposition is also a basic tenet in theories of economic growth. Human capital is an important input in the Solow model. In the new growth theories, technical progress, which incorporates education as also R&D, is endogenous. It is also argued that technical progress depends upon R&D levels. Once again, there is a critical role for education which contributes to R&D as well as learning.[29] Thus, education, which is an essential part of human development, makes a positive contribution to economic growth.[30] The idea can be stretched to incorporate nutrition and health, which also influence productivity. There is obviously a link. But this does not quite establish a connection with macroeconomics.

It is possible to think of a connection, with some causality that may be positive, between human development and macroeconomics. In most developing countries, which are capital scarce, there is surplus labour that is underemployed irrespective of the endowment of land or natural resources. Hence, their most abundant resource, labour, is underutilized. Macroeconomics in developing countries is, at least in part, about mobilizing and creating resources, not only financial resources, but also real resources, for development. Human development, which imparts capabilities to people, can both mobilize and create resources. It constitutes resource mobilization beyond financial resources, which are the usual concern of macroeconomics, in as much as it mobilizes the most abundant yet underutilized resource, people, for development. The absorption of surplus labour in employment, then, is an important source of economic growth. It constitutes resource creation, in so far as it increases the productivity of labour for any given level of technological development, introducing another source of economic growth. The same people, who constitute resources on the supply side, provide markets on the demand side in the process of development. This causation is possible but not automatic or assured. It may not materialize, if employment opportunities are not created or are not sufficient. But if the supply of labour so created is matched by a demand, human development could make macroeconomic management easier and enlarge the space for macroeconomic policies. However, this causation is not a plausible story in the context of industrialized countries. For one, the working population in industrial societies already has the essential attributes of human development in terms of nutrition, literacy and health, even if does not have choices and freedoms in the wider conception of human development. For another, most industrial societies approximate to full employment, even if unemployment rates are high at present, but in so far as there is unemployment it is not attributable to the absence of capabilities in the workforce. Therefore, it is reasonable to infer that the positive causation from human development to macroeconomics is strong in developing countries at low levels of income and low levels of human development, but is weak in industrialized countries at high levels of income and high levels of human development.

It is also possible to think of a connection, with a clear causality that may be negative, between human development and macroeconomics. There is such a negative causation that exists in both developing countries and industrialized countries. In addition, there are two other plausible chains of negative causation that exist only in industrial societies. Consider these in turn.

The common cause is 'jobless growth'. In developing countries, it is possible that proactive policies foster human development and improve the capabilities of people with nutrition, healthcare and education. This, in itself, would improve the quality of life. But if there are no employment opportunities for job seekers, it will only lead to more unemployment, now of the educated or self-employment that is not above subsistence levels. And, if population growth continues, poverty may simply persist. In such situations, investing in people as an approach may be characterized by the same logical flaw as Say's law that 'supply creates its own demand'.[31] In other words, supply without demand or capabilities without opportunities serve little purpose. But that is not all. It is perfectly possible that economic growth is sustained by increases in labour productivity rather than increases in employment. And, human development which imparts capabilities to people makes it possible to use a small number of highly skilled workers at much higher levels of productivity, while much of the workforce is not part of these increments in output. The experience since 1980 suggests that this chain of causation describes the reality in most industrialized economies. It is just as true in many developing countries, in particular the emerging economies, where rapid economic growth has not been associated with commensurate employment creation, as the employment elasticity of output growth has declined almost everywhere in the age of markets and globalization.

This is neither accident nor coincidence. It is the outcome of changes in policies that have stressed more openness in terms of trade, investment and finance. Such a worldview, of which orthodox macroeconomics and financial liberalization are an integral part, has meant an increase in the relative importance of foreign markets as compared to the domestic market, so that countries have sought to stimulate demand through an export surplus rather than demand management at home by governments through fiscal and monetary policies. There is, of course, a fallacy of composition here. It is not possible for all countries to achieve an export surplus at the same time. The export surplus of some must be matched by the import surplus of others. Even for some of the countries that run an export surplus, such policies may turn out to be counterproductive if the contraction in the domestic market turns out to be more than the expansion in external markets.[32] Yet, industrialized countries and emerging economies alike have attempted to be more price competitive than their rivals by reducing unit costs of production. This has been achieved by wage restraint and labour market flexibility on the one hand and raising labour productivity on the other. It is no surprise that integration into world markets has created a strong pressure to reduce costs through the labour market, not simply to attain price competitiveness, but also to attract foreign investment. Such policies have carried the danger of a contraction in domestic demand because wage restraint depresses consumption by workers at a macro level. At the same time, increases in labour productivity, brought about by a downsizing of the workforce through restructuring of firms at a micro level, reinforce this depressive effect.

The rate of employment growth in an economy reflects the difference between output growth and labour productivity growth. It is worth noting that there is a link between output growth and productivity growth which reflects linkages between the supply side and the demand side. The essential idea is that more rapid output expansion leads to the introduction of more productive technologies and the realization of dynamic scale economies, which are a function of cumulative past output or cumulative production experience, and an increase in labour productivity. The cost reduction, passed on to consumers in the form of lower prices, would stimulate demand expansion in domestic and foreign markets. This increase in market size once again facilitates the realization of scale economies, thus bringing about a cost reduction, just as a reduction in costs, hence prices, induces a demand expansion. This cumulative causation, which is complex but virtuous, is termed the Kaldor-Verdoorn Law. However, for any technical change, if the rate of growth of labour productivity is faster than the rate of growth of output, the rate of employment growth declines and could after a point approximate to 'jobless growth'. The cumulative causation then ceases to be virtuous, largely because there is little or no feedback on the demand side, which turns out to be the weak link in the chain. In industrialized countries, this has been the case for the past two decades.[33]

Apart from 'jobless growth', there are two reasons why human development may have a negative effect on macroeconomics in industrial societies. First, it is possible that, in countries at very high levels of income and human development, the welfare state becomes so large that its macroeconomics is unsustainable. Of course, in an era of markets and globalization, this problem may be perceived or portrayed as larger than life by the dominant ideology of our times, which believes that downsizing of governments is both necessary as desirable. But this might be easier said than done in the aftermath of the global economic crisis, which has had an adverse effect on the living standards of vulnerable sections of the population for whom social protection had already been diluted. Second, there is an ageing of industrial societies, more pronounced in some countries than in others, which is partly a consequence of improved healthcare and increased life expectancy in affluent countries. This process has just begun and will gather momentum over the next decade. It could lead to a situation where, in some countries, there are too few producers and too many consumers or too few workers and too many pensioners. Large welfare states and ageing industrial societies may both diminish macroeconomic policy space for governments and make macroeconomic management more difficult.

It is, therefore, plausible to suggest though impossible to prove that the negative causation from human development to macroeconomics may be distinctly stronger in industrialized countries at high levels of income and human development and somewhat weaker in developing countries at low levels of income and human development. Of course, in this respect, there are similarities between the two sets of countries that are attributable to 'jobless growth'.

The political context

Economic policies are neither formulated nor implemented in a vacuum. The design of macroeconomic policies is influenced, often shaped, by constraints embedded in the polity. The quest for policies that promote human development is also influenced, if not shaped, by political compulsions. And policies are an important determinant of outcomes, where perceptions matter as much as reality. There are winners and losers in the economic dimension. Even if the benefits, which accrue to some, are greater than the costs, which are imposed on others, there are political consequences. For, the compensation principle exists only in textbooks on welfare economics. In reality, the gainers do not compensate the losers. The political process is about incentives and disincentives for governments, where ideology, interests and institutions play key roles in an endeavour to shape outcomes. The few who are rich have the voice and the influence to persuade governments to adopt economic policies in conformity with their interests. This process is reinforced by ideology and institutions. Yet, the many ordinary citizens assess the economic performance of governments in terms of the impact on their lives. In democracies, voters exercise their choice at the time of elections, which is shaped, at least in part, by degrees of happiness or unhappiness with outcomes. Even in authoritarian or undemocratic regimes, governments are ultimately accountable to people. Therefore, what governments can or cannot do in the spheres of macroeconomics and human development is also shaped in the realm of politics. This is so not only in developing countries, but also in industrialized countries, even if the nature of politics and levels of income are very different.

The formulation and implementation of macroeconomic policies is subject, everywhere, to constraints embedded in political economy.

Consider, in turn, fiscal policies and monetary policies. In doing so, it is worth noting the similarities and differences between developing and industrialized economies.

In the fiscal domain, governments in developing countries do not have much fiscal flexibility in either revenue or expenditure. Indeed, they find it very difficult to increase their income through tax revenues, because important political constituencies with a voice have the capacity not only to evade or avoid taxes, but also to resist taxes. Orthodoxy does not help matters. For, typically, tax rates are lowered without any systematic effort to improve compliance or broaden the base for taxation. The Laffer curve belief system is not the only culprit. Tax revenues, as a proportion of GDP, also stagnate, if not decline, since import tariffs are systematically reduced in the process of import liberalization, which is an integral part of reform programmes. The same governments find it somewhat less difficult to decrease their expenditure, although there are asymmetries. It is difficult to cut consumption expenditure, so that the axe falls on public investment, which constrains growth, and on social sectors, which hurts the poor. Such cuts are easier because the economic constituencies are not as organized as elsewhere and the consequences are discernible only after a time lag. By contrast, governments in industrialized countries have far more fiscal flexibility, although this is somewhat diminished in the aftermath of the global crisis as deficits and debt have mounted. Yet, outcomes are fairly similar. Ideology and interests, taken together, constitute an almost insurmountable barrier to increasing taxation of the rich, despite efficient tax systems where avoidance and evasion are both difficult. Indeed, the debate is about tax cuts. In economic downturns, the burden then is on expenditure. There are sectors, such as defence, which are hard to cut, while there are other sectors, such as salaries or interest payments, which constitute pre-emptive claims. And there are new claimants, seeking financial bailouts, who are irresistible. It is social sectors, such as health and education, which take the brunt, in part because those who are hurt are not organized as constituencies or do not have a voice, and in part because the consequences are visible only after a lag, by when it is too late.

There is a similar intersection of economics and politics in the sphere of monetary policy. Of course, taken together, the deregulation of domestic financial sectors and capital account liberalization have reduced the space for monetary policy everywhere. But it has also made the financial sector much more influential and powerful in this domain.[34] Ironically enough, as a consequence, monetary policy has become much narrower in its objectives (managing inflation alone) and as an instrument (just interest rates).[35] So much so that inflation targeting seems to be the most important function of central banks and purpose of monetary policy. And, for orthodoxy, the independence of central banks is the fundamental issue in the politics of monetary policy. It would seem that the significant differences between developing countries and industrialized economies, in part about the nature of monetary markets, instruments and institutions and in part about the reach of monetary policy, have become less relevant in this world. In fact, thinking about monetary policy in both sets of countries is now characterized by similarities rather than differences. Indeed, even constraints on the use of interest rates embedded in political economy are almost the same. Property-owning democracies with extensive rentier interests in developing countries, almost as much as in industrial societies, prefer higher interest rates not only because of higher income from financial assets. but also because a wider middle class fears that inflation might erode the real value of their accumulated savings. Countries that rely on foreign capital inflows, both industrialized and emerging economies, also prefer higher interest rates and lower inflation rates. It is not surprising then that any lowering of interest rates is resisted by the rentier class in domestic financial markets which has a political voice, just as any lowering of interest rates is constrained by integration into international financial markets which have become significant political constituencies for finance ministers.

It is clear from the preceding paragraphs that *interests* exercise an enormous influence on macroeconomic policies in the political context. So do *ideology* and *institutions*. The gathering momentum of globalization, associated with an internationalization of financial markets, has led to the formulation of a rationale for orthodox macroeconomic policies that is almost prescriptive. The objectives of price stability and fiscal balance have become sacrosanct, which defines the role of monetary policy and fiscal policy in the narrowest possible sense. Slowly, but surely, this orthodoxy has also come to be embedded in the belief systems of individuals, who influence policy and shape opinion in politics and government. In this process, intellectuals from the world of academia provide the rationale and editors or columnists from the world of media provide the voice. It is no surprise that the orthodox belief system has been transformed into a virtual ideology. The ideology is not abstract. It is embedded in institutions, both international and national. For international financial markets, price stability is almost an article of faith, high interest rates ensure profitability and strong exchange rates impart confidence. Orthodox macroeconomic policies are simply a means to these ends. The same worldview is adopted by multilateral financial institutions, such as the IMF and the World Bank, which exercise enormous influence on policies of economies in crisis. The European Central Bank, indeed most central banks in industrialized countries as institutions, conforms to the same belief system. It is only natural that this thinking is as much an integral part of national institutions, even outside the world of finance. The advocacy may come from domestic financial sectors, but the policies are formulated by finance ministries while the practices are adopted by central banks.

There is an interesting twist in the tale, for those excluded by the economics of markets are included by the politics of democracy.[36] And, citizens in democracies, with a right to vote, do assess the economic performance of their governments. Thus, employment implications and distributional consequences of macroeconomic policies are important underlying factors that influence or shape electoral outcomes. In the ultimate analysis, people judge economic performance of governments in terms of employment possibilities, educational opportunities or health care facilities for themselves and their families. The size of the budget deficit, the internal debt of the government, the external debt of the nation, the balance of payments situation or the expansion of money supply are economic abstractions that are somewhat distant from the daily lives of ordinary people.[37] The poor in developing countries and the vulnerable in industrialized countries, excluded from prosperity in good times and subjected to the brunt in bad times, can exercise their right to vote at election time to eject governments from office. The irony is that, in choiceless democracies, governments that follow are often just as captive of the same interests, ideology and institutions.

Even so, this reality provides access for human development into the political process. There are, of course, those who voice their concerns about the well-being of the poor and the vulnerable. In developing countries, it is social activists, radical intellectuals and concerned citizens who perform this role. In addition, there are some who invoke the MDGs. In industrial societies, it is trade unions, social activists and concerned intellectuals who perform this role. There are political parties in both sets of countries that are committed to the same cause, but they are in general on the fringe rather than in the mainstream. Such people or groups are able to articulate voice but are unable to exercise influence. The sanction of people looms larger for governments, as elections appear on the horizon.

In developing countries, the response of governments could be rhetoric or reality. The rhetoric is mostly statements of good intentions about meeting basic needs, eradicating poverty, creating employment and so on. But there could also be a real effort which allocates more resources for social sectors, improves the delivery of public services and provides safety nets for the poor. There are some examples. In Latin America, the 2000s witnessed the election of social democratic parties to office in several countries which provided left-of-centre governments. This led to a significant increase in public expenditure on social sectors, in particular education, which was supportive of human development, even if did not foster employment creation that could have provided a more sustainable means to improve the well-being of people.[38] In some countries of the developing world, which experienced rapid economic growth that was associated with increasing inequality or persistent poverty, governments discovered the idea of inclusive growth. Some of it remained in the realm of rhetoric. But in a few countries it led to setting aside resources for the poor. In India, it led to the introduction of a National Employment Guarantee Scheme, which assured employment at the minimum wage to one member of every household for 100 days per annum. In Brazil, it led to the introduction of *Bolsa Familia*, cash transfers to poor households that were conditional on sending their girls to school. In both cases, this yielded political dividends to governments that were re-elected. Yet, both countries have miles to go in terms of human development for significant proportions of their populations.

In industrialized countries, following the global economic crisis, unemployment levels are at their highest since the Great Depression. During the past three decades, a large proportion of their workforce has not experienced a significant increase in real wages, while social protection had been progressively diluted. The vulnerable in industrial societies are simply not comparable with the poor in the developing world in income levels or nutrition, healthcare and educational opportunities. Given the affluence around them, however, many live in relative poverty. And, in terms of well-being, many are worse off than earlier. But this has had little impact on political processes. The pursuit of full employment or the strengthening of social protection is not quite on the agenda of governments. This situation is puzzling in the context of democratic societies.

It would seem that processes cannot assure outcomes when ideology and interests compete for political space with voice without influence. For some time, rhetoric can substitute for substance. And governments are adept at finding palliatives that postpone the day of reckoning. Strangely enough, employment, which provides the critical link between macroeconomics and human development, is an object of neglect rather than attention. In the ultimate analysis, however, the interaction of market economy and political democracy does provide some checks and balances. It could, perhaps, create an intersecting space for those who practice macroeconomics and those who are concerned about human development.

Conclusions

This chapter seeks to analyse the relationship between macroeconomics and human development, which is an unexplored domain. It shows that the causation runs in both directions and could be either positive or negative. It also reveals similarities and differences between developing countries and industrialized economies in the nature and strength of the causation.

It would seem that the intersection between macroeconomics and human development has diminished with the passage of time. The concerns of macroeconomics have become narrower, as the focus has shifted from full employment to price stability, from growth to equilibrium, from the long term to the short term and from the real economy to the financial sector. The conception of development has become much wider, starting from just economic growth or increases in per capita income, through basic needs and human development, to freedoms associated with rights, capabilities and opportunities for people. The consequence of changing concerns and shifting emphasis is that the connections between the two do not receive sufficient recognition, let alone attention.

Macroeconomics matters for human development because it determines the level of employment, the degree of social protection and the public provision of services such as healthcare or education. The consequences may be positive where macroeconomic policies pursue full employment, strengthen social protection, provide resources for public entitlements and are conducive to economic growth in the long run. Such policies were, in fact, adopted by the industrialized countries from the late 1940s to the early 1970s, the golden age of capitalism, which contributed to an improvement in the well-being of people in industrial societies. During this era, macroeconomic policies in developing countries were shaped by growth-oriented strategies, which did not create enough employment or significantly reduce poverty, but probably helped create initial conditions and policy space for subsequent progress in terms of human development. Given the differences in levels of income and human development, this positive causation is probably stronger in developing countries and weaker in industrialized countries. The consequences may be negative where macroeconomic policies focus on price stability alone, dilute social protection and cut public expenditure on social sectors. Such policies, driven by orthodox macroeconomics and financial liberalization, were in fact adopted in both developing and industrialized countries starting around 1980. The negative consequences were borne by the poor in developing countries and the vulnerable in industrial societies. Even if the manifestations differ, this negative causation is equally strong in both sets of countries. Financial liberalization, with the shocks or crises it unleashes, tends to reinforce such outcomes everywhere.

Human development has implications and consequences for macroeconomics. In developing countries with surplus labour, human development can enlarge macroeconomic policy space through a mobilization and creation of resources, real rather than financial, provided matching employment opportunities are created. But this causation is not a plausible story for industrial societies, where the working population already has the essential attributes of human development in terms of nutrition, literacy or health, and unemployment is not attributable to the absence of capabilities in the workforce. Thus, the positive causation from human development to macroeconomics is probably strong in developing countries but weak in industrialized countries. There is also a negative causation from human development to macroeconomics, attributable to 'jobless growth' in both developing and industrialized countries. Apart from that, in industrialized countries, large welfare states and ageing of populations could make macroeconomic management difficult and diminish macroeconomic policy space for governments. It is, then, plausible to suggest that such negative causation may be distinctly stronger in industrialized countries at high levels of income and human development, and somewhat weaker in developing countries at low levels of income and human development.

The design of macroeconomic policies is influenced by constraints embedded in the polity, while the quest for policies that promote human development is also influenced by political compulsions not only in developing countries, but also in industrialized countries, even if the nature of politics and levels of income are very different. Macroeconomic policies are often shaped by interests, ideology and institutions taken together. There is, however, an interesting twist in the tale for those excluded by the economics of markets are included by the politics of democracy. This reality provides access for human development into the political process. There is some modest impact in developing countries, often rhetoric rather than substance, but there is almost no discernible impact in industrialized countries, possibly because those concerned can articulate voice but are unable to exercise influence. Yet, the interaction of market economy and political democracy could provide checks and balances. There can be no doubt that employment is absolutely critical in the process. Indeed, this recognition might create an intersecting space for those who practice macroeconomics and those who are concerned about human development.

Acknowledgement

I am indebted to Lance Taylor for helpful discussion and constructive suggestions on the theme of this essay and for valuable comments on a preliminary draft. I would also like to thank Duncan Foley, Sanjay Reddy and Willi Semmler for helpful conversations on the subject.

Notes

1 The distinction between internal balance and external balance was first made by Meade (1951). These were the policy objectives of the model. There were two sets of policy instruments: income adjustments (through fiscal and monetary policies) and price adjustments (through exchange rate variations or wage flexibility).
2 It is worth noting that the United States is perhaps an exception. Even if price stability is the dominant objective, the employment objective remains a part of the mandate of the Federal Reserve Bank. This is reflected in its continued countercyclical stance following the recent global economic crisis even if it is weak or not strong enough, although most other industrialized countries have brought the stimulus to an end and begun to reverse the process in their concerns about government deficits and public debt.
3 This argument is developed, with supporting evidence in Stiglitz et al. (2006).
4 For a detailed discussion, see Nayyar (2007).
5 The most important example, perhaps, is the Keynesian idea that investment is an independent (exogenous) variable to which saving adjusts as a dependent (endogenous) variable, or that exports are autonomous while imports are induced. There are other examples. In a world without capital mobility, capital account transactions in the balance of payments were induced and shaped by the balance on current account, but in a world of capital account mobility, capital account transactions are autonomous and not induced by the current account.
6 These structural differences are discussed at some length elsewhere by the author (Nayyar, 2007). For a discussion on related issues, see Ocampo, Rada and Taylor (2009).
7 See Stiglitz et al. (2006). See also, Nayyar (2008).
8 See, for example, Baster (1972), Seers (1972) and Morris (1979).
9 See Streeten (1981) and Stewart (1985).

10 There is an extensive literature on the subject. For a discussion on the conceptual foundations, see Sen (1989) and Haq (1995). For an analysis of issues related to methodology and measurement, see Anand and Sen (1994). For selected readings on human development, including these, see Fukuda-Parr and Shiva Kumar (2003).
11 See Sen (1999).
12 For a lucid analysis, see Sen (1999).
13 For a detailed discussion on the consequences and implications of the global economic crisis for the developing world, see Nayyar (2011).
14 For a detailed discussion, see Marglin and Schor (1990).
15 For an analysis and evaluation of development experience during this period, see Nayyar (2008b).
16 See UNDP (2010), which presents evidence on progress in terms of the human development index from 1990 to 2010. It shows that the gap between rich and poor countries has narrowed by about one-fifth between 1990 and 2010 and by about one-fourth since 1970. It would seem that there is a convergence in the human development index, even though there is no such convergence in incomes which diverged. Some of this convergence may be attributable to the fact that two indicators which make up the index, such as literacy rates or life expectancy, have natural upper bounds. Even so, health and education outcomes in poor countries registered a clear improvement, which narrowed the gap between rich and poor countries. Obviously, this progress was partly related to the base year or the starting point for the comparison, when levels of human development in most poor countries were low.
17 Such thinking may have been shaped by the experience of hyperinflation in Latin America during the 1980s and in Eastern Europe during the early 1990s. And hyperinflation did indeed mean huge costs and devastating consequences for economies in both Latin America and Eastern Europe. But this hyperinflation was tamed. And countries in Asia, as also Africa, have rarely, if ever, experienced hyperinflation. Indeed, rates of inflation in Asia and Africa, except for the hyperinflation in Vietnam during the late 1960s and the recent hyperinflation in Zimbabwe, have always been moderate.
18 For a discussion, as also evidence, on the propositions outlined in this paragraph, see Stiglitz et al. (2006).
19 During downswings of the business cycle, as the economy slows down, tax revenues fall or do not rise as much as expected. The ability of the government to service public debt diminishes. The interest rate on government borrowing rises. And governments find it not only more expensive, but also more difficult to borrow in order to finance expenditure. During upswings of the business cycle, the opposite happens. Government revenues recover. So does government expenditure. And governments have more access to cheaper credit. But the social costs of procyclical policies are high. For a discussion, see Ocampo (2003). In this context, it is worth noting that, in economies where openness is limited, public and private net borrowing tend to be mutually offsetting and the private sector often leads in an upswing. Of course, capital account liberalization in developing countries makes the story more complicated because capital inflows and outflows are procyclical, which accentuates cyclicality.

20 For an analysis of the impact of such macroeconomic policies in developing countries, as a part of the process of structural adjustment, see Nayyar (2008a).
21 The actual experience of stabilization, adjustment and reform programmes in Sub-Saharan Africa and Latin America during the 1980s, followed by Eastern Europe in the 1990s, guided by the IMF and World Bank, suggests unambiguous outcomes. First, almost without exception, there was an adverse impact on poverty insofar as the burden of adjustment was borne largely by the poor. Second, these programmes, almost as a rule, tended to stifle medium-term or long-run growth prospects. There is an extensive literature on this subject. See, for example, Cornia, Jolly and Stewart (1987), Williamson (1990) and Taylor (1993). For further evidence on the impact of structural adjustment on nutrition, health, education, as also on living standards in developing countries, see Mehrotra and Jolly (1997).
22 For a further discussion, see Stiglitz (2012).
23 This argument outlined in this paragraph is developed, at some length, in Nayyar (2003a).
24 For a broad discussion of these issues, see Ocampo and Stiglitz (2008).
25 In a narrow sense, the poor are people who live below the poverty line of PPP US$ 1.25 per day. In 2005, this number was 1.38 billion people, which is 25 per cent of the developing world's population. However, if the poverty line is drawn at PPP US$ 2 per day, the number of the poor was much larger at 2.56 billion people, which is 50 per cent of the developing world's population. See Ravallion and Chen (2008). It is the population between the two poverty lines, almost as large at 1.2 billion, who are vulnerable in times of crisis because any shock can push them further into poverty. Of course, those already below the poverty line of PPP US$ 1.25 per day are even more vulnerable, as such shocks erode their critical minimum levels of consumption.
26 For example, how does promoting human development or enhancing freedoms influence the setting of interest rates or exchange rates? It could even give the wrong signals, say expansionary appreciation in short run or keeping interest rates low in the context of financial liberalization, thereby setting off a bubble or capital flight.
27 See, for example, Ranis and Stewart (2007), who argue that the causation runs in both directions, so that it is not possible to sustain one without the other.
28 This argument was first set out by Schultz (1964). It was subsequently confirmed in research carried out by several scholars relating to different parts of the developing world.
29 See Romer (1990) and Grossman and Helpman (1991).
30 For a discussion on the relationship between human development and economic growth, see Ranis and Stewart (2007).
31 This idea is developed, at some length, with supporting evidence by Amsden (2010). She argues that poverty alleviation and human development policies will fail unless governments stimulate or create jobs. Human development alone cannot suffice because employment, which should be centre stage in strategies of development, is mostly neglected.
32 For a further discussion, see Bhaduri (2005).

33 For a lucid discussion on this issue, see Taylor (2010). He argues that if aggregate demand is weakly profit-led, where a big change in productivity growth does not stimulate much growth in demand, the outcome would be little employment expansion. It is only if aggregate demand is strongly profit-led, where a big change in productivity growth does stimulate a significant demand expansion, the outcome would be more employment expansion which can at least maintain the rate of growth of employment.
34 The growing influence of the financial sector is analysed further by Stiglitz (2012).
35 In the Unites States, for example, it was Wall Street rentiers in search of capital gains who backed the low interest rates introduced by Alan Greenspan and the financial deregulation implemented by the Clinton and Bush administrations, which led to the bubble. Inflation targeting supported this policy mix.
36 For an analysis of this proposition, see Nayyar (2003b).
37 This hypothesis about how people assess the economic performance of governments, particularly in democracies, is developed at some length in Bhaduri and Nayyar (1996).
38 For a discussion of and evidence on the Latin American experience during the 2000s, see Cornia (2010). See also, the paper by Ocampo in this issue of the journal.

References

Amsden, Alice (2010). 'Say's Law, Poverty Persistence and Employment Neglect', *Journal of Human Development and Capabilities*, Vol. 11, No. 1, pp. 57–66.

Anand, Sudhir and Amartya Sen (1994). 'Human Development Index: Methodology and Measurement', *HDRO Occasional Paper 12*, UNDP, New York.

Baster, Nancy (1972). 'Development Indicators', *Journal of Development Studies*, Vol. 8, No. 3, pp. 1–20.

Bhaduri, Amit (2005). 'Joblessness', in Eric Hershberg and Christy Thornton (eds.), *The Development Alternative: Toward a People-Centered Approach*, Social Science Research Council, New York.

Bhaduri, Amit and Deepak Nayyar (1996). *The Intelligent Person's Guide to Liberalization*, Penguin Books, New Delhi.

Cornia, G. Andrea (2010). 'Income Distribution under Latin America's New Left Regimes', *Journal of Human Development and Capabilities*, Vol. 11, No. 1, pp. 85–114.

Cornia, G. Andrea, Richard Jolly and Frances Stewart (1987). *Adjustment with a Human Face*, Clarendon Press, Oxford.

Fukuda-Parr, Sakiko and A. K. Shiva Kumar (eds.) (2003). *Readings in Human Development*, Oxford University Press, Delhi.

Grossman, G. M. and Helpman, E. (1991). *Innovation and Growth in the Global Economy*, MIT Press, Cambridge, MA.

Haq, Mahbub ul (1995). *Reflections on Human Development*, Oxford University Press, New York.
Marglin, Stephen and Juliet Schor (eds.) (1990). *The Golden Age of Capitalism*, Clarendon Press, Oxford.
Meade, James (1951). *Theory of International Economic Policy: The Balance of Payments*, Oxford University Press, Oxford.
Mehrotra, Santosh and Richard Jolly (eds.) (1997). *Development with a Human Face*, Clarendon Press, Oxford.
Morris, M. D. (1979). *Measuring the Conditions of the World's Poor*, Pergamon Press, Oxford.
Nayyar, Deepak (2003a). 'Globalization and Development Strategies', in John Toye (ed.), *Trade and Development: New Directions for the Twenty-First Century*, Edward Elgar, Cheltenham.
Nayyar, Deepak (2003b). 'The Political Economy of Exclusion and Inclusion: Democracy, Markets and People', in Amitava Krishna Dutt and Jaime Ros (eds.), *Development Economics and Structuralist Macroeconomics: Essays in Honour of Lance Taylor*, Edward Elgar, Cheltenham.
Nayyar, Deepak (2007). 'Macroeconomics in Developing Countries', *Banca Nazionale del Lavoro Quarterly Review*, Vol. LIX, No. 242, September, pp. 249–269.
Nayyar, Deepak (2008a). 'Macroeconomics of Structural Adjustment and Public Finance in Developing Countries: A Heterodox Perspective', *International Journal of Development Issues*, Vol. 7, No. 1, June, pp. 4–28.
Nayyar, Deepak (2008b). 'Learning to Unlearn from Development', *Oxford Development Studies*, Vol. 36, No. 3, September, pp. 259–280.
Nayyar, Deepak (2011). 'The Financial Crisis, the Great Recession and the Developing World', *Global Policy*, Vol. 2, No. 1, January, pp. 20–32.
Ocampo, Jose Antonio (2003). 'Developing Countries Anti-Cyclical Policies in a Globalized World', in Amitava Dutt and Jaime Ros (eds.), *Development Economics and Structuralist Macroeconomics: Essays in Honour of Lance Taylor*, Edward Elgar, Cheltenham.
Ocampo, Jose Antonio, Codrina Rada and Lance Taylor (2009). *Growth and Policy in Developing Countries*, Columbia University Press, New York.
Ocampo, Jose Antonio and Joseph Stiglitz (2008). *Capital Market Liberalization and Development*, Oxford University Press, Oxford.
Ranis, Gustav and Frances Stewart (2007). 'Dynamic Links between the Economy and Human Development', in J. A. Ocampo, K. S. Jomo and S. Khan (eds.), *Policy Matters: Economic and Social Policies to Sustain Equitable Development*, pp. 37–53. Zed Books, London.
Ravallion, Martin and Shaohua Chen (2008). 'The Developing World Is Poorer Than We Thought, but No Less Successful in the Fight Against Poverty', *Policy Research Working Paper 4703*, Development Research Group, World Bank, Washington, DC.
Romer, P. (1990), 'Endogenous Technological Change', *Journal of Political Economy*, Vol. 98, No. 5, pp. S71–S102.

Schultz, T. W. (1964). *Transforming Traditional Agriculture*, Yale University Press, New Haven.

Seers, Dudley (1972). 'What Are We Trying to Measure?', *Journal of Development Studies*, Vol. 8, No. 3, pp. 21–36.

Sen, Amartya (1989). 'Development as Capability Expansion', *Journal of Development Planning*, Vol. 19, pp. 41–58.

Sen, Amartya (1999). *Development as Freedom*, Alfred E. Knopf, New York.

Stewart, Frances (1985). *Planning to Meet Basic Needs*, Macmillan, London.

Streeten, Paul (1981). *First Things First: Meeting Basic Human Needs in Developing Countries*, Oxford University Press, Oxford.

Stiglitz, Joseph, Jose Antonio Ocampo, Shari Spiegel, Ricardo Ffrench-Davis and Deepak Nayyar (2006). *Stability with Growth: Macroeconomics, Liberalization and Development*, Oxford University Press, Oxford.

Stiglitz, Joseph (2012). 'Macroeconomic Fluctuations, Inequality and Human Development', *Journal of Human Development and Capabilities*, Vol. 13, No. 1, pp. 31–58

Taylor, Lance (1993). *The Rocky Road to Reform: Adjustment, Income Distribution and Growth in the Developing World*, MIT Press, Cambridge.

Taylor, Lance (2010). *Maynard's Revenge: The Collapse of Free Market Macroeconomics*, Harvard University Press, Cambridge, MA.

UNDP (2010). *Human Development Report 2010: The Real Wealth of Nations*, Palgrave Macmillan, New York.

Williamson, John (1990). *Latin American Adjustment: How Much Has Happened?* Institute for International Economics, Washington, DC.

4

THE MILLENNIUM DEVELOPMENT GOALS BEYOND 2015

Old frameworks and new constructs

The MDGs, which began life at the turn of the century, are the focus of attention among people for different reasons. Some are concerned with the past to review progress. Some concentrate on the present to consider the implications of the financial crisis and the Great Recession in the world economy. Some think about the future and how to traverse the remaining distance. The conjuncture is obviously important and so are the reasons. But the object of this chapter is different. It seeks to discuss MDGs in prospect rather than retrospect. The object is to reflect on possibilities and options beyond 2015. The structure of the discussion is as follows. First, it sets the stage before the play begins. In doing so, it begins with the origins and significance of MDGs to highlight why they are the object of attention once again. Second, it attempts an evaluation of MDGs. It provides a critical assessment of the conception and design of MDGs. Third, it contemplates the future. It discusses options beyond 2015 in terms of possible choices to explore the necessary and desirable contours of change, which could be the foundations of a modified or alternative framework. Fourth, it examines what developing countries could do in their respective national contexts for the pursuit and attainment of development objectives embedded in the MDGs. The next section is about the international context, where the focus has been narrow and the progress has been slow so far. It highlights possibilities of change for the better, but argues for a different approach and framework which would be conducive for development. The final section concludes.

The setting and the conjuncture

Some of the essential commitments in the Declaration adopted by Heads of Governments at the Millennium Summit of the United Nations in September 2000 were selected, condensed and presented as the MDGs, which sought to eradicate poverty and hunger, achieve universal primary education, promote gender equality, reduce child mortality, improve maternal health, combat common diseases, ensure environmental sustainability and develop a global partnership for development.[1] This was an important watershed. It was the outcome of a long process in the United Nations.[2] The attempt to place poverty reduction and concessional assistance on the international agenda for development continued. It remained the theme at a sequence of conferences and summits during the 1990s where some commitments were made.[3] But it was also an outcome of history in a more substantive sense.[4] The period from 1950 to 1980 witnessed economic growth at a respectable pace across the developing world, which was a radical departure from the stagnation in the colonial era, but this growth did not translate into well-being for ordinary people. The period from 1980 to 2000, the era of markets and globalization, belied expectations and promises of the ideologues. Economic growth across the developing world, except for China and India, was much slower and more volatile than the preceding three decades. What is more, there was a discernible increase in economic inequalities between countries and people, while poverty and deprivation persisted in large parts of the developing world. Thus, it would seem that development experience of the preceding 50 years made 2000 an almost natural conjuncture for the birth of the MDGs.

There were three dimensions to the significance of the MDGs. It was an explicit recognition of the reality that a large proportion of people in the world were deprived and poor. It was a statement of good intentions that sought a time-bound reduction in poverty to improve the living conditions of those deprived and excluded. It was an attempt to place this persistent problem, until then a largely national concern, on the development agenda for international cooperation. Taken together, these attributes of the MDGs introduced a mechanism, even if implicit, to monitor progress in the pursuit of stated objectives. In fact, some of the targets were specified in quantitative terms with respect to stipulated time horizons. Thus, in principle, national governments could be held accountable by their people, just as the international community could be held accountable by national governments.

In retrospect, it is clear that the MDGs, much like the human development index, caught the popular imagination. The reasons are almost obvious. There is a simplicity that is engaging. There are targets that are quantitative. There are objectives that are easy to comprehend. There are good intentions with which no one could possibly disagree. It is no surprise that the MDGs galvanized widespread international support across the entire spectrum of stakeholders. The engagement of the international community was natural, so that multilateral institutions and international organisations provided the meeting space for continuing consultations and monitoring progress. The engagement of national governments was also inevitable, as domestic political processes and civil society organisations entered the picture. In practice, however, accountability of the international community and national governments was limited, because the constituencies – poor countries or poor people – that might have invoked it simply did not have the voice, let alone any power of sanction. What is more, as it turned out the MDGs did not quite serve their larger strategic purpose of changing the discourse on development.[5]

The Millennium Summit in September 2000 set goals for September 2015. An evaluation of progress with respect to the objectives set out in the MDGs is particularly important in view of the experience.[6] At the time of writing this, the MDGs have completed four-fifths of their life span in their present incarnation.[7] But that is not all. There is also a natural concern about the implications of the financial crisis, the food crisis and the environmental crisis, which have roughly coincided in time. This triple crisis is bound to have implications and consequences for the MDGs. It is, therefore, an appropriate time for reflection, or introspection, on what remains to be done before 2015 and what should be done after 2015. This essay is concerned with the latter.

In this context, it must be recognized that the discourse on the MDGs, just as much as the debate on development, is often shaped by ideological perspectives. Therefore, the lessons drawn from experience, particularly in orthodox thinking, are selective and partial. The conventional view is that the MDGs are attainable wherever economic growth is rapid, foreign aid is substantial and governance is good. The moral of the story is that human development is largely growth mediated, aid mediated or governance mediated. In this world view, if countries performed poorly with respect to the MDGs, it was because growth was not enough, aid was not sufficient and governance was poor.[8] This is an oversimplified, if not simplistic, characterization of outcomes. In reality, growth may not trickle down, aid may be marginal if not irrelevant, and the quality of governance might be a consequence rather than a cause of development. The growth, aid and governance arguments have something in common, because they believe that the MDGs agenda is essentially about economic policies and economic development. The underlying belief is that there are best practices in every sphere, which can be replicated or scaled across space and over time. This belief system is based on a convenient but inappropriate abstraction. In fact, economic outcomes are shaped by political processes and social transformation. Therefore, it is a mistake to focus on the economy in isolation from polity and society.

Evaluating the MDGs: conception and design

Any assessment of the MDGs as a framework for thinking about or monitoring progress in development must begin with a focus on their conception and design, which can be followed by an evaluation of their strengths and weaknesses through the lens of experience.

In terms of conception, there are two basic problems. First, the MDGs specify an outcome but do not set out the process which would make it possible to realize the objectives. In other words, the MDGs specify a destination but do not chart the journey. Second, the MDGs are stipulated without any reference to initial conditions, but where a country gets to in any given time horizon depends, at least in part, on where it starts out from. Global goals meant as norms, but often read as targets, also do not recognize that there may be significant differences in national priorities. In sum, the MDGs focus on a comparison between an undesirable state and a desirable state, but do not recognize the importance of the process of change or the transition path from one state to the other. This implicit separation of ends and means compounds the problem. But that is not all. There is another fundamental limitation. The MDGs are set out in terms of aggregates or averages which often conceal as much as they reveal because there is no reference to distributional outcomes. The depiction of social indicators of development as arithmetic means or statistical averages provides a single summary measure, but it cannot reflect the well-being of the poor, most of who are significantly below any line that is drawn on the basis of an average. Therefore, a meaningful assessment of progress in the living conditions of people must recognize rather than ignore the existence of inequality. The 'tyranny of averages' can be deceptive if not misleading. It is essential to disaggregate outcomes so as to reveal rather than conceal distributional realities.[9]

In terms of design, there are three basic limitations. First, there is a multiplicity of objectives. There are 8 goals, 18 quantifiable targets now increased to 21 and 48 indicators now increased to 60. Second, the objectives are specified in many different ways. Some objectives are set out in proportional terms: reducing the proportion of people who live in poverty or hunger by one-half; reducing child mortality rates by two-thirds; reducing maternal mortality rates by three-fourths; or reducing the proportion of people without access to safe drinking water and basic sanitation facilities by one-half. Other objectives are set out in terms of completion: universal primary education; gender equality in school education; productive employment with decent work for all; or universal access to reproductive health. Yet other objectives are set out as statements of intentions: reduce loss in biodiversity or improve the lives of slum dwellers. Third, some indicators, particularly the poverty head count, are inappropriate and could be misleading. The problems associated with these three limitations are almost obvious. Even so, they are worth highlighting.

The multiplicity of objectives means that, apart from duplication and overlap, it is difficult to monitor overall progress. The implicit assumption underlying targets that seek a proportionate reduction is that progress is linear. In fact, it is not. If the object is to reduce the proportion of people living in poverty by one-half, much depends on the initial level whether it is 60 per cent or 20 per cent. Consequently, targets may be set too high for some and too low for others.[10] The problem with targets that seek universal access in terms of completion is that outcomes are characterized as binary, so that it is difficult to differentiate between outcomes where there is little progress and where there is substantial progress. Targets that are set out as statements of intentions mean different things to different people and are exceedingly difficult to monitor. These problems are often compounded by difficulties in measurement which differ across objectives. In some countries and for some indicators, statistics are not good enough. In other countries and for other indicators, statistics are difficult to find. The limitation of inappropriate indicators, such as the proportion of the population below a stipulated poverty line, is somewhat different. These could be misleading because the measurement might miss the point.[11] The problem is not simply that counting the poor is often associated with serious differences because of methodology and statistics, although that often receives much of the attention. The focus on such poverty reduction might be misleading, if it neglects those who are persistently poor or considerably below the poverty line.

The limitations of MDGs as a construct, in conception and in design, provide some basis for an evaluation of the MDGs as a framework. It would mean too much of a digression to attempt a systematic, let alone a complete, evaluation. Nevertheless, it is important to stress some aspects. First, their weakness is their strength. The MDGs are simple, catchy and acceptable, in part, they focus on ends with which no one would disagree. At the same time, this strength is also their weakness, because there is an implicit assumption that one size fits all. Second, the MDGs have been associated with unintended consequences, mostly in the form of misplaced emphasis on stepping up the rate of economic growth and mobilizing external financing for social sectors. Of course, such an emphasis was natural, possibly intended, for conventional economic thinking. The silence on means with a focus on ends meant that orthodox economics simply occupied that vacant space. Given the dominant ideology of our times, it is no surprise. In the process, the essential values underlying the MDGs, which were drawn from the paradigm of human development, have been lost in translation.[12] Third, it would seem that the MDGs have been misunderstood, misused and misappropriated.[13] There is a misunderstanding because global MDG targets are often used as a scale for assessing the performance of different regions or specific countries. But it would have been far more appropriate for the MDGs to be read as collective targets for the world as a whole which did not have to be reached by every country. In fact, countries should have sought to contextualize the MDGs in terms of initial conditions and national priorities. There is a misuse in so far as the MDGs have come to be captured by a donor-centric view of development. This has led to a disproportionate emphasis on the importance of external financing in the pursuit of MDGs. It has also tended to shift the focus of attention away from national governments to the international community. But success or failure in the pursuit of MDGs depends largely upon what happens within countries, where governments are both responsible and accountable for outcomes. There is also a misappropriation of MDGs by the dominant orthodoxy which represents an ideological perspective on development. The MDGs articulate ends. Their silence on means might have been attributable to two reasons, which are understandable: the recognition that development is characterized by specificities in time and in space, and the acceptance that there might be genuine differences of opinion on what are appropriate strategies of development, so that a political consensus on means would be exceedingly difficult if not impossible. But the silence was transformed into an opportunity by orthodoxy, which had voice and exercised influence to focus on faster growth and more aid.

Contemplating the future: what next?

In contemplating the future of MDGs, the first step is to focus on the different possibilities beyond 2015 because there are a number of alternatives. The next step can be an attempt to explore alternative constructs to outline the broad contours of change, even if it is difficult to conceive of an altogether new framework.

Possibilities beyond 2015

There are choices to be made, which can be posed as questions. First, is there any necessity for a framework, such as MDGs, when the stipulated period comes to an end? Second, should it be simply more of the same done better or faster? Third, is there a need to modify the MDGs, plus or minus? Fourth, is it necessary to move away from generalized MDGs to contextualized MDGs because conditions differ across space and over time? The discussion that follows considers these questions in turn.

The answer to the first question is clear. Some framework, even if it is a point of reference, is essential beyond 2015. The MDGs have imparted a focus to concerns about poverty and deprivation, which is the fate of a large proportion of people in the world. The MDGs have also galvanized support for the idea that it is imperative to improve the living conditions of such people in a stipulated time horizon.[14] And, even if we have miles to go in our journey to the destination, the aspiration must remain centre stage.

The answer to the second question is also clear. It cannot simply be more of the same. For one, it would only move the targets farther into the future. This would be an admission of failure. For another, it would negate the possibilities of learning from experience in the pursuit of doing better or moving faster. It might also be possible to do the same things differently or do altogether different things.

The answer to the third question is somewhat more nuanced and complicated. The MDGs can be modified by adding to them or subtracting from them. There might be a strong temptation to opt for a MDG plus scenario.[15] And there are many candidates that range from gender equality, human rights, good governance and climate change, to name just a few. It may also be tempting to introduce a qualitative dimension in the quantitative targets. But it would be wise to hasten slowly in this direction for two reasons. The first is obvious. More targets and more indicators would detract from the simplicity which was the virtue of the MDGs that made them so attractive. The second is not so obvious. Any addition would have to meet a double litmus test of being a sound indicator for which robust data are available. The MDGs minus scenario is also tempting for there are targets that duplicate or overlap. There is a need to minimize such duplication and overlap. It would also be sensible to reduce the number of indicators where the variable is not appropriate or the quality of data is poor. Of course, such a rationalization would mean that the MDGs lose something in coverage. There is an obvious need for prudence in such additions or subtractions. Even so, rethinking about MDGs, plus or minus, should not be stifled or shut out. What is more, it might be worth revisiting indicators of social development and human development, which pick up elements of quality or discrimination, to situate such rethinking in a wider context.[16]

The answer to the fourth question is more straightforward. Generalized MDGs and contextualized MDGs should not be presented as an either-or choice. Indeed, posing them as alternatives creates a false dilemma. Generalized MDGs should be objectives for the world as a whole. And these global goals should be modified in the context of initial conditions and national priorities. But this did not quite happen because the texts were silent on this matter and left the question open to interpretation.[17] However, if global MDGs constitute a set of norms, which provide a framework for national governments to formulate their objectives with reference to specificities in time and in space, country-oriented MDGs can reflect differences in priorities and objectives. Therefore, generalized MDGs and contextualized MDGs are complements rather than substitutes. Of course, it is important to strike a balance, because global goals should allow space for differences in initial conditions and in national priorities. This space cannot be too much and should not be too little.

Exploring alternative constructs

There is a fundamental question that arises. Is it time to think of something different to replace MDGs as a framework? It is difficult to provide an answer. The reason is obvious. A changed paradigm is perhaps too ambitious. Yet, it may be feasible to think about elements of a new framework that might replace the MDGs after 2015. Of course, this is easier said than done. Even so, it is possible to outline some contours of change which would represent departures from or substantial modifications in the existing framework. There are three imperatives that deserve to be highlighted.

First, it is imperative that there is structural flexibility at the national level. It is essential to recognize differences in initial conditions. It is just as important to allow for differences in national priorities. In doing so, it is necessary to recognize the possibilities of some interdependence among objectives and some trade-offs between objectives.

For this purpose, the new framework should state its premises that the MDGs are a norm rather than a floor or a ceiling, and that the MDGs are illustrative rather than exhaustive and that the MDGs are suggestive rather than definitive. It must also be explicitly stated that the MDGs represent objectives for the world as a whole, which are not a scale to measure progress in every country, because national goals must be formulated using global norms as a point of reference.

Second, it is imperative that there is cognition of inequality in any assessment of outcomes. It may be necessary to consider progress towards the stipulated objectives in terms of aggregates, or statistical averages, at the national level. But it cannot be sufficient. It is also necessary to monitor progress at a disaggregated level or compute statistical averages by introducing some weights that reflect the distribution among people. This is essential because inequalities exist and distributional outcomes matter. The simplest method would be to focus on the poorest 25 per cent or the bottom 40 per cent of the population in respect of each of the objectives. This is easier said than done, because statistics on the distribution of income or consumption are often inadequate or sometimes unreliable. But it is not impossible because information, even if imperfect or incomplete, does exist. It is almost as important to recognize the spatial dimensions of inequality within countries. For that purpose, disaggregated data at a provincial or regional level, which establish subnational league tables, are necessary to monitor progress. In fact, such information could help energize the process by emphasizing another aspect of distribution rather than focus on national averages alone. It must be stressed that, in any assessment of outcomes, the reality of economic and spatial inequalities must be explicitly recognized rather than concealed or obscured in the national averages that characterize MDGs. The introduction of structural flexibility at the national level, which contextualizes development needs, is necessary but not sufficient for this purpose, because even if goals are adapted to differ across countries such goals remain at the aggregate level within countries and do not reflect distributional outcomes.

Third, it is imperative that the new framework for the MDGs incorporates something on means rather than simply focus on ends. In other words, something needs to be said not only about outcomes, but also about process. The absence of anything on means or process carries two dangers. For some, it leads to the wrong inference that one size fits all. For others, it provides vacant space in which prescriptive policies can be imposed. Obviously, it is neither feasible nor desirable to specify policies or strategies in the pursuit of MDGs, because development is characterized by specificities in time and in space. There can be no generalized prescriptions or universal blueprints that would deliver the well-being of humankind. In fact, policies and strategies must evolve at a national level as times and circumstances change. But the framework for the MDGs could enunciate some, at least a few, general propositions that might pre-empt misunderstanding or misappropriation. Some examples of such propositions, which are suggestive but cannot be definitive or exhaustive, would suffice. Economic growth is necessary but cannot be sufficient to bring about development. It is necessary to create institutional mechanisms that would transform economic growth into meaningful development by improving the living conditions of people. Public action is an integral part of this process. Employment creation provides the only sustainable means of poverty reduction. Employment creation is also the essential foundation of growth that includes ordinary people. Policies should not be prescribed once and for all, because there are specificities in time and space. External finance is a complement to but cannot be a substitute for domestic resources. The role of the State remains critical in the process of development.

Clearly, it is possible to think of more such propositions, but it would be wise not to increase their number or specify their content. It may also be tempting to be more explicit or specific about means, but that would be a mistake for three reasons. Such an approach could easily become prescriptive and move to the presumption that one size fits all. At the same time, it is bound to constrain degrees of freedom for countries in the formulation of policies, so that it could end up diminishing policy space. What is more, it could lead to more explicit targets which are neither necessary nor desirable. In fact, the suggested propositions are meant as points of reference to provide a framework (which is flexible rather than rigid) that might enable countries to formulate policies and evolve strategies recognizing specificities in time and space. In other words, the idea should be to provide an outline of means, which set out the bare essentials of possible approaches but resist the temptation of setting out specifics of policies. In fact, it is essential to strike a balance. Setting out some propositions on means or process must not encroach upon flexibility or space because national contexts differ. At the same time, a silence on means must not be pre-empted or appropriated by prescriptive views that can surface with ease in a world of unequal partners. Indeed, the discussion that follows shows that such propositions, which are no more than a statement of some priors, could help countries adopt policies and strategies suitable for and appropriate in their respective national contexts that are conducive to the pursuit of development objectives embedded in the MDGs.

The national context

The recognition of poverty and deprivation with an emphasis on human development in the MDGs served a valuable purpose. But it was not enough because nothing was said about strategies to meet this challenge of development. There was another basic shortcoming. People are not just beneficiaries of development. It is only if people are centre stage in the process of development as the main actors that development can empower people to participate in decisions that shaped their lives. The significance of this proposition is highlighted by the medieval distinction between agents and patients, which is invoked by Amartya Sen. He argues that the freedom-centred understanding of the process of development is very much an agent-oriented view. This is because individuals with adequate social opportunities can effectively shape their own destiny and help each other. They must not be seen primarily as patients or passive recipients of the benefits of cunning development programmes.[18]

In the national context, the near obsession with economic growth and economic efficiency as objectives is misplaced and must change. These are simply means. It is the well-being of people that is an end. Therefore, it is imperative that the end is not lost sight of in the concern for means. And there are two forgotten essentials that should form an integral part of any attempt to attain objectives set out in the MDGs.[19] First, it must be recognized that economic growth is necessary but not sufficient to bring about a reduction in poverty. It cannot suffice to say that the outcomes of economic policies should be moderated by social policies. It is important to create institutional mechanisms that mediate between economic growth and social development. Second, it must be recognized that the well-being of humankind is the essence of development. It follows that distributional outcomes are important so that the problem of increasing inequality needs to be addressed rather than accepted as a fact of life. Similarly, employment and livelihoods are also important. After all, employment creation is not only the most important means of reducing poverty, but also the only sustainable solution in the long term. Moreover, employment is also essential for the well-being and dignity of people. In the national context, therefore, it is necessary to reformulate policies, redesign strategies and rethink development.

In reformulating policies, there is a strong need to reflect on macroeconomic objectives and macroeconomic policies.[20] Such a reformulation must begin by redefining policy objectives. In the short term or in crisis situations, the prime concern should not be the stability of prices alone. The stability of output and employment is just as important. In the medium term or in normal times, the essential objective of macroeconomic policies cannot simply be the management of inflation and the elimination of macroeconomic imbalances. It should be just as much, if not more, about fostering employment creation and supporting economic growth. The reformulation must also extend to reconsidering policy instruments. Fiscal policy cannot be reduced to a means of reducing government deficits or restoring macroeconomic balances. It is a powerful instrument in the quest for full employment and economic growth. Monetary policy cannot be reduced to a means of controlling inflation through interest rates. It is a versatile instrument, where both the price and volume of credit can be most effective in the pursuit of development objectives. In sum, it is essential to return to a developmental approach to macroeconomic policies, which is based on an integration of short-term countercyclical fiscal and monetary policies with long-term development objectives. Economic growth with full employment should be the fundamental objective of macroeconomic policies, which must be an integral part of the mandate for central banks and finance ministries. In the longer term, poverty reduction is possible only with such an approach. In the interim, for people who remain unemployed, there is need for employment programmes and social protection, both of which require sensible macroeconomics. Even when people are employed, often with low incomes, their private consumption needs to be supplemented by social consumption. For this purpose, governments need to allocate resources for expenditure in social sectors, to create supply through higher investments and demand through lower user charges, both of which require macroeconomic policy space.

In redesigning strategies, it is necessary to introduce correctives and interventions that prevent or minimize the exclusion of people from development.[21] The object of correctives should be to foster inclusion. The inclusion of poor people requires the spread of education and an increase in social consumption. It also requires a substantial investment in infrastructure, particularly in rural areas. The object of interventions should be to curb exclusion. The extent of exclusion can be limited by providing public goods and services to regions or groups that are vulnerable, marginalized or excluded. For the people who remain excluded despite such interventions, it is essential to widen and strengthen safety nets such as anti-poverty programmes. The role of government is vital in every sphere. It is not sufficient to speak about inclusive growth as governments often do. It is necessary to ensure that the process of growth is pro-poor. Employment creation is the obvious foundation of pro-poor growth. At the same time, resources that become available to governments through growth should be used, in part, to provide public services for the poor in terms of both access and delivery. The MDGs would be easier to reach if governments decide that, in some critical spheres, access for all is provided within stipulated time horizons. The choice would, of course, differ across countries. But some obvious possibilities for such national development priorities are: the provision of safe drinking water, the creation of sanitation facilities, the immunization of children and the completion of primary education.

In rethinking development, it is important to recognize the relevance of the balance between domestic and external factors and the critical importance of public action. It must be stressed that the developmental role of the State is critical across the entire spectrum of what needs to be done. For this purpose, it is imperative to restore the moral authority of the State, which was eroded by the virtual ideology of market fundamentalism associated with globalization in a prescriptive mode. The reason is simple enough. If governments do badly, it is not possible to dispense with them or replace them with markets. Governments must be made to perform better.

It is essential to rethink the relative importance of the external and the internal in the process of development, in terms of market and in terms of resources. It is necessary to recognize that the domestic market is critical in the process of development and that external markets are at best complements, but cannot be substitutes for the domestic market even in smaller countries. Of course, the validity of this argument depends, in part, on the size of a country. Even so, domestic markets are, at one level, constitutive of development because it means that ordinary people have purchasing power and are, at another level, instrumental in the process of development because they can drive processes of growth. Similarly, it is desirable to rely more on domestic resources for investment and think of external resources as complements rather than substitutes.

The time has come to recognize that there is a complex relationship between the State and the market.[22] Both market failure and government failure are facts of life. For neither markets nor governments are, or can ever be, perfect. Indeed, markets are invariably imperfect and governments are without exception fallible. But these failures are seldom absolute. A reasonable degree of correction is possible in either case, particularly where the coexistence of the two institutions provides mutual checks and balances. The State and the market are complements rather than substitutes. What is more, the relationship between the State and the market cannot be defined once and for all. In fact, the State and the market must adapt to each other as time and circumstances change. Development experience during the second half of the 20th century suggests that successes have come in countries that have found this right blend of State and market. It is time to give up the belief in the magic of the market to consider a more proactive role for the State. If development is to be people-friendly, it does mean that the State has to play a critical role in terms of providing investment in infrastructure, which is not forthcoming from the private sector, whether domestic or foreign players. The state has also to focus on expenditure on social sectors, because if development is about improving living conditions of people, allocating resources to support social consumption is both constitutive of and instrumental in development. But this cannot suffice. The State should also attempt to ensure that economic growth creates employment and livelihoods for people. Most important, perhaps, it is vital to redress the balance in the respective role of the market and the State for the pendulum had swung to one end, because the exclusion of large proportions of the population from well-being cannot even sustain growth, let alone lead to development. And there is a developmental role for the State. So much of what needs to be done can only be done by the State. The reason is simple. Governments are accountable to people. Markets are not.

It is clear that the living conditions of poor people, in terms of poverty reduction and human development, will be shaped largely by what is done or what remains undone within countries. Thus, MDGs after 2015 must create a framework that allows, indeed encourages, countries to reformulate policies, redesign strategies and rethink development in the national context. The essential objective must be the well-being of people. This, in turn, will require employment creation that provides sustained livelihoods to support private consumption, combined with the public provision of services, such as education and health care, to support social consumption. The desired outcome will be ensured by the process, if governments are accountable to people and if people are actors rather than beneficiaries. In fact, participatory development can provide the connect between national development and the global agenda. And it is not necessary for the global agenda to incorporate incentives or disincentives. The very existence of a framework, such as MDGs, would serve that purpose, in so far as the juxtaposition of the international community with national governments can provide checks and balances which create accountability to people without voice. The focus of the global agenda, as argued in what follows, must be different. For one, it should enlarge rather than diminish policy space for poor countries, so that participatory development becomes possible. For another, it should think of poor countries not as recipients or beneficiaries of largesse but as partners in development.

The international context

The international aspects of the MDGs are set out in Goal 8, which seeks to develop a global partnership for development. This aspiration has multiple dimensions, which range from addressing the special needs of the LDCs, through providing a comprehensive solution to the debt problem of the developing world, to creating a multilateral trading system and international financial system that are conducive to development. There are several reviews that attempt to monitor the uneven and inadequate progress in this sphere.[23] The objectives enunciated in the MDGs are long on words. But it would seem that outcomes have been short on substance. And Goal 8 has turned out to be simply inadequate.

It would be no exaggeration to state that the pursuit of multilateral development cooperation has been characterized by a selective focus, if not a misplaced emphasis, on concessional development assistance. This is attributable, in large part, to a donor-centric world view with a focus on aid that dominates the discourse. This is also attributable, in part, to a concern that the volume, effectiveness and architecture of aid leave much to be desired. It is clear that the international community needs to do better at this unfinished business, for its completion is not even on the distant horizon. But it must be recognized that far more needs to be done. Even if the targets for development assistance set out in the MDGs are met, and that is most unlikely, it is not obvious how this would ensure development outcomes. Evidence and experience suggest that aid is a mixed blessing. Indeed, it is possible to go further and argue that aid often turns out to be the equivalent of a natural resource course. That may be a contested proposition. But there can be little doubt that the availability of aid tends to ease the pressure on governments to implement change or reform that is necessary for development. And it is more than plausible to argue that aid often becomes a soft option for governments, so that domestic resource mobilization does not receive the attention it deserves as a means of financing the MDGs. In fact, for developing countries, remittances from migrants are a much larger and more stable source of external financing than aid inflows.[24] Thus, it might be worth thinking about policies and mechanisms that could more effectively use remittances for development. In any case, it is clear that, for developing countries, access to markets in the form of trade and access to knowledge in the form of technology is far more important in their quest for development than foreign aid could ever be. The bottom line is clear. It must be recognized that foreign aid is not all there is to external finance, and that external finance is not all there is to development. This recognition alone will reduce some of the asymmetries in the existing framework of MDGs. And it could provide a starting point for thinking about a new global agenda built upon partnerships in development.

Reviews of progress on the MDGs in LDCs suggest that it will not be enough to reach global targets. This is surprising, at least on surface, because economic growth in LDCs during the 2000s, until the financial crisis, was rapid and quite unprecedented as it exceeded most projections, thanks to the boom in prices of primary commodities, the abundance of cheap capital (even if some of it was footloose money) and the great bubble in the world economy. There could be three plausible explanations: the targets were set too high, the growth was not enough or the growth was not inclusive. Obviously, the task has been made more difficult by the financial crisis and the Great Recession in the world economy. Even without these setbacks, however, the MDGs would not have been attainable in the LDCs, partly because the targets were too ambitious and partly because national strategies were neither adequate nor appropriate. The irony is that the LDCs were not quite allowed, let alone enabled, to move beyond what was set out in Poverty Reduction Strategy Papers (PRSPs). The strategy in PRSPs was to focus on economic growth – assuming that it will trickle down – and on investment in social sectors – assuming that the services so produced would reach the poor.[25] This approach, advocated by orthodoxy, which was nothing new, almost assumed away the problem. But there was little, if any, thinking on how economic growth or social sectors could be made more inclusive or, even better, pro-poor. In fact, the emphasis on social development meant that governments in LDCs relied on external resources to finance expenditure on social sectors but did not mobilize domestic resources to finance investment in infrastructure, agriculture or productive activities. There is need to transform such thinking. Macroeconomic policies need to be integrated with long-term development objectives rather than be shaped by the objective of price stability in the short term. Domestic resources need to be mobilized to step up investment in infrastructure and in agriculture that enhances production capacities. The approach to poverty reduction needs to be reoriented away from compartmentalization in social sectors into an integration with development strategies that seek to combine economic growth with employment creation and participatory development. This is not only about reformulating policies, but also about rethinking development in the LDCs. Clearly, the time has come to depart from this past and think anew about MDGs in LDCs.

Going beyond the LDCs, to consider the entire spectrum of developing countries, it is clear that, during the first quarter of the 21st century, development outcomes would be shaped, at least in part, by the international context. It is also clear that unfair rules of the game in the contemporary world economy would encroach upon policy space so essential for development.[26] Many of these rules are a part of the WTO regime, while several are implicit in IMF-World Bank conditionalities. Similar conditions are increasingly imposed, particularly on LDCs, by donor countries that provide foreign aid. And the problem is compounded by integration into international financial markets, as portfolio investment flows exercise a disproportionate influence on macroeconomic policies and exchange rates. This situation needs to be corrected. The correctives should endeavour to make existing rules less unfair, introduce new rules where necessary and recognize that even fair rules may not suffice.[27] In reshaping unfair rules, the nature of the solution depends upon the nature of the problem. Where there are different rules in different spheres, it is necessary to make the rules symmetrical across spheres. Where there are rules for some but not for others, it is necessary to ensure that rules are uniformly applicable to all. Where the agenda for new rules is partisan, it is imperative to redress the balance in the agenda. But that is not all. There are some spheres where there are no rules such as environmental sustainability, international financial markets or cross-border movements of people. Climate change is on the agenda even if there is little progress. The time has come to introduce some rules that govern international financial markets. Similarly, it is worth contemplating a multilateral framework for consular practices and immigration laws that would govern the movement of people across borders.[28] Rules that are fair are necessary but not sufficient. For a game is not simply about rules, it is also about players. If one of the teams or one of the players does not have adequate training or preparation, it will simply be crushed by the other. For countries at vastly different levels of development, there should be more flexibility instead of complete rigidity in the application of uniform rules. Indeed, uniform rules for unequal partners can only produce unequal outcomes. And there is a need for positive discrimination, if not affirmative action, in favour of poor countries, particularly but not only for the LDCs that are latecomers to development.

In sum, the object of change, whether reshaping unfair rules, introducing new rules or allowing exceptions to existing rules in the world economy, should be to address the problems associated with the constraints on poor countries implicit in the presence or absence of rules, so as to enlarge the policy space available for the pursuit of national development objectives. This alone can provide the foundations for what is described as a global partnership in development. Of course, such a global partnership will also require a change in the asymmetrical relationship between rich and poor countries that has unfolded as the reality in the present agenda for global development cooperation, read by some as no more than performance criteria for developing countries, even if the intentions underlying the MDGs were noble. In this quest, there is need for a more equal partnership between industrialized countries and developing countries. There is just as much need for a partnership among the latter at different levels of development, particularly between the emerging economies and the LDCs.

The possibilities of cooperation among developing countries provide a new window of opportunity at this juncture in time. So far, this has been in the world of rhetoric rather than reality, words rather than substance. But this subset is an integral part of the logic of international collective action. What is more, the world has changed. In 2005, developing countries accounted for 81 per cent of the world population and 22 per cent of world income (almost 45% of world GDP in PPP terms). But that is not all. In the same year, 2005, developing countries accounted for 34 per cent of world exports, 33 per cent of world manufactured exports, 25 per cent of world manufacturing value added and 30 per cent of the stock of inward foreign direct investment in the world economy.[29] It needs to be said that much of the significance is concentrated in 12 developing countries, which account for 60 per cent of the population and 68 per cent of the income in the developing world.[30] Even so, this changed situation opens up possibilities. In the international context, where the distribution of economic and political power is so unequal, the increased economic significance and political influence of developing countries provides an opportunity to reshape rules and institutions even in the world of unequal partners. At the same time, the large emerging economies – say Brazil, China, India and South Africa – taken together may be able to exercise significant influence through multilateralism, whether institutions or rules, in the global context.[31] The United Nations, the World Bank, the IMF and the WTO are among the most important multilateral institutions in which the large emerging economies could exercise influence on behalf of the developing world.

Even if developing countries cannot change the world by articulating their voice or by using their bargaining power as a group or subset of a group, there are possibilities of cooperation among developing countries for themselves in many spheres. The institutional mechanisms might be inter-regional or intra-regional arrangements that pool markets and resources for development. The institutional mechanisms could also be bilateral or plurilateral forms of assistance, where some developing countries, learning from their experience, can help other countries that have to traverse a similar path. In fact, cooperation among developing countries may be particularly important in the pursuit of the MDGs, because it is about learning from each other in spheres where countries in the industrialized world simply do not have the experience.

In reflecting on the MDGs after 2015, there is an almost obvious need to think again and start afresh on the international aspects of MDGs. In doing so, it is imperative not simply to adapt, modify or transform the existing Goal 8, but also to reformulate, indeed redefine, the global agenda for development cooperation beyond the confines of Goal 8. This reflection should be concerned with three dimensions of the international context. First, it is necessary to remove the asymmetries implicit in the relative importance of different issues and in the relationship between rich and poor countries. Second, it is essential to enlarge the policy space available to countries that are latecomers to development, which has been encroached upon and significantly diminished by unfair rules for unequal partners in the contemporary world economy. Third, it is time to move away from unidirectional or asymmetrical relationships to evolve partnerships in development between industrialized countries and developing countries, as also among developing countries, in keeping with the logic and the spirit of international collective action.

Conclusions

The limitations of MDGs as a construct, in conception and in design, provide some basis for an evaluation of the MDGs as a framework. In terms of conception, there are some basic problems. The MDGs specify an outcome but do not set out the process which would make it possible to realize the objectives. The MDGs are stipulated without any reference to initial conditions, but where a country gets to in any given time horizon depends, at least in part, on where it starts out from. The MDGs are set out in terms of aggregates or averages which often conceal as much as they reveal, because there is no reference to distributional outcomes. In terms of design, there are some serious limitations. There is a multiplicity of objectives both quantitative and qualitative that span a wide range. The objectives are specified in many different ways: in proportions, to completion or just intentions. Some indicators are inappropriate and could be misleading. An evaluation of MDGs as a framework for monitoring progress in development highlights shortcomings. There is an implicit, albeit incorrect, presumption that one size fits all. There are unintended consequences, mostly in the form of misplaced emphasis, on stepping up the rate of economic growth and mobilizing external financing for social sectors. What is more, it would seem that the MDGs have been misunderstood, misused and misappropriated. These problems are attributable, in large part, to the silence on means, with a focus on ends, which in turn might have been attributable to two reasons that are understandable: the recognition that development is characterized by specificities in time and in space, and the acceptance that there might be genuine differences of opinion on what are appropriate strategies of development so that a political consensus on means would be exceedingly difficult if not impossible. But the silence was transformed into an opportunity by orthodoxy which simply occupied that vacant space. It had the voice and the influence to focus on faster growth, more aid and better governance. In the process, the essential values underlying the MDGs have been lost in translation.

In contemplating the future of MDGs beyond 2015, this chapter suggests some important conclusions. Such a framework is necessary even if it is point of reference. But it cannot simply be more of the same. The MDGs should be modified, but there is need for prudence in additions or subtractions while ensuring that such rethinking is not stifled. Generalized MDGs and contextualized MDGs are complements rather than substitutes, so that global goals should allow space for differences in initial conditions and in national priorities. Indeed, the time has come to reflect on contours of change which would represent departures from or substantial modifications in the existing framework. There are three imperatives that deserve to be highlighted. First, there should be structural flexibility at the national level. It must be made explicit that MDGs represent objectives for the world as a whole, which are not a scale to measure progress in every country because national goals must be formulated using global norms as a point of reference.

Second, there should be a clearly enunciated cognition of inequality in any assessment of outcomes. This is essential because inequalities exist and distributional outcomes matter. Hence, the focus of any such exercise to monitor progress must be on the poorest 25 per cent or bottom 40 per cent of the population. At the same time, there should be some attempt to consider spatial inequality within countries and monitor progress through disaggregated data at provincial or regional levels. Third, the new framework for the MDGs must incorporate some priors on means rather than simply focus on ends. The idea should be to provide an outline of the means, which sets out the bare essentials of possible approaches as points of reference but resists the temptation of setting out the specifics of policies. Indeed, the framework must be flexible so that countries have the freedom to formulate policies and evolve strategies recognizing specificities in time and space.

The recognition of poverty and deprivation with an emphasis on human development in the MDGs served a valuable purpose. But it was not enough because nothing was said about strategies to meet this challenge of development. The well-being of humankind is the essence of development, so that employment and livelihoods are essential while distributional outcomes are just as important. In the national context, therefore, it is necessary to reformulate policies, redesign strategies and rethink development. In reformulating policies, there is a strong need to reflect on macroeconomic objectives and macroeconomic policies. In redesigning strategies, it is necessary to introduce correctives and interventions that prevent or minimize the exclusion of people from development. The object of correctives should be to foster inclusion. In rethinking development, it is important to recognize the relevance of the balance between domestic and external factors and the critical importance of public action. It must be stressed that the developmental role of the state is critical across the entire spectrum of what needs to be done.

In the international context, the focus of MDGs is much too narrow. The misplaced emphasis on concessional development assistance, attributable to a donor-centric world view, dominates the discourse. Clearly, the international community needs to do better at this unfinished business, but far more needs to be done. Moreover, aid is a mixed blessing. There are other sources of external financing such as remittances from migrants that need to be explored. In any case, for developing countries, access to markets in trade and access to technology for development are far more important than foreign aid could ever be. Similarly, there is need to transform thinking on LDCs which seems to stress economic growth – assuming that it will trickle down – and investment in social sectors – assuming that it would reach the poor. The approach to poverty reduction needs to be reoriented away from compartmentalization in social sectors into an integration with development strategies that seek to combine economic growth with employment creation and participatory development. Most important, perhaps, it must be recognized that unfair rules of the game in the contemporary world economy encroach upon policy space so essential for development. This situation needs to be corrected. Even rules that are fair are necessary but not sufficient. And there is a need for positive discrimination, if not affirmative action, in favour of poor countries, particularly the LDCs that are latecomers to development. The possibilities of cooperation among developing countries at this juncture provides a new window of opportunity, through better bargaining and collective action, for reshaping some existing rules or creating new rules that are at least less unequal if not fair.

Acknowledgement

I am indebted to Sakiko Fukuda-Parr, Gustav Ranis and Jan Vandemoortele for helpful discussion and constructive suggestions on the theme of this essay. And I am grateful to Yilmaz Akyuz, Diana Alarcon, Seeta Prabhu, A. K. Shivakumar, Rob Vos and Guanghua Wan for valuable comments on presentations at different stages.

Notes

1 See United Nations (2000).
2 There were two resolutions in the United Nations in 1970, on the International Development Strategy for the Second United Nations Development Decade, which set out the objective that official development assistance (ODA) to developing countries should reach a level of 0.7 per cent of GDP of industrialized countries by middle of the decade (United Nations, 1970).
3 For a discussion on MDGs in historical perspective, see Jolly (2010).
4 In retrospect, it is clear that turning points in thinking about development during the second half of the 20th century, which reshaped strategies, were strongly influenced by history and conjuncture, reinforced by the dominant political ideology of the times. This hypothesis is developed, at some length, elsewhere by the author (Nayyar, 2008a).
5 See Vandemoortele (2010) and Fukuda-Parr (2010).
6 There is an extensive literature on the subject that attempts to provide an assessment of progress on MDGs. See, for example, United Nations (2009), UNDP (2010a), ESCAP-ADB-UNDP (2010), United Nations (2010a,b). See also, Vandemoortele (2010) and Fukuda-Parr and Greenstein (2010).

It would mean too much of a digression to enter into a discussion here because the purpose of this paper is somewhat different.

7 Studies carried out by the United Nations, which review the experience so far, suggest some correctives in the MDGs agenda for the period 2010–2015. See, in particular, UNDP (2010a) and UNDP(2010b). See also United Nations (2009), United Nations (2010a) and ESCAP-ADB-UNDP (2010).

8 For a lucid and critical analysis of this worldview, see Vandemoortele (2010).

9 For a more detailed discussion on the importance of inequality in the context of MDGs, see Fukuda-Parr (2010) and Vandemoortele and Delamonica (2010).

10 It has been convincingly argued that the MDGs set the bar too high for countries in Sub-Saharan Africa. See, for example, Easterly (2009). See also Vandemoortle and Delamonica (2010), who highlight this problem with the MDGs in a pointed manner: '. . .(this) begs the question whether Africa is missing the targets or the world is missing the point'.

11 See Gaiha (2003) and Reddy and Heuty (2008). There is substance in such critiques. Yet, it must be recognized that the problem arises in part from the definition of poverty in the headcount measure. For any given poverty line, those below are poor and those above are not. If the definition is binary, so is the target.

12 See Saith (2006).

13 For a detailed discussion, see Vandemoortele and Delamonica (2010). See also, Vandemoortele (2010).

14 The results of a survey of civil society organizations in developing countries suggest strong support for something like the MDGs (Pollard et al., 2011).

15 See, for example, Sumner and Tiwari (2009).

16 The earliest discussion on social indicators of development is in Baster (1972). This was followed by a focus on meeting basic human needs. See, for instance, Streeten (1981) and Stewart (1985). There is now an extensive literature on possible indicators of human development. See, for example, Fukuda-Parr and Shivakumar (2003) and UNDP(2010b).

17 For a discussion, see Manning (2009). See also, Fukuda-Parr and Greenstein (2010).

18 For a lucid analysis, see Sen (1999).

19 For a more detailed discussion, see Nayyar (2007).

20 See Nayyar (2011). See also, Stiglitz et al. (2006).

21 These correctives and interventions are discussed, at greater length, in Nayyar (2003).

22 For a more detailed discussion, see Nayyar (1997). See also, Bhaduri and Nayyar (1996).

23 See United Nations (2008) and United Nations (2010b). See also, UNDP (2010a).

24 See Nayyar (2008b).

25 For a more detailed discussion, see Fukuda-Parr (2010).

26 This proposition is developed, at some length, in Nayyar (2007).

27 The discussion that follows in this paragraph, on rules of the game in the world economy, draws upon earlier work of the author (Nayyar, 2002a, 2003).

28 For a discussion on the rationale for such a multilateral framework to govern cross-border movements of people, see Nayyar (2002b).
29 This evidence on the significance of developing countries in the world economy is from Nayyar (2009).
30 For more detailed evidence on this concentration, see Nayyar (2009).
31 The implications and consequences of the emerging significance of Brazil, China, India and South Africa in the wider context of the world economy are analysed, at some length, in a recent paper by the author. For a detailed discussion, see Nayyar (2010).

References

Baster, Nancy (ed.) (1972). *Measuring Development*, Frank Cass, London.

Bhaduri, Amit and Deepak Nayyar (1996). *The Intelligent Person's Guide to Liberalization*, Penguin Books, New Delhi.

Easterly, William (2009). 'How the Millennium Development Goals Are Unfair to Africa', *World Development*, Vol. 37, No. 1, pp. 26–35.

ESCAP-ADB-UNDP (2010). *Achieving the Millennium Development Goals in an Era of Global Uncertainty*, United Nations, Bangkok, and Asian Development Bank, Manila.

Fukuda-Parr, Sakiko (2010). 'Reducing Inequality – The Missing MDG: A Content Review of PRSPs and Bilateral Donor Policy Statements', *IDS Bulletin*, Vol. 41, No. 1, pp. 26–35.

Fukuda-Parr, Sakiko and J. Greenstein (2010). 'How Should MDG Implementation Be Measured: Faster Progress or Meeting Targets?', *IPC-IG Working Paper*, International Policy Centre for Inclusive Growth, Brasilia.

Fukuda-Parr, Sakiko and A. K. Shiva Kumar (eds.) (2003). *Readings on Human Development*, Oxford University Press, Delhi.

Gaiha, R. (2003). 'Are Millennium Goals of Poverty Reduction Useful', *Oxford Development Studies*, Vol. 31, No. 1, pp. 59–84.

Jolly, Richard (2010). 'The MDGs in Historical Perspective', *IDS Bulletin*, Vol. 41, No. 1, pp.48–50.

Manning, Richard (2009). *Using Indicators to Encourage Development: Learning Lessons from the Millennium Development Goals*, Danish Institute of International Studies, Copenhagen.

Nayyar, Deepak (1997). 'Themes in Trade and Industrialization', in Deepak Nayyar (ed.), *Trade and Industrialization*, Oxford University Press, Delhi.

Nayyar, Deepak (2002a). 'The Existing System and the Missing Institutions', in Deepak Nayyar (ed.), *Governing Globalization: Issues and Institutions*, Oxford University Press, Oxford.

Nayyar, Deepak (2002b). 'Cross-Border Movements of People', in Deepak Nayyar (ed.), *Governing Globalization: Issues and Institutions*, Oxford University Press, Oxford.

Nayyar, Deepak (2003). 'Globalization and Development Strategies', in John Toye (ed.), *Trade and Development*, Edward Elgar, Cheltenham.

Nayyar, Deepak (2007). 'Development through Globalization?', in George Mavrotas and Anthony Shorrocks (eds.), *Advancing Development: Core Themes in Global Economics*, Palgrave, London.

Nayyar, Deepak (2008a). 'Learning to Unlearn from Development', *Oxford Development Studies*, Vol. 36, No. 3, pp. 259–280.

Nayyar, Deepak (2008b). 'International Migration and Economic Development', in Narcis Serra and Joseph Stiglitz (eds.), *The Washington Consensus Reconsidered: Towards a New Global Governance*, Oxford University Press, Oxford.

Nayyar, Deepak (2009). 'Developing Countries in the World Economy: The Future in the Past?', *WIDER Annual Lecture 12*, UNU-WIDER, Helsinki.

Nayyar, Deepak (2010). 'China, India, Brazil and South Africa in the World Economy: Engines of Growth?', in Amelia Santos-Paulino and Guanghua Wan (eds.), *Southern Engines of Global Growth*, Oxford University Press, Oxford.

Nayyar, Deepak (2011). 'Rethinking Macroeconomic Policies for Development', *Brazilian Journal of Political Economy*, Vol. 31, No. 2, April–June, pp. 339–351.

Pollard, Amy, Andy Sumner, Monica Polato-Lopes and Agnes de Mauroy (2011). *100 Voices: Southern Perspectives on What Should Come after the Millennium Development Goals*, CAFOD, London and IDS, Sussex.

Reddy, Sanjay and Antoine Heuty (2008). 'Global Development Goals: The Folly of Technocratic Pretensions', *Development Policy Review*, Vol. 26, No. 1, pp. 5–28.

Saith, Ashwani (2006). 'From Universal Values to Millennium Development Goals: Lost in Translation', *Development and Change*, Vol. 37, No. 6, pp. 1167–1199.

Sen, Amartya (1999). *Development as Freedom*, Alfred E. Knopf, New York.

Stewart, Frances (1985). *Planning to Meet Basic Needs*, Macmillan, London.

Stiglitz, Joseph E., Jose Antonio Ocampo, Shari Spiegel, Ricardo Ffrench-Davis and Deepak Nayyar (2006). *Stability with Growth: Macroeconomics, Liberalization and Development*, Oxford University Press, Oxford.

Streeten, Paul (1981). *First Things First: Meeting Basic Human Needs in Developing Countries*, Oxford University Press, Oxford.

Sumner, Andy and Meera Tiwari (2009). 'After 2015: What Are the Ingredients of an MDG Plus Agenda for Poverty Reduction?', *Journal of International Development*, Vol. 21, No. 6, pp. 834–843.

UNDP (2010a). *What Will It Take to Achieve the Millennium Development Goals?*, United Nations, New York.

UNDP (2010b). *Human Development Report 2010*, United Nations, New York.

United Nations (1970). *International Development Strategy for the Second United Nations Development Decade*, General Assembly, Resolution A/RES/2626, United Nations, New York.

United Nations (2000). *Millennium Declaration*, DPI/2163, United Nations, New York.

United Nations (2008). *Delivering on the Global Partnership for Achieving the Millennium Development Goals*, The MDG Task Force Report 2008, New York.

United Nations (2009). *The Millennium Development Goals Report 2009*, United Nations, New York.

United Nations (2010a). *The Millennium Development Goals Report 2010*, United Nations, New York.

United Nations (2010b). *The Global Partnership for Development at a Critical Juncture, The MDG Task Force Report 2010*, United Nations, New York.

Vandemoortele, Jan (2010). Changing the Course of MDGs by Changing the Discourse, Real Instituto Elcano, available from http://www.realinstitutoelcano.org

Vandemoortele, Jan and Enrique Delamonica (2010). 'Taking the MDGs beyond 2015: Hasten Slowly', *IDS Bulletin*, Vol. 41, No. 1, pp. 60–69.

Part II

GROWTH AND DEVELOPMENT

5

THE WEST AND THE REST IN THE WORLD ECONOMY

The next transformation?

The world has changed. Sixty years ago, *circa* 1950, soon after the end of the Second World War and at the beginning of the post-colonial era, there were two sharp divides in the world: the East-West divide between communist and capitalist countries and the North-South divide between rich and poor countries. The distinction between East and West vanished with the collapse of communism in 1990, as capitalism emerged triumphant. The world of competing political ideologies was replaced by a world with a single dominant political ideology. The distinction between the North and the South has also become more diffused with the passage of time, as the reality has changed during the past three decades. The financial crisis of the late 2008, which led to the Great Recession, turned out to be the deepest crisis in capitalism since the Great Depression more than 75 years ago. The recovery is fragile and the prospects are uncertain. This has eroded the triumph of capitalism. But it has also reinforced the shift in the balance of economic power somewhat more towards the South. This process began some time ago, but is now more discernible. Even so, perceptions have changed slowly. There are oversimplified pictures of one billion people in rich countries and six billion people in poor countries, although there are poor people in rich countries and rich people in poor countries. It is time for a dispassionate analysis of how much this reality has changed.

The object of this chapter is to analyse the evolution of developing countries in the world economy situated in a long-term historical perspective, but with a focus on the second half of the 20th century and the first decade of the 21st century. Developing countries are made up of Africa, Asia (excluding Japan) and Latin America (including the Caribbean). The discussion highlights the overwhelming significance of the three continents, now described as the developing world, in the world economy until two centuries ago, and traces their decline and fall during the period from 1820 to 1950. The six decades since 1950 witnessed an increase in the share of developing countries not only in world population and world income, but also in international trade, international investment, industrial production and manufactured exports, which gathered momentum after 1980. The divergence in per capita incomes came to a stop in 1980. This was followed by a modest convergence beginning around 1990, which became more discernible after 2000, but it was clearly visible only in Asia. The ongoing catch up is driven by industrialization and economic growth. However, this impressive performance in the aggregate is characterized by uneven development. There is an exclusion of countries and people from the process. The catch up is concentrated in a few countries. Growth has often not been transformed into meaningful development that improves the well-being of people. Yet, the economic balance of power in the world is beginning to shift. In this context, the essay contemplates the future of developing countries in the world economy, which is obviously uncertain and unpredictable, to consider whether this catch up is sustainable and how it might reshape the international context.

Overwhelming significance

In the span of world history, the distinction between industrialized and developing economies, or rich and poor countries, is relatively recent. It surfaced in the last quarter of the 19th century. In fact, 1,000 years ago, Asia, Africa and South America, taken together, accounted for more than 80 per cent of world population and world income. This was attributable in large part to Asia, where just two countries, China and India, accounted for approximately 50 per cent of world population and world income. The overwhelming significance of these three continents in the world economy continued for another five centuries until 1500.

The beginnings of change are discernible from the early 16th century to the late 18th century. The voyages of discovery and the colonization of the Americas were critical turning points, as the consequent mercantile expansion of trade, supported by State power and naval power, combined with social, political and institutional change in Europe, created the initial conditions for capitalist development. Even so, in the mid-18th century, the similarities between Europe and Asia were far more significant than the differences. Indeed, demography, technology and institutions were broadly comparable. The Industrial Revolution in Britain during the late 18th century, which spread to Europe over the next 50 years, exercised a profound influence on the shape of things to come. Yet, in 1820, less than 200 years ago, Asia, Africa and Latin America still accounted for almost three-fourths of world population and around two-thirds of world income. The share of China and India, taken together, was 50 per cent even in 1820.

Decline and fall

The dramatic transformation of the world economy began around 1820. Slowly but surely, the geographical divides in the world turned into economic divides. The divide rapidly became a wide chasm. The economic significance of Asia, Africa and Latin America witnessed a precipitous decline such that, by 1950, there was a pronounced asymmetry between their share of world population at two-thirds and their share of world income at about one-fourth. In sharp contrast, between 1820 and 1950, Europe, North America and Japan increased their share in world population from one-fourth to one-third and in world income from more than one-third to almost three-fourths. The rise of 'The West' was concentrated in Western Europe and North America. The decline and fall of 'The Rest' was concentrated in Asia, much of it attributable to China and India, while Latin America was the exception, as its shares in world population and income were not only symmetrical throughout, but also rose over time.

The Great Divergence in per capita incomes was, nevertheless, the reality. In a short span of 130 years, from 1820 to 1950, as a percentage of GDP per capita in Western Europe and North America, GDP per capita in Latin America dropped from three-fifths to two-fifths, in Africa from one-third to one-seventh and in Asia from one-half to one-tenth. But that was not all. Between 1830 and 1913, the share of Asia, Africa and Latin America in world manufacturing production, attributable mostly to Asia, in particular China and India, collapsed from 60 per cent to 7.5 per cent, while the share of Europe, North America and Japan rose from 40 per cent to 92.5 per cent, to stay at these levels until 1950. The industrialization of Western Europe and the deindustrialization of Asia during the 19th century were two sides of the same coin. It led to the Great Specialization, which meant that Western Europe, followed by the United States, specialized in and exported manufactured goods, while Asia, Africa and Latin America specialized in and exported primary commodities.

The century from 1850 to 1950 witnessed a progressive integration of Asia, Africa and Latin America into the world economy, through international trade, international investment and international migration, which created and embedded a division of labour between countries that was unequal in its consequences for development. The outcome of this process was the decline and fall of Asia and a retrogression of Africa, although Latin America fared much better in its post-colonial era, except for the divergence in incomes, so that by 1950 the divide between rich industrialized countries and poor underdeveloped countries was enormous.

Divergence ends: convergence begins?

During the six decades from 1950 to 2010, changes in the share of developing countries in world output and in levels of per capita income relative to industrialized countries provide a sharp contrast. In terms of Maddison PPP statistics, the share of developing countries in world output stopped its continuous decline *circa* 1960, when it was about one-fourth, to increase rapidly after 1980, so that it was almost one-half by 2008, while the divergence in GDP per capita also came to a stop in 1980 and was followed by a modest convergence thereafter, so that as a proportion of GDP per capita in industrialized countries it was somewhat less than one-fifth in 2008. In current prices at market exchange rates, between 1970 and 2010, the share of developing countries in world GDP doubled from one-sixth to one-third, while their GDP per capita as a proportion of that in industrialized countries recorded a modest increase from one-fourteenth to one-eleventh. Differences in GDP growth rates underlie the rising share of developing countries and the falling share of industrialized countries in world GDP.

During the period 1951–1980, GDP growth rates in developing countries were somewhat higher than in industrialized countries. This performance was impressive, because these three decades coincided with the golden age of capitalism when the industrialized world experienced unprecedented rapid growth. For developing countries, such growth rates provided a sharp contrast with their performance in the preceding 100 years, and were also much higher than growth rates in industrialized countries at comparable stages of their development.

During the period 1981–2008, GDP growth rates in developing countries were almost double those in industrialized countries. Until 1980, growth rates of GDP per capita in developing countries were lower than in industrialized countries because of high population growth rates, but this was reversed after 1980 as their GDP growth was so much higher and population growth rates slowed down. These differences underlie the end of divergence in per capita incomes *circa* 1980, followed by the beginnings of a very modest convergence that is discernible after 1990 and more visible in the 2000s.

The idea that latecomers to industrialization catch up with countries that are leaders, over time, exists in unconventional economic history and orthodox economic theory. In reality, there is nothing automatic about convergence, just as there is nothing automatic about growth. Convergence and divergence are often simultaneous. Convergence is also uneven across space and over time. This is borne out by the experience of developing countries in the world economy since 1950. It is clear that there were the modest beginnings of convergence in Asia and growing divergence in Africa, while Latin America stayed roughly where it was. Of course, it is difficult to generalize at the level of continents. But it is possible to draw conclusions about convergence or divergence with reference to particular countries. And evidence for selected countries confirms these inter-regional differences. Even so, it does not quite validate the convergence hypothesis.

The engagement of developing countries with the world economy witnessed a decline during the period from 1950 to 1980, particularly when compared with the past, but revived *circa* 1980 and grew rapidly thereafter. However, this deeper engagement was a matter of choice, in sharp contrast with the compulsion of the past. Their share in world merchandize trade, exports and imports more than doubled, from less than 20 per cent in 1970 to more than 40 per cent in 2010. Similarly, their share of international trade in services registered a substantial increase to reveal their comparative advantage in exports of services. During the 1990s and 2000s, the share of developing countries in the stock and flows of inward, as also outward, foreign direct investment in the world economy increased at the expense of industrialized countries, although they were more important as countries of destination than as countries of origin.

The movement of people from developing to industrialized countries emerged as a significant form of engagement, despite draconian immigration laws and restrictive consular practices, with new forms of mobility such as guest workers, illegal immigrants and professional persons, driven by markets and globalization. Such international migration exercised an important influence on the world economy. It was an important factor underlying productivity increase and economic dynamism in industrialized countries. Remittances from migrants were an important source of external finance in developing countries that eased constraints on growth, although the brain drain was an obvious negative consequence, but return migration could transform this into a brain gain.

It is clear that, during the second half of the 20th century and the first decade of the 21st century, there was a substantial catch up on the part of developing countries. Some comparisons of their relative importance in the world economy at present with the past are instructive. In 2008, the share of developing countries in world GDP was close to their share around 1850, while their GDP per capita as a proportion of that in industrialized countries was about the same as in 1900. The share of developing countries in world trade even in 1970 was the same as it was in 1913. And the significance of foreign investment for developing countries at the end of the 20th century was about the same as it was at the end of the 19th century. The share of developing countries in world industrial production remained at its 1913 level until 1970, but returned to its 1880 level around 1990. In 2010, this share was higher than it was in 1860 and possibly close to its level around 1850.

On the whole, it is plausible to suggest that the significance of developing countries in the world economy *circa* 2010 is about the same as it was in 1870 or a little earlier. Given this situation in 2010, which is an outcome of the catch-up process since 1950, it is also plausible to suggest that the significance of developing countries in the world economy *circa* 2030 would be about the same as it was in 1820.

Catch up in industrialization

It is clear that there was a significant catch up in industrialization for the developing world as a whole beginning around 1950 that gathered momentum in the early 1970s. Structural changes in the composition of output and employment, which led to a decline in the share of agriculture with an increase in the shares of industry and services, were an important factor underlying this process. There was a dramatic transformation in just four decades from 1970 to 2010. The share of developing countries in world industrial production jumped from one-twelfth to one-third in constant prices and from one-eighth to two-fifths in current prices, so that in 2010 it was close to its level in the mid-19th century. Similarly, their share in world exports of manufactures rose from one-twelfth to two-fifths. Industrialization also led to pronounced changes in the composition of their trade, as the share of primary commodities and resource-based products fell while the share of manufactures (particularly medium-technology and high-technology goods) rose in both exports and imports. However, this industrialization was most uneven between regions. Asia led the process in terms of structural change, share in industrial production, rising manufactured exports and changing patterns of trade, while Latin America witnessed relatively little change and Africa made almost no progress.

The observed outcome in terms of industrial production was attributable, in important part, to development strategies and economic policies in the post-colonial era that created the initial conditions and laid the essential foundations in countries, which were latecomers to industrialization. The import substitution led strategies of industrialization, much maligned by orthodoxy that was concerned with comparative statics rather than economic dynamics, performed a critical role in this process of catch up. Of course, a complete explanation would be far more complex, as it would need to recognize specificities and nuances. All the same, it is clear that the role of the State in evolving policies, developing institutions and making strategic interventions, whether as a catalyst or a leader, was also central to the process. Indeed, even among the small East Asian countries, success stories that orthodoxy portrayed as role models of markets and openness, development was more about the visible hand of the State rather than the invisible hand of the market, particularly in South Korea and Taiwan, but perhaps even in Singapore.

Thus, industrialization was not so much about getting-prices-right as it was about getting-state-intervention-right. Indeed, it is plausible to suggest that, for a time, it might even have been about getting-prices-wrong. It may be argued that State intervention in the form of industrial policy should recognize and exploit potential comparative advantage, but it is just as plausible to argue that instead of climbing the ladder step-by-step it could be rewarding to jump some steps in defiance of what comparative advantage might be at the time. In either case, state intervention is critical. Apart from an extensive role for governments, the use of borrowed technologies, an intense process of learning, the creation of managerial capabilities in individuals and technological capabilities in firms, the nurturing of entrepreneurs and firms in different types of enterprises were important factors underlying the catch up in industrialization.

The creation of initial conditions was followed by a period of learning to industrialize so that outcomes in industrialization surfaced with a time lag. This accounts for the acceleration in the growth of manufacturing output that became visible in the early 1970s.

The share of developing countries in world manufacturing value added was higher than their share of world manufactured exports through the 1970s, in the process of learning to industrialize, but his difference narrowed through the 1980s as some countries became increasingly competitive in some sectors, such as labour-intensive consumer goods. The two shares moved in tandem from the late 1980s to the early 1990s, as developing countries became competitive in the world market for manufactures. The share of developing countries in manufactured exports exceeded their share in manufacturing value added in the world economy from 1992 to 2008, possibly as a consequence of their increasing international competitiveness and their growing engagement with the world economy driven partly by the internationalization of production and the activities of global value chains. It is not surprising that the two shares moved in tandem once again thereafter in the aftermath of the financial crisis that led to an economic downturn in the industrialized countries, which provided the markets for manufactured exports from developing countries.

Clearly, it was not the magic of markets that produced the sudden spurt in industrialization. It came from the foundations that were laid in the preceding quarter century. In this context, it is important to note that much the same can be said about the now industrialized countries, where industrial protection and state intervention were just as important, at earlier stages of their development when they were latecomers to industrialization.

Uneven development

The distribution of catch up in industrialization and development was uneven not only among regions, but also between countries within regions. There was a high degree of concentration among a few: Argentina, Brazil, Chile and Mexico in Latin America; China, India, Indonesia, Malaysia, South Korea, Taiwan, Thailand and Turkey in Asia; and Egypt and South Africa in Africa. In fact, the economic significance of these countries, termed the Next-14, in the developing world was overwhelming in terms of their size reflected in GDP and population; their engagement with the world economy reflected in trade, investment and migration; and industrialization reflected in manufactured exports and industrial production. The determinants of such concentration are size, growth and history. There was also enormous diversity within the few, characterized by an unequal distribution, in terms of the same attributes that revealed the concentration among them. In comparison with per capita income levels in the industrialized world, country-level evidence confirms regional differences. The eight Asian countries brought an end to divergence and saw the beginnings of convergence, while the four Latin American countries stayed roughly where they were and the two African countries experienced a continuing divergence.

There were also differences between the Next-14 in settings (abundant or scarce in land and natural resources), drivers (primary commodities or cheap labour), emphases, (domestic or external markets and resources), transitions (patterns of structural change) and models (domestic or foreign capital, technology and markets). Yet, despite their apparent diversity, it is possible to group them into clusters based on similarities in terms of geographical location, country size, economic characteristics and development models. They had even more in common across clusters in terms of three factors that put them on the path to industrialization: initial conditions, enabling institutions and the role of governments as catalysts or leaders in the process. The essential differences with other countries in the developing world, apart from a history of manufacturing experience, also lie in these three common factors. But many of the laggards in industrialization may not be very different from what these leaders in industrialization were 50 years ago. Indeed, there is much that they can learn from the experience of the Next-14 in creating initial conditions, establishing enabling institutions and nurturing supportive governments. But these efforts must be contextualized. In the catch-up process, there are two essential challenges for late industrializers – leaders and followers alike. It is necessary to create control mechanisms embodied in institutions that impose discipline on economic behaviour not only of individuals and firms, but also of governments. It is necessary to develop technological capabilities in firms and in the economy, which can advance the technology frontier in at least a few industries or sectors.

Emerging divergences

The era of catch up from 1950 to 2010 has been associated with emerging divergences in the world economy. First, international inequality between countries and people remained at high levels. Inequality between countries diminished slowly if modestly, but if China and India are excluded it increased rapidly after 1980. Much of this was attributable to inequality between rich industrialized countries and the poor developing world, although there was some increase in inequality within the latter. Inequality among people in the world, which increased sharply during the period from 1820 to 1950 as a consequence of the Great Divergence, persisted at somewhat higher levels through the second half of the 20th century. Second, the process of catch up was associated with an exclusion of countries and regions within countries in the developing world from the process of development. There was a massive divergence in per capita incomes between LDCs and the rest of the developing world, while there was a significant convergence in per capita incomes for the Next-14 with the rest of the developing world. But there was an exclusion of regions within the Next-14 from this convergence process. Third, rapid economic growth in the developing world, underlying the catch up in terms of aggregate income, was not always transformed into meaningful development, which improved the well-being of ordinary people. During the period from 1981 to 2008, the proportion of the population below the specified international poverty lines declined steadily, more for the lower than for the higher poverty line, but these proportions remain significant. Moreover, the absolute number of people below both poverty lines remains large, while the number of people between the two poverty lines, who are vulnerable, doubled over this period. The number of poor people in 2010 is large not only in Sub-Saharan Africa, but also in Asia despite its rapid economic growth, rising share of world income and catch up in industrialization. This is because economic inequality between people has been high or rising in these countries (particularly in the Next-14) that have led the catch-up process. Indeed, a disproportionately large part of increments in income may have accrued to the super-rich or the ultra-rich in the population.

The emerging divergences within the developing world are striking and deserve emphasis. It is perfectly clear that LDCs experienced a sharp divergence in their per capita incomes when compared with other parts of the developing world, which suggests that this set of countries were largely excluded from the catch-up process. It is also worth noting that there was a similar exclusion of regions within countries, particularly in countries that were an integral part of the catch-up process. Income inequality between people within countries was driven up everywhere by markets and globalization. Developing countries were no exception to this global trend, so that there was an exclusion of people from the catch up in terms of GDP aggregates. In most of the Next-14, which led the process of catch up, income inequality increased in some countries, where it was low to start with, and remained at high levels in other countries, even if it decreased from higher initial levels. It would seem that the modest convergence of incomes with the outside world was associated with a divergence of incomes between countries, as also between regions and people within countries.

In conclusion

The changes in the significance of developing countries in the world economy, which started in 1950 to gather momentum after 1980, are beginning to chip away at the economic dominance and political hegemony of the leading industrialized countries. This hegemony was reinforced for a time following the collapse of communism *circa* 1990, but has been diluted in the aftermath of the financial crisis in 2008. There is an important lesson that emerges from history. Dominant powers are reluctant to cede economic or political space to newcomers. Thus, the emergence of new centres of production in economics and new centres of power in politics does have a profound effect on hegemonic powers in terms of political economy. Such processes are always slow, and the present conjuncture represents an interregnum because the resurgence of Asia, particularly China, is not large enough in the context of the world economy, at least so far, to shift the hegemonic balance. But the beginnings of change with some erosion of hegemony are discernible. This is complex rather than simple as a phenomenon and will be played out over a long period of time. Both the duration and the outcome of this process are unpredictable. Even so, it is possible to contemplate or speculate about possible future scenarios.

The economic determinants of potential growth in the developing world are a source of good news. And, in principle, developing countries may be able to sustain high rates of growth for some time to come. There are three reasons. Their population size is large, which is a possible source of growth, and their income levels are low, which means that the possibilities of growth are greater. Their demographic characteristics, in particular the high proportion of young people in the population, which would mean an increase in their workforce and savings rates for some time to come, are conducive to economic growth, provided education spreads across society to create capabilities among people. Their wages are significantly lower than in the world outside, which is an important source of competitiveness for some time to come.

In practice, developing countries may not be able to realize this potential for growth because of constraints that may differ across space and surface over time. There are country-specific constraints. There are general constraints, common to most developing countries such as poor infrastructure, underdeveloped institutions, inadequate education, unstable politics or poor governance. There are constraints that may arise from the process of growth such as economic exclusion, social conflict and environmental stress. And there are some constraints that may be external such as worsening terms of trade, restricted market access for exports, inadequate sources of external finance or a crisis in the world economy.

The biggest challenge to the rise of developing countries lies within. They must ensure that the benefits of catch up are distributed in a far more equal manner between people and regions within countries. It will not be possible to sustain economic growth in the long run if it does not improve the living conditions of people. In the pursuit of development, poverty eradication, employment creation and inclusive growth are an imperative. This is the only sustainable way forward because it would enable them to mobilize their most abundant resource, people, for the purpose of development and reinforce the process of growth through cumulative causation. Therefore, developing countries must endeavour to combine economic growth with human development and social progress. In this process, political democracy can provide the much-needed checks and balances.

It is essential to recognize that the significance of developing countries in the world would be shaped not only in the sphere of economics, but also in the realm of politics. Their emerging significance in the world economy is attributable in part to their share in world population and in world income and in part to their engagement in the world economy through international trade, international investment and international migration. In the economic sphere, their potential importance in future far exceeds their actual importance at present. In the political sphere, their importance is more discernible at the present juncture, which is attributable in part to their size in terms of population (that is young rather than old) and in part to their size in terms of geographical space. The end of the first decade in the 21st century is perhaps a turning point. It is plausible to argue though impossible to prove that this represents the beginnings of a profound change in the balance of economic and political power in the world.

History may not repeat itself. But it would be wise to learn from history. The early 19th century was a turning point in the world economy. It was the beginning of the end of Asia's overwhelming significance in the world economy. And it was the beginning of the rise of Europe, in particular Britain, to dominance in the world. The early 20th century was the next turning point. It was the beginning of the end of Britain's dominance in the world. And it was the beginning of the rise of the United States to dominance in the world. The catch up and the transformation spanned half a century. The early 21st century, perhaps, represents a similar turning point. It could be the beginning of the end of the dominance of the United States in the world. The emergence of countries outside North America and Western Europe, particularly the powerhouse economies not only in Asia, but also in other continents of the developing world, constitutes a striking transformation. The rise of Asia and the decline of Western Europe, in a relative rather than absolute sense, are discernible. There is an irony in this emerging situation when compared with the past of Asia and Western Europe in history.

The outcome, 50 years later, is likely to be a multipolar world in which dominance might not be so striking. Of course, in times to come, the continued rise of the Next-14, or countries that follow in their footsteps or the developing world as a whole, is not quite predictable and far from certain. It would depend, in large part, on whether developing countries can transform themselves into inclusive societies where economic growth, human development and social progress move in tandem. This catch up and transformation, if it materializes, could span at least half a century if not longer. Yet, the beginnings of a shift in the balance of power are discernible. And the past could be a pointer to the future.

Acknowledgement

This chapter is based on the author's book, *Catch Up: Developing Countries in the World Economy*, Oxford University Press, Oxford, 2013. For details, including statistical sources and bibliographic references, readers should consult the book.

6

CHINA, INDIA, BRAZIL AND SOUTH AFRICA IN THE WORLD ECONOMY

Engines of growth?

Introduction

The object of this chapter is to analyze the economic implications of the rise of China, India, Brazil and South Africa situated in the wider context of the world economy. The structure of the chapter is as follows. The first section sketches a profile of China, India, Brazil and South Africa in the world economy. It sets the stage by outlining the broad contours of their significance in the past, present and future. The next section asks whether these countries could be the new engines of growth for the world, beginning with history and statistics to touch upon the underlying economic causation. The third section examines the possible impact of rapid growth in the four economies on the world economy, the industrialized countries and the developing countries. The penultimate section considers the main forms of engagement and channels of interaction for these countries with the world economy, with a focus on international trade, international investment, international finance and international migration. The final section discusses the potential influence of China, India, Brazil and South Africa on institutions in the global context, which would obviously extend beyond economics into politics and range from bilateralism through plurilateralism to multilateralism.

China, India, Brazil and South Africa in the world economy

The significance of China, India, Brazil and South Africa (CIBS) in the global context has changed over time. The discussion in this section provides a historical perspective of the past, a snapshot of the present and an extrapolated scenario for the future.

The past

The emerging significance of CIBS in the world economy must be situated in historical perspective. Table 6.1, which is based on estimates made by Angus Maddison, presents evidence on the shares of CIBS in world population and in world income for selected years during the period 1820–2001. It shows that in 1820, CIBS accounted for 57 per cent of world population and almost 50 per cent of world income. There was a dramatic change in the next 150 years. In 1973, the share of CIBS in the world population was significantly lower, at about 40 per cent, but their share in the world income collapsed to less than 11 per cent, which was a small fraction when compared with 150 years earlier. The next 30 years witnessed some recovery. While the share of

Table 6.1 China, India, Brazil and South Africa in the world economy: share in world population and world GDP, 1820–2001

Year	*China*	*India*	*Brazil*	*South Africa*
	Percentage share of world population			
1820	36.6	20.1	0.4	0.1
1870	28.1	19.9	0.8	0.2
1913	24.4	17.0	1.3	0.3
1950	21.7	14.2	2.1	0.5
1973	22.5	14.8	2.6	0.6
2001	20.7	16.5	2.9	0.7
	Percentage share of world income			
1820	32.9	16.0	0.4	0.1
1870	17.1	12.1	0.6	0.2
1913	8.8	7.5	0.7	0.4
1950	4.5	4.2	1.7	0.6
1973	4.6	3.1	2.5	0.6
2001	12.3	5.4	2.7	0.5

Notes: The percentages in this table have been calculated from estimates of population and GDP in Maddison (2003). The data on GDP are in 1990 international Geary–Khamis dollars, which are PPPs used to evaluate output that are calculated based on a specific method devised to define international prices. This measure facilitates inter-country comparisons over time.

Source: Maddison (2003).

CIBS in world population remained in the range of 40 per cent, their share in world income rose to almost 21 per cent in 2001. These aggregates not only reveal the essential contours, but also conceal some aspects of the story. There are similarities between China and India, just as there are similarities between Brazil and South Africa; however, there are significant differences between the two sets of countries. For much of the time, China and India had dominant shares.[1]

Beginning in 1820, the share of China and India in world population declined steadily until 1973, but over the same period the decline in their share of world income was considerably more pronounced. Consequently, during the period 1820–1973, there was a sharp increase in the asymmetries or disproportionalities between the shares of China and India in world population and in world income. The partial recovery in their share of world income during the period 1973–2001 has reduced the asymmetry, but the disproportionality remains significant. For much of the time, the shares of Brazil and South Africa were far smaller. However, there were also other important differences: the shares of Brazil and South Africa in world population and in world income increased, even if slowly for some of the time throughout this period; the shares of Brazil and South Africa in world population and in world income were symmetrical and proportional throughout this period.

The present

It is possible to juxtapose this past with the present. Table 6.2 outlines a profile of GDP, population and GDP per capita in CIBS in 2000 and 2005, as compared with developing countries, industrialized countries and the world. It shows that the population of the world is more than 6 billion, of which slightly fewer than 1 billion are in the industrialized countries, somewhat more than 5 billion are in the developing countries and more than 2.5 billion are in CIBS. Thus, 40 per cent of the population in the world and 50 per cent of the population in developing countries live in CIBS. There are two sets of figures on GDP and GDP per capita: at constant prices with market exchange rates and in terms of PPPs.

At market exchange rates, between 2000 and 2005, the share of CIBS increased from 7 per cent to 9 per cent of world GDP and from 39 per cent to 43 per cent of GDP in developing countries. Over the same period, at market exchange rates, GDP per capita in China was about the same, GDP per capita for India was less than half, while GDP per capita in Brazil and South Africa was more than double the average GDP per capita in developing countries. It is worth noting that

Table 6.2 GDP, population and GDP per capita: China, India, Brazil and South Africa, 2000 and 2005

Country	*GDP*				*Population*		*PPP-GDP*			
	($ billion)		*($ per capita)*		*(million)*		*($ billion)*		*($ per capita)*	
	2000	*2005*	*2000*	*2005*	*2000*	*2005*	*2000*	*2005*	*2000*	*2005*
China	1,198	1,890	949	1,449	1,263	1,305	4,973	7,842	3,939	6,012
India	460	644	453	588	1,016	1,095	2,402	3,362	2,364	3,072
Brazil	602	670	3,461	3,597	174	186	1,251	1,393	7,193	7,475
South Africa	133	160	3,020	3,406	44	47	386	463	8,764	9,884
Total	2,393	3,364			2,496	2,632	9,011	13,061		
Developing countries	6,058	7,813	1,191	1,440	5,085	5,427	18,818	25,322	3,701	4,666
(CIBS as percentage of)	(39.5)	(43.1)			(49.1)	(48.5)	(47.9)	(51.6)		
Industrialized countries	24,542	27,148	27,304	29,251	899	928	25,157	27,898	27,988	30,058
World	31,756	36,352	5,241	5,647	6,060	6,438	45,144	54,573	7,450	8,477
(CIBS as percentage of)	(7.5)	(9.3)			(41.2)	(40.9)	(20.0)	(23.9)		

Notes: GDP and GDP per capita are measured in constant US$ 2000. PPP-GDP and PPP-GDP per capita are measured in constant 2000 international dollars.

Source: World Bank (2007).

CIBS are far below GDP per capita in the industrialized countries and significantly below GDP per capita in the world as a whole. The picture is somewhat different if the comparison is in terms of PPPs. Between 2000 and 2005, the CIBS share increased from 20 per cent to 24 per cent of world PPP-GDP and from 48 per cent to 52 per cent of the PPP-GDP of developing countries. It would seem that, for CIBS, taken together, these shares in world income are now much more symmetrical with their share in world population. Over the same period, in PPP terms, GDP per capita in China moved ahead of GDP per capita in developing countries, whereas GDP per capita in India was about two-thirds of GDP per capita in developing countries. In contrast, GDP per capita in Brazil and South Africa was more than double the GDP per capita in developing countries and close to the world average.

This snapshot situates CIBS in the world economy at the present juncture. However, the observed reality has been shaped by their economic performance in the past. Table 6.3 sets out rates of growth in CIBS GDP and GDP per capita during the period 1951–1980 and 1981–2005 in comparison with regions within the developing world, the developing countries, the industrialized countries and the world economy.[2]

It is worth noting that time series data on GDP and GDP per capita for the entire period from 1951 to 2005 are not available from a single source. The figures for the period 1951–1980 are based on the Maddison data, as United Nations data are not available before 1971. The figures for the period 1981–2005 are based on United Nations data because Maddison data are not available after 2001. These two sources are not strictly comparable. However, it is possible to resolve the problem, as data are available from both sources for the period 1981–2000. To facilitate a comparison, Table 6.3 also presents figures on growth rates during 1981–2000, computed separately from Maddison data and United Nations data. A comparison of the two sets of growth rates during the period 1981–2000, for which both sources are available, shows that the numbers correspond closely, except in the figures for China, where UN data suggest much higher growth rates than Maddison data. Even so, it is reasonable to infer that the growth rates for the periods 1951–1980 and 1981–2005, even if computed from different sources, are comparable, with the exception of China. In interpreting the data on China, where the step-up in growth rates between these two periods is probably overstated, some downward adjustment might be needed.

A study of Table 6.3 clearly shows that growth in GDP and GDP per capita during 1981–2005 was much slower than during 1951–1980.

Table 6.3 Growth performance of China, India, Brazil and South Africa, 1951–1980 and 1981–2005, comparison with regions and country-groups (percentage per annum)

	Maddison data		*United Nations data*	
	1951–1980	*1981–2000*	*1981–2000*	*1981–2005*
	GDP			
China	5.0	7.4	9.8	9.7
India	3.6	5.7	5.5	5.8
Brazil	6.8	2.1	2.0	2.0
South Africa	4.5	1.5	1.6	2.0
Asia	6.3	4.0	3.9	4.1
Latin America	4.7	2.0	2.1	2.3
Africa	4.1	2.4	2.6	3.0
Developing countries	4.8	2.7	2.7	3.0
Industrialized countries	4.4	2.6	2.6	2.5
World	4.8	2.6	2.7	3.0
	GDP per capita			
China	3.0	6.0	8.5	8.5
India	1.4	3.6	3.5	3.8
Brazil	3.9	0.3	0.2	0.3
South Africa	1.9	–0.3	–0.6	0.0
Asia	2.9	1.6	1.4	1.6
Latin America	2.1	0.2	0.2	0.4
Africa	1.7	–0.2	–0.1	0.4
Developing countries	2.2	0.4	0.4	0.8
Industrialized countries	3.5	2.0	2.1	2.0
World	2.4	0.7	0.7	1.0

Notes: The growth rates for each period are computed as geometric means of the annual growth rates in that period. The Maddison data and the United Nations data on GDP and GDP per capita are not strictly comparable. The Maddison data on GDP and GDP per capita, which are in 1990 international Geary–Khamis dollars, are PPPs used to evaluate output which are calculated based on a specific method devised to define international prices. This measure facilitates intercountry comparisons. The United Nations data on GDP and GDP per capita are in constant 1990 US dollars. The figures in this table for the world economy cover 128 countries, of which 21 are industrialized countries and 107 are developing countries. Latin America includes the Caribbean.

Sources: Maddison (2003) and United Nations (2006b, 2006c).

This was so for the world economy, for industrialized countries and for developing countries. Almost everywhere, growth in GDP was in the range of 4–5 per cent per annum during 1951–1980 and in the range of 2–3 per cent per annum during 1981–2005, except in Asia, where it was 6 per cent and 4 per cent per annum, respectively. Growth in GDP per capita slowed down considerably, even in the industrialized countries, from 3.5 per cent per annum to 2 per cent per annum, but the slowdown was more pronounced for developing countries, from 2.2 per cent per annum to 0.8 per cent per annum. In Latin America and Africa during 1981–2005, growth in GDP per capita was less than 0.5 per cent per annum, while Asia fared better at more than 1.5 per cent per annum.

The economic performance of China, Brazil and South Africa presents a mixed picture, which does not quite conform to the trends observed in the aggregate. The most striking contrast is that China and India were the clear exceptions to this worldwide slowdown in growth. In both countries, growth rates in the second period were much higher than the perfectly respectable growth rates in the first period. So much so that, between 1951–1980 and 1981–2005, average annual growth in GDP per capita almost trebled in both China and India. This was attributable, in part, to higher GDP growth rates and lower population growth rates. Unlike China and India, however, Brazil and South Africa were a part of the worldwide slowdown in growth. In both countries, growth rates in the second period were much lower than the impressive growth rates in the first period. So much so that, during 1981–2005, average annual growth in GDP per capita was almost negligible in both Brazil and South Africa. However, it is also worth noting that, during 1951–1980, average annual growth in GDP and GDP per capita in Brazil was significantly higher than that in China and India. The growth performance of South Africa during 1951–1980 was also better than that of India, although it did not quite match that of China. This suggests that, during the period 1981–2005, growth performance in China and India may have been better, in part, because their growth was on a lower base than that in Brazil and South Africa.

It might also be worthwhile comparing the growth performance of CIBS with the growth performance of other latecomers to industrialization, such as Japan and Korea, at comparable stages of development. Figure 6.1 attempts such a comparison. It shows the GDP growth trajectories in China (starting in 1979), India (starting in 1980), Brazil (starting in 1964) and South Africa (starting in 1990) compared with Japan (starting in 1960) and Korea (starting in 1965). The selected years coincide, as far as possible, with points at which rapid economic growth began in these countries. In Japan, rapid growth started around the mid-1950s, but comparable data for the period before 1960 are not available. In South Africa, it is not possible

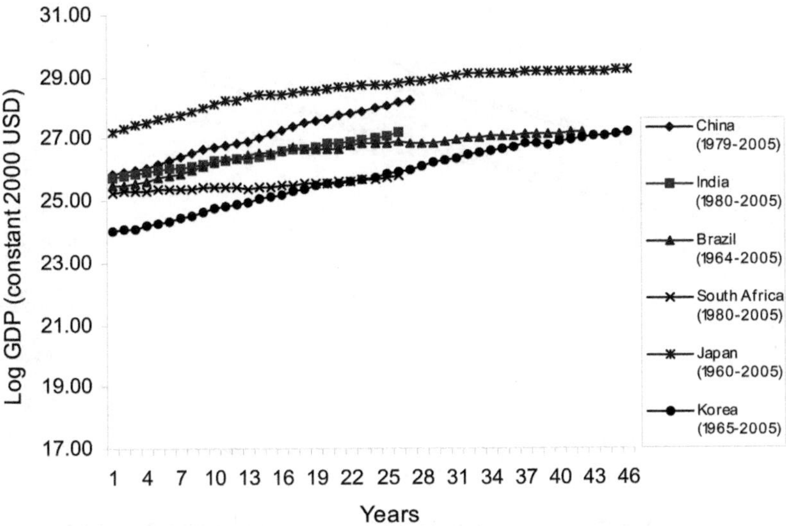

Figure 6.1 GDP growth trajectories in China, India, Brazil and South Africa compared with Japan and Korea

Source: World Bank (2007).

to discern any turning point in economic growth, but 1990 may be the most appropriate choice as the economic and political situation stabilized around that time. It is worth noting that, in Figure 6.1, the year of origin for each country is different, which makes it possible to compare their growth trajectories at similar stages of development. It would seem that China's growth performance is discernibly better, while India's growth performance is roughly comparable with that of Japan and Korea. Brazil's growth performance, until about 1980, was also broadly comparable with that of Japan and Korea at similar stages, but lagged behind thereafter. South Africa, it would seem, is the exception in so far as its growth performance is simply not comparable with that of other latecomers to industrialization. Interestingly, a comparison of growth in exports of goods and services, shown in Figure 6.2, reveals that export performance in China (beginning in 1979), India (starting in 1980) and Brazil (beginning in 1964 but only until 1980) was roughly comparable with that in Japan (beginning in 1960) and Korea (starting in 1965), although export growth in Japan and Korea was discernibly higher in the first decade. Once again, South Africa does not fit into this picture.

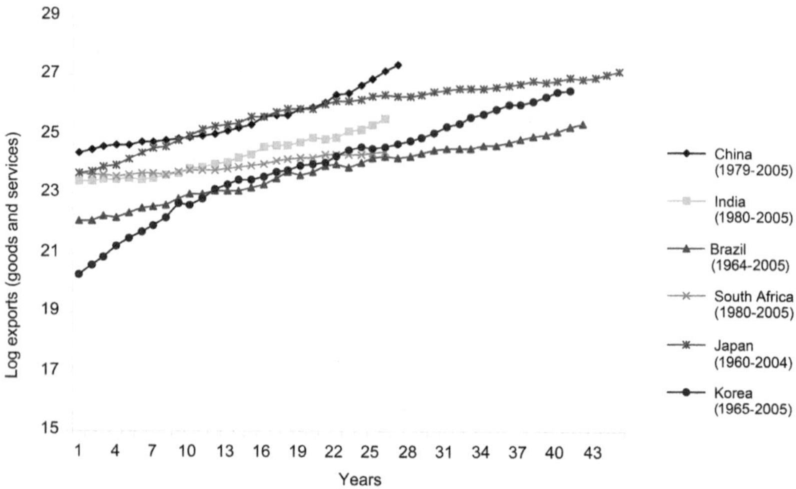

Figure 6.2 Export growth in China, India, Brazil and South Africa compared with Japan and Korea

Source: World Bank (2007).

The future

Most growth scenarios for the future are based on an extrapolation of growth from the past. In attempting such projections, most exercises assume that growth rates in China and India, as also in the industrialized countries, would remain at levels observed in the recent past while growth rates in Brazil would step up once again. Of course, it is Russia rather than South Africa that is an integral part of projections for and scenarios in 2050. And even if South Africa has some potential, it is not yet on a trajectory of rapid economic growth.

The construction of future scenarios began with the Goldman Sachs study, which attempted to project levels of GDP and GDP per capita for Brazil, Russia, India and China (BRIC) in 2050.[3] The exercise is based on a simple model of capital accumulation and productivity growth combined with demographic projections. The broad conclusions of the study[4] are that in 2000 the GDP of these four economies was less than 15 per cent of the GDP of the G6: the United States, Japan, Germany, the United Kingdom, France and Italy. By 2025, in terms of GDP, BRIC would be more than 50 per cent of the G6. In 2040, BRIC economies together would have a larger GDP than the G6. In terms of GDP, each of the BRIC economies would overtake each of these G6 economies, except the United States, by 2040. And by 2050, of the G6, only the United States and Japan would remain among the six largest economies in the world. It is estimated that about two-thirds of the increase in BRIC GDP, measured in US dollars, would come from real growth, while the remaining one-third would be attributable to currency appreciation. BRIC catch up is expected to be at its most dramatic until 2030. Thereafter, BRIC growth would also slow down and only India might have growth rates higher than 3 per cent per annum in 2050. The catch up would be less marked in terms of GDP per capita. On average, with the exception of Russia, BRIC citizens are likely to be poorer than citizens in the G6. It must be stressed that the projected BRIC growth path, even in the Goldman Sachs study, depends on critical assumptions about policies and institutions, and also the capacities of these countries to resolve their problems: outcomes are therefore neither predictable nor certain.[5]

In a more sophisticated exercise for China and India that uses simple convergence equations, Robert Rowthorn (2006) projects that, in 2050, at PPP, per capita income in China would be 63 per cent of per capita income in the USA, while per capita income in India would be 45 per cent of per capita income in the USA. It is also projected that both China and India should comfortably overtake the USA in GDP measured at PPP. This catch up is not confined to PPP-GDP comparisons. The Rowthorn projections show that, even at market exchange rates, by 2050 the total output in China would be 60 per cent larger than in the United States, while total output in India and the United States would be roughly equal.[6]

It must be said that these projections suggest broad orders of magnitude rather than precise predictions. Even so, such projections highlight the power of compound growth rates – for growth rates do, indeed, matter. If GDP grows at 10 per cent per annum, national income doubles in seven years. If GDP grows at 7 per cent per annum, national income doubles in 10 years. If GDP per capita grows at 5 per cent per annum, per capita income doubles in 14 years. Growth rates in China and India have been in this range for some time. Also, growth rates in India have accelerated during the early 2000s. Growth rates in Brazil were also in this range during the period 1951–1980 and could return to that path once again. If such growth rates are sustained, their cumulative impact over time is no surprise. However, growth is not simply about arithmetic. In fact, it is about more than economics. Therefore, it is necessary to consider the economic determinants of growth.

In principle, China and India might be able to sustain high rates of economic growth for some time to come for several reasons. Brazil might also be able to attain high rates of growth for similar reasons, although their relative importance could be different. First, the population in these countries is large and income levels are low. Second, their demographic characteristics – in particular, the high proportion of young people in the population, which would mean an increase in the workforce for some time to come – are conducive to growth. Third, in China and India, more so than in Brazil, wages are significantly lower than in the world outside, while there are large reservoirs of surplus labour. Fourth, emerging technological capabilities have the potential to support an increase in productivity. In practice, however, China, India and Brazil might not be able to sustain their high rates of growth because of constraints that are already discernible. In China, the declining productivity of investment at the margin and the sustainability of the political system are both potential constraints. In India, the crisis in agriculture, the bottlenecks in infrastructure and the limited spread of education in society are potential constraints. In Brazil, the level and the productivity of investment, both of which are low, constrain growth at a macro level. Of course, these constraints are illustrative rather than exhaustive. And there are many other problems in these countries that could slow down the process of growth. Even if growth slows, however, a catch-up scenario is plausible, but it would require a greater length of time.

Engines of economic growth in the world

Globalization is associated with increasing economic openness, growing economic interdependence and deepening economic integration in the world economy. In such a world, growth prospects would be significantly influenced, if not shaped, by the growth performance of lead economies. The discussion that follows asks whether CIBS could be new engines of growth, to consider the underlying causation and mechanisms.

Engines of growth

History provides obvious examples. Britain in the 19th century and the United States in the 20th century were engines of growth for the world economy. Statistical analysis for the period since the early 1960s provides confirmation.[7] It is widely accepted that GDP growth in the United States leads GDP growth in the world. A statistical analysis of long-term trends in economic growth for the period 1963–2001, with five-year moving averages for both sets of growth rates, yields a correlation coefficient of 0.82, while a simple lead–lag analysis shows that the US economy leads the world economy by one year. Evidence available also reveals that developing countries, excluding China, follow the trends in world economic growth, and hence trends in the economic growth of the United States. It is worth noting that economic growth in developing countries follows economic growth in the United States with a lag, but with more pronounced swings in cyclical ups and downs.

In reflecting on the future, is it possible to think of CIBS as engines of growth for the developing world, even if not for the world economy? The answer depends, in large part, on the size of the four economies and their rates of growth. There are some pointers in recent experience. Statistical analysis shows that, since 1980, the Chinese economy has also led world GDP with a lag of one or two years, although the correlation coefficient is much smaller than that for the United States.[8] This is not surprising: consider that, in 2005, China accounted for 5 per cent of world GDP at market exchange rates and 14 per cent of world GDP in PPP terms. Also, GDP growth in China has been at approximately 9 per cent per annum for 25 years. By these criteria, India is not an engine of growth – at least, not yet. This is also not surprising. In economic terms, it is smaller than China and its growth rate is not as high. For example, in 2005, India accounted for only 2 per cent of world GDP at market exchange rates and 6 per cent of world GDP in PPP terms. Additionally, GDP growth in India has been in the range of 6 per cent per annum for 25 years. Even so, India is a potential engine of growth in terms of both attributes. Brazil presents a mixed picture. Its economic size is significant. In 2005, Brazil accounted for 2.5 per cent of world GDP, both at market exchange rates and in PPP terms. However, GDP growth has been just 2 per cent per annum for the past 25 years. Brazil has the economic size to exercise some influence on, even if it cannot drive growth in the world economy, but it does not have the growth rate to do so. South Africa provides a sharp contrast. In 2005, it accounted for only 0.6 per cent of world GDP at market exchange rates and 0.8 per cent of world GDP in PPP terms, and GDP growth has only been at 2 per cent per annum for the past 25 years. Clearly, South Africa meets neither criterion, whether size or growth. Of course, given their economic size in relation to most developing countries, taken together, CIBS could be a possible engine of growth for the developing world, but that would depend on the degree and nature of linkages.

Rapid economic growth in lead economies drives economic growth elsewhere in the world by providing markets for exports, resources for investment, finances for development and technologies for productivity. The classic examples – Britain in the 19th century and the United States in the 20th century – provide confirmation of the suggested economic causation and the possible transmission mechanisms. Indeed, during their periods of dominance in the world, both Britain and the United States were engines of growth, in so far as they provided the rest of the world not only with markets for exports and resources for investment, but also with finances for development and technologies for productivity. And, despite the diminished dominance, the US economy continues to be an engine of growth for the world. At this juncture, China is not quite an engine of growth in every dimension. Economic growth in China provides a stimulus to economic growth elsewhere, in large part as a market for exports. So far, India and Brazil cannot be characterized as engines of growth in any dimension, perhaps not even as markets for exports. But, along with China, India and Brazil have some future potential in terms of markets for exports, resources for investment and technologies for productivity. South Africa is the obvious outlier in this picture, although it could provide some impetus to the growth process in Africa if linkages develop appropriately. In this context, it is worth noting that the four CIBS economies could, in times to come, provide a significant impetus to the growth process in their respective regions. What is more, even if these CIBS economies cannot be a substitute for the United States, as an engine of growth for the world economy, they could be an important complement to the older engine in driving global growth.

Causation and mechanisms

The economic causation outlined above is necessary but not sufficient. The overall effects of economic growth in lead economies on economic growth elsewhere depend on: (i) whether such growth is complementary or competitive; (ii) whether the direct effects are reinforced or counteracted by the indirect effects; and (iii) whether, on balance, the impact is positive or negative.[9]

In principle, economic growth in lead economies might be complementary or competitive to economic growth elsewhere. It might be complementary in so far as it increases the demand for exports, but it might be competitive in so far as it develops alternative sources of supply. It might be complementary, if it provides resources for investment or finances for development, but it might be competitive if it pre-empts such resources for investment or finances for development. It might be complementary if it provides technologies to others, but it might be competitive if it stifles the development of technologies elsewhere. This distinction between the complementary and the competitive aspects is widely recognized. However, the distinction between direct effects and indirect effects is less clear because the latter sometimes are difficult to discern, let alone measure. In situations where direct effects are complementary, indirect effects could be reinforcing if complementary, but counteracting if competitive. Some examples might be illustrative. The direct effects might be complementary if the lead economies – say, CIBS – provide cheap wage goods to other developing countries, but the indirect effects might be competitive if competition from firms in lead economies squeezes out local firms in other developing countries. The direct effects might be complementary if firms from these lead economies invest in other developing countries, but the indirect effects might be competitive if firms from industrialized countries relocate production and invest in CIBS rather than in other developing countries. The direct effects might be complementary if these lead economies provide cheaper inputs for manufactured exports from other developing countries, but the indirect effects might be competitive if competition from the lead economies squeezes out manufactured exports from other developing countries in the markets of industrialized countries. In principle, then, the impact of economic growth in lead economies on economic growth elsewhere, in different spheres, could be positive or negative or a combination of both. Therefore, on balance, such impact could be either positive or negative. The outcomes could differ across space and change over time, so generalizations are difficult.[10]

The main mechanisms of interaction through which outcomes would be shaped are international trade, investment and finance. These are considered later in the chapter. In this context, however, it is worth noting that domestic developments within such large countries could also have international consequences. For instance, macroeconomic policies in China, India and Brazil, once these countries become lead economies, might exercise an important influence on economic growth elsewhere. If such policies are countercyclical, which has been the case for the United States, these would be supportive of economic growth elsewhere. However, if these policies are procyclical, which is common in developing countries, these could be disruptive for economic growth elsewhere. Similarly, exchange rates and interest rates in lead economies could exercise a significant influence, either positive or negative, on economic growth elsewhere in the world. For example, an undervalued exchange rate in China, which has persisted for quite some time, constrains the prospects for labour-intensive manufactured exports from other developing countries, thereby limiting the potential demand stimulus to economic growth that could be provided by exports. Similarly, the combination of a high interest rate and a strong exchange rate, which has been the case for some time in both India and Brazil (albeit for different reasons), pre-empts possible foreign capital inflows, thereby limiting the potential external finance necessary to support economic growth in other developing countries.

Possible impact of rapid growth in CIBS

Rapid economic growth in China and India, if it is sustained at the projected rates, is bound to exercise considerable influence on prospects for the world economy, the industrialized countries and the developing countries. This impact could be either positive or negative.

World economy

The consequences for the world economy could be positive if, as the old engine of growth slows down, CIBS emerge as new engines of growth that drive the process. Ultimately, it is possible that the new engines replace the old engines of growth. This is, at best, a scenario for the future. The preceding discussion suggests that rapid growth in China supports, but does not yet lead, growth in the world economy. India and Brazil have the potential to provide similar support, but this has not materialized so far. South Africa does not even exhibit such potential. It is clear that, for some time to come, the US economy would continue to be the engine of growth for the world economy. But this dominance is bound to diminish as rapid growth in the large emerging economies of the developing world slowly, yet surely, changes the balance of economic power in the world.

The impact of rapid economic growth in CIBS on the world economy could also be negative in the form of consequences for the environment and the labour market. Much of the literature tends to focus on the environmental consequences of rapid economic growth in China and India. The energy needs of these two mega-economies are enormous. This is not surprising, as levels of consumption per capita are low and income elasticities of demand are high. In absolute terms, China's demand for oil is catching up rapidly with that of Europe and the United States, while China's carbon dioxide emissions are now only exceeded by the United States. India lags behind China, but the catch-up process has commenced. Energy consumption in Brazil and South Africa is also likely to grow, even if not as rapidly as in China and India. It would mean too much of a digression to enter into a discussion of this complex issue here.[11]

In the context of the world economy, the other issue that has received attention is the consequences for the labour market. The focus, once again, is on China and India. It has been argued by Richard Freeman that entry into the world economy by China, India and the erstwhile socialist countries of Europe has had a dramatic impact on the size of the global workforce. He argues that, if nothing had changed, the world labour force would have increased from almost 1 billion people in 1980 to about 1.5 billion people in 2000 – attributable, in large part, to population growth. In fact, however, he concludes that the world labour force in 2000 was double the size, at 3 billion, attributable largely to the economic integration of China, India and the transition economies with the world.[12] Freeman believes that this transformation is good for workers in low-income countries and bad for workers in high-income countries. The conclusion drawn is not protectionist. It is much more nuanced. Freeman suggests that government intervention, in the national and international contexts, would be conducive to a more harmonious integration of China and India (to which could be added Brazil and South Africa) into the world economy. In pursuit of this objective, he suggests that it would be important to follow the good examples of integration, such as the integration of Western Europe and Japan into the world economy after the Second World War, rather than the bad examples of integration, such as the integration of the southern part of the United States into the United States after the Civil War or the integration of East Germany into Germany after unification. This proposition is clearly sensible. Even so, it is important to recognize two essential limitations of the Freeman hypothesis:[13] (i) it seeks to focus far too much on the supply side in terms of labour market consequences in the world economy, while it neglects the demand side in so far as rapid economic growth in China and India, as well as Brazil, could also provide an impetus to growth in the world economy; (ii) it underestimates the strength and dynamism of the US economy embedded in history that provides it with a competitive edge even in the early 21st century.

Industrialized countries

The impact of rapid economic growth in CIBS on the industrialized countries could be either positive or negative.

There are three reasons why the impact might be negative. First, rapid economic growth in CIBS might worsen the terms of trade for industrialized countries. The burgeoning demand from CIBS could drive up the prices of primary commodities in the world market. At the same time, rising wages in CIBS could drive up prices of labour-intensive manufactured goods in the world market. Both could turn the terms of trade against industrialized countries. Rowthorn (2006), who examines this issue in some depth, argues that terms of trade for industrialized countries might worsen over time, but that the consequences would be easy to absorb because the process would be spread over a long period.[14] What is more, its impact in terms of loss of real income in the industrialized world would be modest.

Second, for the industrialized countries, CIBS could emerge as new destinations that could become a source of competition for investment. This might happen if firms from the industrialized countries, whether the United States or Europe, relocate production in CIBS. Even if they do not, it would strengthen capital and weaken labour in terms of bargaining power, thereby exercising some outward pressure on wages. Rowthorn, who also examines this issue in depth, concludes that it is a limited phenomenon so far and is not likely to happen on a larger scale for quite some time to come.[15]

Third, the economic rise of CIBS might lead to a downward pressure on employment levels and real wages in the industrialized countries. It needs to be said that this concern is somewhat exaggerated. It is important to recognize that the stagnation in real wages and the high levels of unemployment in the industrialized countries are attributable to the nature of technical progress, which is replacing several unskilled workers with a few skilled workers, and the impact of macroeconomic policies, which have sought to maintain price stability at the expense of full employment. The source of these problems lies within the industrialized countries and not in their trade with developing countries.[16] And even if the expansion of such trade in manufactured goods with CIBS could exert some downward pressure on employment levels or real wages in industrialized countries, such pressures are bound to diminish with the ageing of industrial societies.[17] There are two other reasons, stressed by Rowthorn (2006) and Singh (2007), which confirm that such concerns about employment and wages are probably exaggerated. There is the Krugman proposition that 'economic history offers no examples of a country that experienced long-term productivity growth without a roughly equal rise in real wages'.[18] Thus, in the long run, productivity increase in China and India would also be followed, after a time, by a commensurate increase in real wages. Also, a coordination of macroeconomic polities, reinforced by the logic of international collective action, could be an important means of minimizing the social costs for workers in the industrialized countries during the transition period in which CIBS integrate into the world economy.

It is just as important to recognize that rapid economic growth in CIBS could have a positive impact on the industrialized countries.[19] First, starting from low levels of income per capita juxtaposed with high-income elasticities of demand, higher incomes associated with rapid growth would create expanding markets for exports from industrialized countries. Second, these emerging economies could be a source of cheap manufactured goods that could help reduce inflationary pressures in industrialized countries, thereby enabling them to maintain higher levels of output and employment than would otherwise be possible. Third, these emerging economies could be a source of new technologies in the future that could help extend production possibility frontiers and consumer possibility frontiers in the industrialized economies.

Developing countries

During the first quarter of the 21st century, economic growth in CIBS could have a positive impact on developing countries if it improves terms of trade, provides appropriate technologies and creates new sources of finance for development, whether investment or aid.

It is clear that, for some time to come, the positive impact on developing countries would be transmitted through an improvement in their terms of trade.[20] Rapid economic growth in China and India is bound to boost the demand for primary commodities exported by developing countries. The reasons are simple enough. Both China and India have large populations. That is not all, however. In both countries, levels of consumption per capita in most primary commodities are low, while income elasticities of demand for most primary commodities are high. This burgeoning demand will almost certainly raise prices of primary commodities in world markets and thereby improve the terms of trade for developing countries. It would benefit Brazil and South Africa, as exporters of primary commodities, while the revival of growth in Brazil and South Africa, when it happens, would reinforce this process. What is more, China already is while India and Brazil are likely to become sources of manufactured goods in the world market. Such manufactures – particularly wage goods, but also capital goods from China, India and Brazil – are likely to be cheaper than competing goods from industrialized countries. At the same time, Brazil and South Africa could provide cheaper natural resource-based manufactures. This would also improve the terms of trade for developing countries.

The positive impact of CIBS on developing countries through the other potential channels of transmission is not as clear. We do not, yet, have either the evidence or the experience. In principle, it is possible that CIBS would develop technologies that are more appropriate for the factor endowments and the economic needs of developing countries. But it is too early to come to a judgement on this matter. Similarly, CIBS are potential sources of finance for development. Their foreign aid programmes, particularly in Africa, constitute a modest beginning.[21] However, so far, their contribution in terms of foreign direct investment is limited.

The emergence of CIBS in the world economy could also have a negative impact on developing countries, if these economies provide developing countries with competition in markets for exports or as destinations for investment.

At this juncture, China is clearly the largest supplier of labour-intensive manufactured goods in the world market. Similarly, India is also a significant supplier, though not as large as China. Brazil and South Africa are important suppliers of natural resource-based manufactures. China, India and Brazil are emerging suppliers of capital goods. There can be little doubt that manufactured exports from CIBS span almost the entire range of manufactured exports in which other developing countries could have a potential comparative advantage. Hence, it is plausible to argue – though impossible to prove – that, on balance, CIBS possibly could have a negative impact on manufactured exports from other developing countries that have to compete with these four economies for export markets in industrialized countries.[22] This can change if and when China and India vacate their space in the international trade matrix, in much the same way as latecomers to industrialization in Asia, such as Japan, Korea, Hong Kong, Taiwan and Singapore, vacated their space in the market for simple labour-intensive manufactures for countries that followed in their footsteps. It is not likely, at least in the medium term, because both China and India have large reservoirs of surplus labour at low wages not only in the rural hinterlands, but also in the urban informal sectors. Brazil and South Africa might not have such large reservoirs of surplus labour, but given their abundance in primary commodities and natural resources, it is not likely that they would vacate their space in the market for processed products or resource-based manufactures for other developing countries that have similar natural endowments.

The evidence, presented later in the chapter, shows that CIBS absorb a significant proportion of inward foreign direct investment in developing countries in terms of both stocks and flows. Given that China, India and Brazil are now among the most attractive destinations for transnational firms seeking to locate production in the developing world, it is once again plausible to suggest that perhaps foreign direct investment in China, India and Brazil might be at the expense of developing countries. South Africa might not have the same attraction as a destination, but it might draw foreign direct investment that could have gone to developing countries in Africa. At the same time, the share of CIBS in outward foreign direct investment in the world economy, as also from developing countries, is modest in both stocks and flows, so that firms from these four countries do not compensate with foreign direct investment in other developing countries.

The implicit barriers to change in the traditional division of labour and specialization in production are a less discernible but more significant negative impact of the four economies, particularly China, on developing countries. For example, China and India might pre-empt opportunities for other developing countries to industrialize through exports of labour-intensive manufactures, which is attributable to their surplus labour and low wages and which might continue for some time to come. Further, Brazil and South Africa might pre-empt opportunities for other developing countries to industrialize through agro-based or resource-intensive manufactures, which is attributable to their abundance in primary commodities and natural resources. But this is no more than a plausible hypothesis about possible future developments and one that cannot be tested.

The problem has, however, surfaced in one dimension. China's present division of labour with the developing world, reflected in the composition of trade flows, is not different from the old North–South pattern of trade, in so far as Chinese imports from the developing world are largely primary commodities, while Chinese exports to the developing world are largely manufactured goods.[23] China's trade with countries in Southeast Asia is the exception to this rule. But Chinese trade with and investment in Africa conforms even more closely to this caricature of a neocolonial pattern. It should be recognized that such traditional patterns of trade can neither transform the structure of production in developing countries, nor make for a new international division of labour. Indeed, such trade can only perpetuate the dependence of developing countries on exports of primary commodities without creating opportunities to increase value added before export or entering into manufacturing activities characterized by economies of scale.

Such path-dependent specialization can only curb the possibilities of structural transformation in developing countries. Trade with China can sustain growth and support industrialization in developing countries, only if there is a successful transition from a complementary to a competitive pattern of trade, so that inter-sectoral trade is gradually replaced by intra-sectoral or intra-industry trade and specialization.

Channels of engagement and transmission

The preceding discussion is largely in terms of macroeconomic aggregates. It is also necessary to consider the forms of engagement with the world economy, through which the impact of rapid economic growth in CIBS, whether positive or negative, is transmitted elsewhere. The obvious and most important channels of transmission are international trade, international investment, international finance and international migration.

International trade

International trade is, perhaps, the most important form of engagement with the world economy, not only for CIBS, but also for developing countries. Available evidence provides confirmation. Exports and imports of goods and services as a proportion of GDP rose from 44 per cent to 69 per cent in China, from 28 per cent to 45 per cent in India, from 23 per cent to 29 per cent in Brazil, from 53 per cent to 56 per cent in South Africa and from 56 per cent to 67 per cent in developing countries.[24] Table 6.4 presents evidence on trade in goods for CIBS, with the developing countries, the industrialized countries and the world as a whole in 2000 and 2005. It shows the relative importance of CIBS, as markets for exports and sources of imports for the world. During this brief period, the CIBS share in world trade almost doubled, from 5.7 per cent in 2000 to about 9.8 per cent in 2005. Their share in the trade of developing countries increased from 19 per cent to 27 per cent and in the trade of industrialized countries increased from 6 per cent to 10 per cent.[25] The emerging significance is clear. In 2005, CIBS, taken together, accounted for about one-tenth of merchandize trade in the world, more than one-quarter of the merchandize trade of developing countries and one-tenth of the merchandize trade of industrialized countries. It is worth noting that these aggregate proportions could be somewhat deceptive, because in 2005 China accounted for as much as 72 per cent, India accounted for 12 per cent, Brazil accounted for 10 per cent and South Africa accounted for only 6 per cent of CIBS trade with the world. The respective shares of these

Table 6.4 Trade flows: China, India, Brazil and South Africa, 2000 and 2005 (US$ billion)

	Total exports		*Total imports*	
	2000	*2005*	*2000*	*2005*
China	249	762	225	660
India	42	100	52	139
Brazil	55	118	59	78
South Africa	30	52	30	62
Total above	377	1,031	365	939
World	6,444	10,441	6,642	10,712
(CIBS as percentage of)	(5.8)	(9.9)	(5.5)	(8.8)
	Exports to developing countries		*Imports from developing countries*	
China	102	317	104	330
India	17	52	17	45
Brazil	21	56	24	38
South Africa	8	15	9	22
Total above	148	440	154	434
Developing countries	803	1,614	791	1,664
(CIBS as percentage of)	(18.4)	(27.3)	(19.4)	(26.1)
	Exports to industrialized countries		*Imports from industrialized countries*	
China	144	421	106	254
India	23	44	21	46
Brazil	31	54	37	41
South Africa	14	31	20	38
Total above	212	550	184	380
Industrialized countries	3,161	4,645	3,151	4,553
(CIBS as percentage of)	(6.7)	(11.9)	(5.8)	(8.3)

Notes: The figures in this table are on merchandize trade, exports and imports, in US$ billion at current prices.

Source: UNCTAD, *UNCTAD Handbook of Statistics Online*.

countries in CIBS trade with developing countries and industrialized countries were about the same.[26]

International investment

The picture of international investment is different. In the global context, the relative importance of CIBS is mixed. Table 6.5 sets out

Table 6.5 Foreign direct investment: stocks and flows (US$ billion), 2000 and 2005

	Stocks				*Flows (average per annum)*	
	Inward		*Outward*		*Inward*	*Outward*
	2000	*2005*	*2000*	*2005*	*2001–2005*	*2001–2005*
China	193	318	28	46	57	4
India	18	45	2	10	6	2
Brazil	103	201	52	72	16	3
South Africa	43	69	32	39	3	0
Total above	357	634	114	166	82	8
Developing countries	1,697	2,655	856	1,268	225	80
(CIBS as percentage of)	(21.1)	(23.9)	(13.3)	(13v.1)	(36.6)	(10.3)
Developed countries	4,035	7,219	5,593	9,278	476	602
World	5,803	10,130	6,471	10,672	727	691
(CIBS as percentage of)	(6.2)	(6.3)	(1.8)	(1.6)	(11.3)	(1.2)

Source: *UNCTAD*, Foreign Direct Investment Database.

evidence on foreign direct investment, inward and outward in CIBS, compared with developing countries, industrialized countries and the world. The figures on stocks are for 2000 and 2005, while the figures on flows are annual averages for the period 2001–2005. In the early 2000s, CIBS accounted for 20–25 per cent of the inward stock of foreign direct investment in developing countries and about 6 per cent of that in the world. During the period 2001–2005, CIBS accounted for about 37 per cent of inward flows of foreign direct investment in developing countries and about 11 per cent of those in the world. In the early 2000s, CIBS accounted for about 13 per cent of the outward stock of foreign direct investment from developing countries and less than 2 per cent of that in the world. During the period 2001–2005, CIBS accounted for 10 per cent of the outward flows of foreign direct investment from developing countries and about 1 per cent of those from the world. These aggregate proportions could also be deceptive, but the distribution of the stock of foreign direct investment, whether inward or outward, among CIBS was not as unequal as it was in trade and China was not as dominant. In 2005, China accounted for 50 per cent of the inward stock but only 27 per cent of the outward stock,

India accounted for just 7 per cent of the inward stock and 6 per cent of the outward stock, Brazil accounted 32 per cent of the inward stock and 43 per cent of the outward stock, while South Africa accounted for 11 per cent of the inward stock and 24 per cent of the outward stock.[27] It is possible to draw three inferences from this evidence. First, foreign direct investment in and from CIBS is small as a proportion of both stocks and flows in the world. Second, for CIBS, inward foreign direct investment is much more significant than outward foreign direct investment in terms of both stocks and flows. Third, it would seem that CIBS are more competition for rather than a source of foreign direct investment for developing countries.[28]

International finance

International finance is, perhaps, the most limited form of engagement for CIBS with the world economy, at least so far, but this could change. In principle, these four countries could be potential sources of finance for development through current account surpluses, foreign exchange reserves and foreign aid flows.

The current account surplus in the balance of payments is significant for China, but this is not the case for India, Brazil and South Africa. In China, the current account surplus, as a proportion of GDP, increased from 2.3 per cent during 1996–2000 to 3.5 per cent during 2001–2005.[29] In India, there was a modest current account surplus during 2001–2005, the equivalent of 0.9 per cent of GDP, while there was a current account deficit during 1996–2000, the equivalent of 1.1 per cent of GDP. In Brazil, the current account deficit decreased from 4 per cent of GDP during 1996–2000 to 0.4 per cent of GDP during 2001–2005. In South Africa, the current account deficit, as a proportion of GDP, increased from 1 per cent during 1996–2000 to 1.4 per cent during 2001–2005. These figures are quinquennial averages that might conceal fluctuations over time. Figure 6.3 outlines the trends in the current account balances for these countries, as a percentage of GDP, during the period 1996–2005. It shows that, during 2001–2005, the current account balance improved rapidly in China and Brazil, while it worsened slowly in India and South Africa. These trends are easily explained in a wider macroeconomic context (Figure 6.4). Throughout the period 2001–2005, as a proportion of GDP, gross domestic savings exceeded gross capital formation in China and Brazil. This was also the case in South Africa for three of the five years, which is puzzling on the surface but is probably attributable to low levels of investment rather than high levels of saving. In India, however, gross

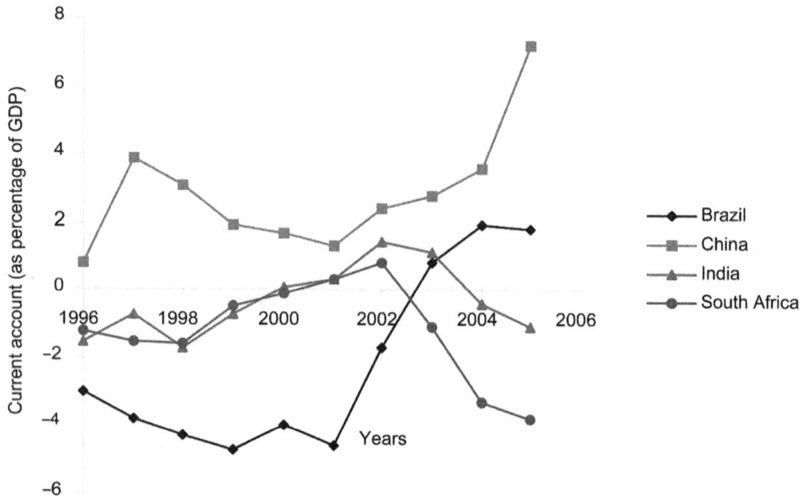

Figure 6.3 Current account balance in China, India, Brazil and South Africa, 1996–2006

Source: World Bank (2007).

capital formation exceeded gross domestic savings.[30] This evidence suggests that China is a potential source of international finance for developing countries, but that India, Brazil and South Africa are not, at least not yet.

In the sphere of foreign exchange reserves, however, the similarities are greater than the differences. Table 6.6 outlines the trends in foreign exchange reserves from 1996 to 2005 for CIBS, developing countries and the world. It shows that both China and India accumulated international reserves at a rapid rate. In Brazil, international reserves went down, and then recovered. In South Africa, international reserves increased slowly but remained at modest levels. Between 1996 and 2005, the share of CIBS in the total foreign exchange reserves of developing countries rose from 22 per cent to 35 per cent, while their share of foreign exchange reserves in the world as a whole more than doubled from 11.1 per cent to 24 per cent. Once again, it is important to note that these aggregates are deceptive, because in 2005 China accounted for 80 per cent of the international reserves held by the four countries taken together, whereas India accounted for 13 per cent, Brazil just 5 per cent and South Africa a mere 2 per cent. The substantial importance of China, India and Brazil in foreign exchange reserves held by

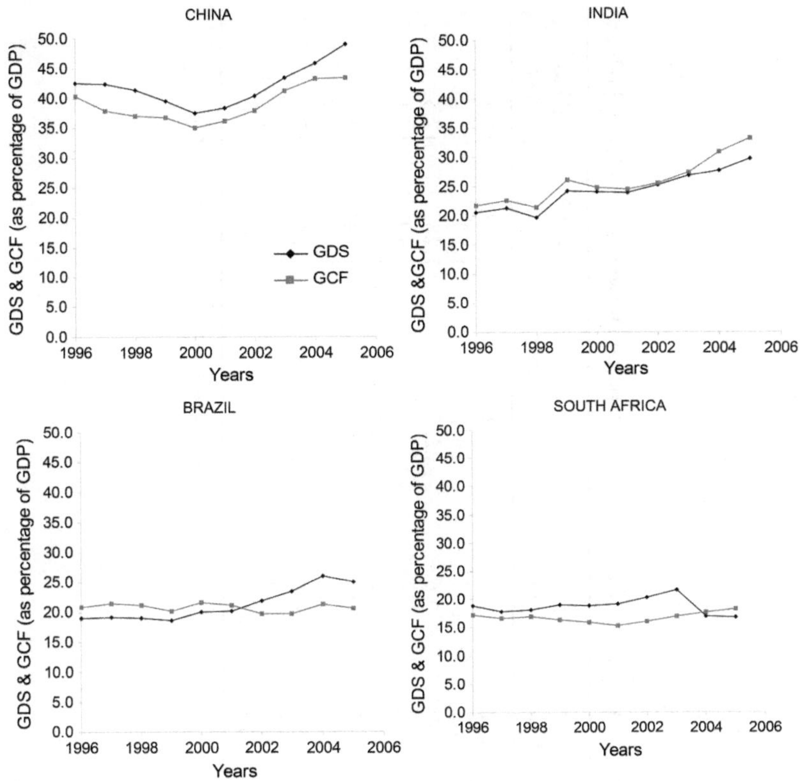

Figure 6.4 Gross domestic savings (GDS) and gross capital formation (GCF) in China, India, Brazil and South Africa, 1996–2005

Source: World Bank (2007).

central banks, however, does not quite translate into a potential source of finance for developing countries. This is so for two reasons. First, an overwhelming proportion of these foreign exchange reserves are held in the form of fiduciary deposits or government bonds in industrialized countries, so that actual placements are not put to any strategic use, let alone provide a potential source of finance for development. Second, even these massive foreign exchange reserves are marginal in relation to transactions in international finance, given that daily transactions in foreign exchange in world markets are perhaps as large as the foreign exchange reserves held by all the central banks in the world.[31]

Table 6.6 Foreign exchange reserves: China, India, Brazil and South Africa, 1996–2005 (Special Drawing Rights [SDRs] billion)

Years	*China*	*India*	*Brazil*	*South Africa*	*Total CIBS*	*Developing countries*	*CIBS as percentage of*	*World*	*CIBS as percentage of*
1996	75	14	41	1	131	601	21.8	1,178	11.1
1997	106	19	38	4	166	691	24.1	1,297	12.8
1998	106	20	30	3	160	706	22.7	1,282	12.5
1999	115	24	25	5	170	786	21.6	1,405	12.1
2000	130	29	25	5	189	902	20.9	1,586	11.9
2001	172	37	28	5	242	1,022	23.7	1,741	13.9
2002	215	50	28	5	297	1,127	26.4	1,890	15.7
2003	275	67	33	5	380	1,306	29.1	2,155	17.6
2004	396	82	34	9	521	1,588	32.8	2,521	20.7
2005	575	93	37	13	719	2,035	35.3	3,000	24.0

Note: The data relate to international reserves held by the central banks of countries or country-groups at the end of the calendar year.

Source: IMF, *International Financial Statistics Online Database*.

The possibilities are much greater in the sphere of foreign aid and development assistance. CIBS are emerging as donors, with a significant presence in Africa. The thrust of China's aid programmes is development finance, whereas the focus of India's aid programmes is technical assistance. Evidence on foreign aid flows from CIBS to developing countries is not readily available. However, it is clear that foreign aid from these four countries is relatively small compared with foreign aid provided by the industrialized countries.[32] Yet, it is possible that the multiplier effects of aid from CIBS, as also from other emerging donors such as Korea, could be significant for two reasons. For one, technical assistance might alleviate infrastructural constraints in developing countries. For another, emerging donors could be a catalyst for aid flows from the industrialized countries in much the same way as foreign aid from the socialist countries was a catalyst in the Cold War era.

International migration

International migration is, possibly, a significant form of engagement with the world economy, particularly for India and, to some extent, China, but much less so for Brazil and almost negligible for South Africa. In the contemporary world economy, it is possible to distinguish between four categories of cross-border movements of people. The traditional category is emigrants who move to a country and settle there permanently. The new categories are guest workers, illegal migrants and professionals. Guest workers are people who move to a country on a temporary basis for a specified purpose and a limited duration. Illegal migrants are people who enter a country without a visa, take up employment on a tourist visa or simply stay after their visa has expired. Professionals are people with high levels of education, experience and qualifications, whose skills are in demand everywhere and who can move from country to country, temporarily or permanently. Both China and India have always been, and continue to be, important countries of origin for international migration. Globalization has, however, increased the mobility of labour in the new categories.[33] India and China – and possibly Brazil – are also countries of origin for such cross-border movements of people.

Remittances are, perhaps, the most important source of development finance associated with international migration.[34] Indeed, for India, remittances are a substantial source of external finance.[35] This is not so for China, Brazil and South Africa. During the period 1996–2005, remittance inflows were the equivalent of 2.7 per cent of GDP in

India, but only 0.15 per cent of GDP in China, 0.26 per cent of GDP in Brazil and 0.08 per cent of GDP in South Africa.[36] In this context, it is important to note that India, China and Brazil export labour to rather than import labour from the outside world. Consequently, remittances from India, China and Brazil cannot simply enter the picture as a source of development finance. The engagement of India and China with the world, through international migration, is attributable in the past to the diaspora. In the present, the engagement of India, China and Brazil with the world economy, through cross-border movements of people, is attributable to globalization.

The diaspora has historical origins. Following the abolition of slavery in the British Empire, starting around the mid-1830s and for a period of 50 years, about 50 million people left India and China to work as indentured labourers in mines, plantations and construction in the Americas, the Caribbean, South Africa, Southeast Asia and other distant lands.[37] This was probably close to 10 per cent of the total population of India and China *circa* 1880. The migration from India and China continued, in somewhat different forms, during the first half of the 20th century, particularly in the period between the two world wars. There is, consequently, a significant presence of the diaspora from China and India across the world, not only in the industrialized countries, but also in the developing countries. This is associated with entrepreneurial capitalisms, Chinese and Indian, in developing countries as well as the industrialized world, where the migration stream has aged.

The second half of the 20th century also witnessed significant waves of international migration from India, comprising permanent emigration to the industrialized countries and temporary migration to the oil-exporting countries in the Middle East.[38] The international migration from China, however, was limited during this period. Of course, such migration, particularly to the industrialized countries, is now constrained by immigration laws and consular practices. But the gathering momentum of globalization during the past two decades has led to a significant increase in the new categories of cross-border movements of people. In this sphere, the engagement of India with the world economy is much more than that of China, Brazil or South Africa. The advent of globalization – which has also made it easier to move people across borders – is associated with managerial capitalisms, especially with professionals from India and, to some extent, Brazil, who can migrate permanently, live abroad temporarily or stay at home and travel frequently for business. These people are almost as mobile across borders as capital.

The global context

It is necessary to recognize that the significance of CIBS in the world would be shaped not only in the sphere of economics, but also in the realm of politics. Their emerging significance in the world economy is attributable, in part, to their share in world population and world income and, also in part, to their engagement with the world through international trade, investment and finance. The early 2000s are perhaps a turning point. Even so, in the economic sphere, their potential importance in the future far exceeds their actual importance at present. In the realm of politics, however, their importance is more discernible at the present juncture, which is attributable partly to their size and partly to their rise. It is plausible to argue that this represents the beginnings of a profound change in the balance of economic and political power in the world. History does not repeat itself; it would, however, be wise to learn from history. The early 20th century was a turning point. It was the beginning of the end of Britain's dominance in the world. And it was the beginning of the rise of the United States to dominance in the world. The catch up and the transformation spanned half a century. The early 21st century perhaps represents a similar turning point. It could be the beginning of the end of the dominant status of the United States in the world. The emergence of countries outside North America and Western Europe, particularly the powerhouse economies in Asia, which began with the East Asian success stories and is now manifest in the rise of China and India, represents a striking transformation. In addition, there are emerging economies in other continents of the developing world, among which Brazil and South Africa deserve mention. Of course, in the decades to come, the continued rise of these countries is not predictable and is by no means certain. This catch up and transformation might also span a half century, or longer. Yet, the beginnings of a shift in the balance of power are discernible.

This is going to shape the international politics of nation states in the future, not only through bilateralism, but also through plurilateralism. CIBS are each engaged in a bilateralism that is both intra-regional and inter-regional. There are intra-regional initiatives led by China and India in Asia, by Brazil in Latin America and by South Africa in Africa. There are also some inter-regional initiatives on the part of these countries, such as China taking a lead in forging APEC and India seeking a partnership with ASEAN. CIBS are also beginning to engage in a plurilateralism. There are two striking examples. At one level, India, Brazil and South Africa have constituted a plurilateral group, the G3 (or IBSA), attempting to develop a strategic alliance that would foster partnership between them, promote cooperation with developing countries and articulate a collective voice in international politics. At another level, CIBS, together with Mexico, constitute the Outreach 5, who have been invited to the G8 Summit in recent years. There is a hint of discontent about their status as observers peripheral to deliberations and decisions, and the Outreach 5 are now seeking a place at the high table with the G8.

From the perspective of the developing world, CIBS, together, might be able to exercise significant influence in the global context through multilateralism, whether through institutions or rules. The United Nations, the World Bank, the IMF and the WTO are among the most important multilateral institutions.[39]

Of CIBS, only China is a permanent member of the United Nations Security Council with a right to veto. China is also a member of the P5. However, India, Brazil and South Africa are engaged in knocking at the door, seeking permanent membership of the Security Council, with or without a right to veto. There can be little doubt that, if and when there is an increase in the number of permanent members of the Security Council in the United Nations, these three countries would have the strongest claim to permanent membership.

In the Bretton Woods institutions, the World Bank and the IMF, CIBS are permanent members of the Executive Boards. The industrialized countries might be the principal shareholders, but the developing countries are the principal stakeholders. Given the democratic deficit in these institutions, which is embedded in unequal voting rights, CIBS, together, could influence decisions or even reshape rules. So far, however, there is only limited, if any, coordination among CIBS for this purpose.[40] They have neither articulated a collective voice nor exercised collective influence.

The situation in the WTO is different. India and Brazil have been long-standing advocates of developing countries in the WTO. China has a low profile, possibly because of its recent accession. South Africa is not quite part of the strategic alliance among developing countries. However, India and Brazil, along with the United States and the European Union, are now members of the Quad, which is the principal institutional mechanism for resolving differences and finding solutions.

In conclusion, it would seem that CIBS have a considerable potential for articulating a collective voice in the world of multilateralism. Coordination and cooperation among them carries a significant potential for exercising influence on multilateral institutions, which could reshape rules and create policy space for countries that are latecomers to development. Such coordination and cooperation, which is in the realm of possibility, has not yet surfaced. There could be two reasons for the near absence of coordination and cooperation so far. In the early stages of change, these countries might not have recognized their potential for exercising collective influence. Also, their relationship with each other might be characterized more by rivalry, economic or political, and less by unity. It is obviously difficult to predict how reality might unfold in the future. Even so, it is important to recognize that once these countries become major players, there is a danger that they might opt for the pursuit of national interest rather than the spirit of solidarity among developing countries or the logic of collective action.

Acknowledgement

The author would like to thank Ananya Ghosh-Dastidar for valuable assistance.

Notes

1 The dominance was even greater earlier. During the period from 1000 to 1700, China and India, taken together, accounted for 50 per cent of world population and 50 per cent of world income. Two thousand years ago, in 1 AD, China and India accounted for almost 60 per cent of world population and world income. For a more detailed discussion, see Nayyar (2008b).
2 The evidence in Table 6.3 and the discussion that follows draw upon earlier work by the author. See Nayyar (2008c).
3 See O'Neill et al. (2004).
4 For a discussion of the methodology, assumptions and conclusions, see Wilson and Purushothaman (2004).
5 The authors recognize this limitation to state: 'there is a good chance that our projections are not met, either through bad policy or bad luck' (Wilson and Purushothaman, 2004: 25).
6 For a detailed discussion, see Rowthorn, who explains the methodology underlying these projections (Rowthorn, 2006 appendix 1: 17–18).
7 For a more detailed discussion on the statistical evidence and analysis cited in this paragraph, see United Nations (2006a).
8 See United Nations (2006a: 22–3).
9 For a detailed discussion, see Kaplinsky (2006). The literature on this subject is limited. However, the implications and consequences of rapid growth in China and India, for the developing world, are analysed in Kaplinsky and Messner (2008).
10 There is a clear need for more systematic research on the subject, where information and understanding are both limited.
11 For some evidence and discussion on this issue, see Rowthorn (2006) and Kaplinsky (2006).

12 For a more detailed discussion on this proposition, see Freeman (2005).
13 For a critical, yet nuanced, evaluation of the Freeman hypothesis, see Singh (2007).
14 It is argued that such a loss could be quite severe if all of it came at the same time, but if it were spread over many years it would have only a marginal impact. For instance, if the United States experienced deterioration in its terms of trade that lowered real income by the equivalent of 5 per cent of GDP over a period of 25 years, per capita income would grow by 1.6 per cent per annum instead of its present trend rate of 1.8 per cent per annum (Rowthorn, 2006: 9).
15 For a discussion, see ibid. It must also be recognized that the high mobility of capital combined with the low mobility of labour in the contemporary world economy have already strengthened capital and weakened labour, so that any observed downward pressure on wages cannot be attributed to trade with CIBS alone.
16 This argument is developed, at length, in Nayyar (1996).
17 For a discussion and some evidence, see Nayyar (2002a).
18 Krugman (1994). This argument is developed further, in the China–India context, by Rowthorn (2006) and Singh (2007).
19 The underlying factors mentioned in this paragraph are also emphasized by Singh (2007) and Rowthorn (2006), with reference to China and India.
20 This proposition is stressed by Kaplinsky (2006), Rowthorn (2006) and Singh (2007).
21 For a discussion on China's trade with and aid to Africa, see Toye (2008).
22 Kaplinsky and Morris (2008) show that China's emergence as a large exporter of manufactured goods in the world economy poses severe problems for export-oriented growth in Sub-Saharan Africa, particularly in textiles and clothing.
23 An unpublished study by Rhys Jenkins and Chris Edwards on China's trade with 18 developing countries (6 in Asia, 6 in Africa and 6 in Latin America), cited at United Nations (2006b: 22), shows that countries that had significant trade with China were exporting mostly agricultural or extractive primary commodities. A study on China's economic interaction with Latin America and the Caribbean also confirms the traditional pattern of trade, importing mostly primary commodities and exporting mostly manufactured goods (Inter-American Development Bank, 2005). Another study on the impact of China's trade with and foreign direct investment in Latin America and the Caribbean shows that there are winners and losers that can be identified: primary commodity-producing sectors and countries are the winners, while sectors and countries producing or exporting manufactured goods are the losers (Jenkins, Peters and Moreira, 2008).
24 These figures, obtained from data reported in World Bank (2007), relate to exports *and* imports of goods *and* services as a proportion of GDP. Even so, it needs to be said that for large countries, such as China and India, these trade: GDP ratios are high and might not be sustainable in the long term. Merchandize trade flows, presented in Table 6.4 and discussed in this paragraph, are perhaps the more appropriate indicator.
25 The shares of CIBS in the trade of developing countries, industrialized countries and the world, reported in this paragraph, are calculated from

the data in Table 6.4 and relate to total trade: that is, the sum total of exports and imports.

26 The share of South Africa was somewhat higher in trade with industrialized countries and somewhat lower in trade with developing countries.

27 The distribution of flows among the CIBS was different. During the period 2001–2005, China accounted for 70 per cent of the inflows and 45 per cent of the outflows, Brazil accounted for 20 per cent of the inflows and 33 per cent of the outflows, while India accounted for 7 per cent of the inflows and 22 per cent of the outflows. The residual share of South Africa was only 3 per cent in inflows and negligible in outflows. It would seem that the relative importance of China in inflows and outflows of FDI from CIBS registered an increase during the early 2000s.

28 In this context, it is worth noting that the sectoral composition and geographical distribution of outward FDI from India provides two sharp contrasts with that from developing countries: three-fifths of international investment from India is in manufacturing activities while this proportion is about one-eighth for developing countries; almost three-quarters of international investment from India is in industrialized countries, while this proportion is less than one-fifth for developing countries. The proportions for China are similar to those for developing countries as a group. In fact, FDI from China is probably even more concentrated in primary commodities and developing countries. For a discussion, see Nayyar (2008a).

29 The data on the current account balance, as a percentage of GDP, for China, India, Brazil and South Africa, cited in this paragraph, are obtained from World Bank (2007).

30 During the period 2001–2005 in China, gross domestic saving was 43.4 per cent of GDP and gross capital formation was 40.4 per cent of GDP; in India, gross domestic saving was 26.7 per cent of GDP and gross capital formation was 28.4 per cent of GDP; in Brazil, gross domestic saving was 23.3 per cent of GDP and gross capital formation was 20.5 per cent of GDP; and in South Africa, gross domestic saving was 19 per cent of GDP and gross capital formation was 16.8 per cent of GDP. These averages for the period are calculated from data reported in World Bank (2007).

31 In April 1997, for example, the average turnover in foreign exchange markets in the world was the equivalent of US$ 1,490 billion per day, while at the end of 1997 the combined foreign exchange reserves of all the central banks in the world totalled US$ 1,550 billion (Nayyar, 2006).

32 During the period 2001–2005, net official development assistance (ODA) disbursements from Development Assistance Committee (DAC) countries were US$ 73,200 million per annum, while net ODA disbursements from non-DAC donors were a mere US$ 575 million per annum. For the annual statistics, see http://stats.oecd.org/Index.aspx. It is worth noting that non-DAC donors include Saudi Arabia, Korea, Turkey, Kuwait, United Arab Emirates, Czech Republic, Hungary and Poland, among others, but net ODA disbursements from China, India, Brazil and South Africa are not even reported in these OECD statistics on foreign aid.

33 The changing nature of international migration is analysed, at some length, in Nayyar (2002a).

34 See Nayyar (2008d) and Solimano (2005).

35 For an analysis of the macroeconomic significance of remittances in India, see Nayyar (1994).
36 These percentages have been calculated from data on remittances obtained from the IMF balance of payments statistics online database and from data on GDP in World Bank (2007).
37 See Lewis (1977) and Tinker (1974). See also Nayyar (2002a).
38 For a discussion of and evidence on international migration from India, see Nayyar (1994).
39 For a detailed discussion on the possibilities of reform and change in these multilateral institutions, in the wider context of global governance, see Nayyar (2002b).
40 There is, perhaps, a modest beginning in the G20, where India, Brazil and South Africa, with some participation from China, have made an attempt to coordinate their stance on reform and change in the IMF. But this is no more than a beginning. It has not influenced, let alone shaped, outcomes.

References

Freeman, R. B. (2005). 'What Really Ails Europe and America: The Doubling of the Global Workforce', *Globalist*, 3 June.

IMF, *International Financial Statistics Online Database*, available from http://imf.org/external/data.htm

Inter-American Development Bank (2005). *The Emergence of China: Opportunities and Challenges for Latin America and the Caribbean* (Washington, DC: IADB).

Jenkins, R., E. D. Peters and M. M. Moreira (2008). 'The Impact of China on Latin America and the Caribbean', *World Development*, 36: 235–53.

Kaplinsky, R. (ed.) (2006). 'Asian Drivers: Opportunities and Threats', *IDS Bulletin*, 37, 1–11.

Kaplinsky, R. and D. Messner (2008). 'The Impact of the Asian Drivers on the Developing World', *World Development*, 36: 197–209.

Kaplinsky, R. and M. Morris (2008). 'Do the Asian Drivers Undermine Export-Oriented Industrialization in SSA?', *World Development*, 36: 254–73.

Krugman, P. (1994). 'Competitiveness: A Dangerous Obsession', *Foreign Affairs*, 73: 28–44.

Lewis, W. A. (1977). *The Evolution of the International Economic Order* (Princeton, NJ: Princeton University Press).

Maddison, A. (2003). *The World Economy: Historical Statistics* (Paris: OECD).

Nayyar, D. (1994). *Migration, Remittances and Capital Flows: The Indian Experience* (Delhi: Oxford University Press).

Nayyar, D. (1996). 'Free Trade: Why, When and for Whom?', *Banca Nazionale del Lavoro Quarterly Review*, 49 (198): 333–50.

Nayyar, D. (2002a). 'Cross-Border Movements of People', in D. Nayyar (ed.), *Governing Globalization: Issues and Institutions* (Oxford: Oxford University Press for UNUWIDER).

Nayyar, D. (2002b). 'The Existing System and the Missing Institutions', in D. Nayyar (ed.), *Governing Globalization: Issues and Institutions* (Oxford: Oxford University Press for UNU-WIDER).

Nayyar, D. (2006). 'Globalization, History and Development: A Tale of Two Centuries', *Cambridge Journal of Economics*, 30: 137–59.

Nayyar, D. (2008a). 'The Internationalization of Firms from India: Investment, Mergers and Acquisitions', *Oxford Development Studies*, 36: 111–31.

Nayyar, D. (2008b). 'Learning to Unlearn from Development', *Oxford Development Studies*, 36(3): 259–80.

Nayyar, D. (2008c). 'The Rise of China and India: Implications for Developing Countries', in P. Artesis and J. Eatwell (eds.), *Issues in Economic Development and Globalization* (Basingstoke: Palgrave Macmillan).

Nayyar, D. (2008d). 'International Migration and Economic Development', in J. Stiglitz and N. Serra (eds.), *The Washington Consensus Reconsidered: Towards a New Global Governance* (Oxford: Oxford University Press).

O'Neill, J., S. Lawson, D. Wilson, R. Purushothaman, M. Buchanan, and L. Griffiths (eds.) (2004). *Growth and Development: The Path to 2050* (London: Goldman Sachs).

Rowthorn, R. (2006). 'The Renaissance of China and India: Implications for the Advanced Economies', *UNCTAD Discussion Paper 182* (Geneva: UNCTAD).

Singh, A. (2007). 'Globalization, Industrial Revolutions in India and China and Labour Markets in Advanced Countries: Implications for National and International Economic Policy', *ILO Working Paper* 81 (Geneva: Policy Integration Department, ILO).

Solimano, A. (2005). 'Remittances by Emigrants: Issues and Evidence', in A. B. Atkinson (ed.), *New Sources of Development Finance* (Oxford: Oxford University Press for UNU-WIDER).

Tinker, H. (1974). *A New System of Slavery: The Export of Indian Labour Overseas, 1830–1920* (Oxford: Oxford University Press).

Toye, J. (2008). 'China's Impact on Sub-Saharan African Development: Trade, Aid and Politics', in P. Artesis and J. Eatwell (eds.), *Issues in Economic Development and Globalization* (Basingstoke: Palgrave Macmillan).

UNCTAD, *Foreign Direct Investment Database*, available from http://www.unctad.org/Templates/Page.asp?intItemID=1923

UNCTAD, *UNCTAD Handbook of Statistics Online*, available from http://www.unctad.org/Templates/Page.asp?intItemID=1890

United Nations (2006a). *Diverging Growth and Development, World Economic and Social Survey 2006* (New York: United Nations).

United Nations (2006b). *National Accounts Main Aggregates Database* (New York: UN-DESA Department of Economic and Social Affairs), available from http://unstats.un.org/unsd/snaama/Introduction.asp

United Nations (2006c). *Demographic Yearbook* (New York: UN-DESA, Department of Economic and Social Affairs), available from http://unstats.un.org/unsd/demographic/products/dyb/dyb2.htm

Wilson, D. and R. Purushothaman (2004). 'Dreaming with BRICS: The Path to 2050', in J. O'Neill, S. Lawson, D. Wilson, R. Purushothaman, M. Buchanan, and L. Griffiths (eds.), *Growth and Development: The Path to 2050*, Chap. 2 (London: Goldman Sachs).

World Bank (2007). *World Development Indicators 2007* (Washington, DC: World Bank).

7

THE EMERGING ASIAN GIANTS AND ECONOMIC DEVELOPMENT IN AFRICA

The last two decades of the 20th century, beginning *circa* 1980, witnessed rapid economic growth in China and India. In the first decade of the 21st century, the rapid growth has sustained in China and accelerated in India. This remarkable growth performance provides a sharp contrast to the world economy over the same period and to the preceding 100 years in these two Asian giants. Indeed, except for Japan and the East Asian Four, economic history provides few parallels of such rapid and sustained growth. The past quarter of a century has thus witnessed the return of the forgotten dragon and the vanishing tiger to the world economy. So much so that it is no longer possible to consider prospects for the world economy in 2025 or 2050 without placing China and India at centre stage. During the period since 1980, Africa provides a sharp contrast. Its economic performance ranged from retrogression to stagnation.

The object of this chapter is to analyse the economic implications of the rise of China and India for Africa, situated in the wider context of the world economy. The first section sketches a profile of China, India and Africa in the world economy. It sets the stage by outlining the broad contours of their significance in the past, present and future. The following section considers the main forms of engagement and channels of interaction for China and India with Africa. Its focus is on international trade, with some discussion on international investment, international aid and international migration. The next part examines the implications of rapid economic growth in China and India for economic development in Africa. In doing so, it asks whether these two Asian giants could be the new engines of growth, touches upon the underlying economic causation and explores their possible impact on Africa. The final section draws together some conclusions.

China, India and Africa in the world economy

The significance of China, India and Africa in the global context has changed over time. This section provides a historical perspective of the past and a snapshot of the present. It also sets out an extrapolated scenario of the future for China and India.

The past

The emerging significance of China, India and Africa in the world economy must be situated in historical perspective. Table 7.1, which is based on estimates made by Angus Maddison (2003), presents evidence on the shares of China, India and Africa in world population and in world income for selected years, from 1820 to 2001. It shows that in 1820, China and India accounted for 57 per cent of the world population and 49 per cent of world income.[1] A dramatic change took place in the next 150 years. In 1973, the share of China and India in the world population was significantly lower at 37 per cent, but their share in world income had collapsed to less than 8 per cent, a small fraction of what it was 150 years earlier. Over the same period, the significance of Africa in the world economy also changed, but nowhere near as much. In 1820, Africa accounted for 7 per cent of world population and 4.5 per cent of world income. In 1973, the share of Africa

Table 7.1 China, India and Africa in the world economy (percentage share in population and income)

Year	*Share of world population*			*Share of world income*		
	CHINA	*INDIA*	*AFRICA*	*CHINA*	*INDIA*	*AFRICA*
1820	36.6	20.1	7.1	32.9	16.0	4.5
1870	28.1	19.9	7.1	17.1	12.1	4.1
1913	24.4	17.0	7.0	8.8	7.5	2.9
1950	21.7	14.2	9.0	4.5	4.2	3.8
1973	22.5	14.8	10.0	4.6	3.1	3.4
2001	20.7	16.5	13.4	12.3	5.4	3.3

Source: Maddison (2003).

Note: The percentages in this table have been calculated from estimates of population and GDP in Maddison (2003). The data on GDP are in 1990 international Geary–Khamis dollars, which are PPPs used to evaluate output that are calculated based on a specific method devised to define international prices. This measure facilitates inter-country comparisons over time.

in world population was distinctly higher at 10 per cent, although its share in world income was somewhat lower at 3.4 per cent. The next 30 years witnessed some recovery in China and India, but not in Africa. While the share of China and India in world population remained in the range of 37 per cent, their share in world income rose to almost 18 per cent in 2001. On the other hand, the share of Africa in world population rose further to 13 per cent, while its share in world income remained almost unchanged at 3.3 per cent. The essential contours of this story are clear enough. Beginning in 1820, China and India's share in world population declined steadily until 1973, but over the same period, the decline in their share of world income was much more pronounced. Consequently, during the period from 1820 to 1973, there was a sharp increase in the asymmetries or disproportionalities between the shares of China and India in world population and in world income. The partial recovery in their share of world income from 1973 to 2001 has reduced the asymmetry, but the disproportionality remains significant. However, this trend suggests that China and India have re-entered the world economy. For Africa, this asymmetry increased throughout the period. In 2001, its share in world population had nearly doubled, while its share in world income was less than three-fourths what it was in 1820. This trend suggests a decline in the significance of Africa in the world economy, which was clearly discernible during the last quarter of the 20th century.

The present

It is possible to juxtapose this past with the present. Table 7.2 outlines a profile of GDP, population and GDP per capita in China, India and Africa as compared to developing countries, industrialized countries and the world in 2000 and 2005. It shows that the population of the world is more than six billion, of which a little less than one billion people live in industrialized countries, while somewhat more than five billion people live in developing countries. Of the latter, 1.3 billion live in China, 1.1 billion live in India and 0.9 billion live in Africa. Thus, 51 per cent of the population in the world and 60 per cent of the population in developing countries live in China, India and Africa. There are two sets of figures on GDP and GDP per capita: at constant prices with market exchange rates and in terms of PPPs. Consider each in turn. At market exchange rates, from 2000 to 2005, in world GDP, the share of China increased from 3.8 per cent to 5.2 per cent, the share of India increased from 1.4 per cent to 1.8 per cent and the share of Africa increased from 1.9 per cent to 2 per cent. The share of

Table 7.2 GDP, population and GDP per capita in China, India and Africa, 2000 and 2005

Country	*GDP*				*Population*		*PPP-GDP*			
	($ billion)		*($ per capita)*		*(million)*		*($ billion)*		*($ per capita)*	
	2000	*2005*	*2000*	*2005*	*2000*	*2005*	*2000*	*2005*	*2000*	*2005*
China	1,198	1,890	949	1,449	1,263	1,305	4,973	7,842	3,939	6,012
	(3.8)	*(5.2)*			*(20.8)*	*(20.3)*	*(11.0)*	*(14.4)*		
India	460	644	453	588	1,016	1,095	2,402	3,362	2,364	3,072
	(1.4)	*(1.8)*			*(16.8)*	*(17.0)*	*(5.3)*	*(6.2)*		
Africa	588	727	731	810	804	897	1,635	2,016	2,033	2,247
	(1.9)	*(2.0)*			*(13.3)*	*(13.9)*	*(3.6)*	*(3.7)*		
Developing countries	6,058	7,813	1,191	1,440	5,085	5,427	18,818	25,322	3,701	4,666
Industrialized countries	24,542	27,148	27,304	29,251	899	928	25,157	27,898	27,988	30,058
World	31,756	36,352	5,241	5,647	6,060	6,438	45,144	54,573	7,450	8,477

Source: World Bank (2007).

Notes: (a) GDP and GDP per capita are measured in constant 2000 US dollars. (b) PPP-GDP and PPP-GDP per capita are measured in constant 2000 international dollars. (c) Figures in parentheses are the totals for China, India and Africa as a percentage of totals for the world economy.

China, India and Africa, taken together, increased from 37 per cent to 42 per cent of the GDP of developing countries. Over the same period, at market exchange rates, GDP per capita in China was about the same, GDP per capita in India was less than half and GDP per capita in Africa was more than half the average GDP per capita in developing countries. It is worth noting that China, India and Africa are far below the GDP per capita of the industrialized countries and significantly below GDP per capita in the world as a whole. The picture is somewhat different if the comparison is in terms of PPPs. From 2000 to 2005, in world PPP-GDP, the share of China increased from 11 per cent to 14.4 per cent, the share of India increased from 5.3 per cent to 6.2 per cent and the share of Africa changed little from 3.6 per cent to 3.7 per cent. The share of China, India and Africa, taken together, increased from 48 per cent to 52 per cent of the PPP-GDP of developing countries. Over the same period, in PPP terms, GDP per capita in China surpassed GDP per capita in developing countries by a significant margin, whereas GDP per capita in India was about two-thirds and GDP per capita in Africa was less than one-half of GDP per capita in developing countries.

This snapshot situates China, India and Africa in the world economy at present. However, the observed reality has been shaped by their economic performance in the past. Table 7.3 sets out rates of growth in GDP and GDP per capita, from 1951 to 1980 and from 1981 to 2005, for China, India and Africa in comparison with the developing countries, the industrialized countries and the world economy.[2]

It is worth noting that time series data on GDP and GDP per capita for the entire period, from 1951 to 2005, are not available from a single source. The figures for the period 1951–1980 are based on Maddison data, because United Nations data are not available for years prior to 1971. The figures for the period 1981–2005 are based on United Nations data, because Maddison data are not available for years after 2001. These two sources are not strictly comparable. However, it is possible to resolve the problem, as data are available from both sources for the period 1981–2000. To facilitate a comparison, Table 7.3 also presents figures on growth rates from 1981 to 2000, computed separately from Maddison data and United Nations data. A comparison of the two sets of growth rates during the period 1981–2000, for which both sources are available, shows that the numbers correspond closely, except in the figures for China, where the UN data suggest much higher growth rates than the Maddison data. Even so, it is reasonable to infer that the growth rates for the periods 1951–1980 and 1981–2005, even if computed from different sources, are

Table 7.3 Growth performance of China, India and Africa, 1951–1980 and 1981–2005, comparison with country-groups (percentage per annum)

	Maddison data		*United Nations data*	
	1951–1980	*1981–2000*	*1981–2000*	*1981–2005*
	GDP			
China	5.03	7.36	9.80	9.73
India	3.57	5.68	5.54	5.79
Africa	4.12	2.42	2.60	2.97
Developing countries	4.84	2.65	2.74	3.04
Industrialized countries	4.40	2.56	2.59	2.50
World	4.77	2.64	2.72	2.95
	GDP per capita			
China	3.01	6.01	8.46	8.51
India	1.40	3.62	3.50	3.83
Africa	1.66	–0.17	–0.06	0.39
Developing countries	2.19	0.39	0.42	0.80
Industrialized countries	3.50	2.04	2.06	1.96
World	2.40	0.66	0.69	0.99

Sources: Maddison (2003) and United Nations (2006b, 2006c).

Notes:

1 The growth rates for each period are computed as geometric means of the annual growth rates in that period.

2 The Maddison data and the United Nations data on GDP and GDP per capita are not strictly comparable.

3 The Maddison data on GDP and GDP per capita, which are in 1990 international Geary–Khamis dollars, are PPPs used to evaluate output, which are calculated based on a specific method devised to define international prices. This measure facilitates intercountry comparisons.

4 The United Nations data on GDP and GDP per capita are in constant 1990 US dollars.

5 The figures in this table for the world economy cover 128 countries, of which 21 are industrialized countries and 107 are developing countries.

6 Latin America includes the Caribbean.

comparable, with the exception of China. In interpreting the data on China, where the step up in growth rates between these two periods is probably overstated, some downward adjustment might be needed.

A study of Table 7.3 shows that growth in GDP and GDP per capita during 1981–2005 was much slower than it was during 1951–1980. This was the case for the world economy, for industrialized countries and for developing countries. Growth in GDP was in the range of 5 per cent per annum from 1951 to 1980 and in the range of 3 per cent per annum from 1981 to 2005 almost everywhere, including

Africa, except in China and India where it was much higher. Growth in GDP per capita slowed considerably even in the industrialized countries, from 3.5 per cent per annum to 2 per cent per annum, but the slowdown was more pronounced for developing countries, from 2.2 per cent per annum to 0.8 per cent per annum. In Africa, however, during 1981–2005, growth in GDP per capita was less than 0.4 per cent per annum.[3] It is worth stressing that China and India were the exceptions to this worldwide slowdown in growth. In both countries, growth rates in the second period were much higher than the perfectly respectable growth rates in the first period. So much so that, between 1951 and 1980 and between 1981 and 2005, average annual growth in GDP per capita almost trebled in both China and India. This was attributable in part to higher GDP growth rates and in part to lower population growth rates.

The future

Most growth scenarios for the future are based on an extrapolation of growth from the past. The construction of future scenarios began with the Goldman Sachs study that attempted to project levels of GDP and GDP per capita for BRICs in 2050.[4] In attempting such projections, most exercises assume that growth rates in China and India, as in the industrialized countries, would remain at levels observed in the recent past. In a more sophisticated exercise that uses simple convergence equations, Robert Rowthorn (2008) projects that, in 2050, at PPP, the per capita income in China will be 63 per cent of per capita income in the United States, while per capita income in India will be 45 per cent of per capita income in the United States. It is also projected that both China and India should comfortably overtake the United States in GDP measured at PPP. This catch up is not confined to PPP-GDP comparisons. The Rowthorn projections show that, even at market exchange rates, by 2050 total output in China will be 60 per cent larger than in the United States, while total output in India and the United States will be roughly equal.[5]

It needs to be said that these projections suggest broad orders of magnitude rather than precise predictions. Even so, such projections highlight the power of compound growth rates – for growth rates do indeed matter. If GDP grows at 10 per cent per annum, national income doubles in seven years. If GDP per capita grows at 7 per cent per annum, per capita income doubles in 10 years. If GDP grows at 7 per cent per annum, national income doubles in 10 years. If GDP per capita grows at 5 per cent per annum, per capita income doubles in 14 years. Growth rates in China and India have been in this range for some time. And growth rates in India have accelerated in the early 2000s. If such growth rates are sustained, their cumulative impact over time is no surprise. However, growth is not simply a matter of arithmetic. In fact, it is about more than economics; therefore, it is necessary to consider the economic determinants of growth.

In principle, China and India may be able to sustain high rates of economic growth for some time for the following reasons. First, their populations are large and income levels are low. Second, their demographic characteristics, which indicate an increase in the workforce for some time to come, are conducive to growth.[6] Third, in both countries, wages are significantly lower than in the world outside and there are large reservoirs of surplus labour. In practice, however, China and India may not be able to sustain their high growth rates because of constraints that are already discernible. In China, the declining productivity of investment at the margin and the sustainability of the political system are both potential constraints. In India, the crisis in agriculture, the bottlenecks in infrastructure and the limited spread of education are potential constraints. In a longer term perspective, environmental degradation and climate change could impose serious constraints on growth in both countries. Of course, these constraints are illustrative rather than exhaustive. And there are many others in both countries, which could slow down the process of growth. Even if growth slows down, however, a catch-up scenario is still plausible, but it would require a longer period of time.

It is far more difficult to construct future scenarios for Africa, in part, because it is a continent comprising a large number of countries that are significantly different from each other in geographical size, level of income and stage of development. What is more, there are substantial differences in growth performance across countries. Thus, meaningful analyses or projections are possible only at a disaggregated level for particular countries. Even so, in principle, Africa has a considerable potential for economic growth. Its population is large and income levels are low. Its demographic characteristics, in particular a young population, are a possible advantage. It has low wages combined with surplus labour. And it is abundant in natural resources. Yet, there are dominant constraints: the infrastructure is poor; the spread of education in society is limited; institutions are missing or underdeveloped; and political systems are not conducive to good governance. But these constraints are neither insurmountable nor immutable. Economic policies and development strategies, appropriately designed and effectively implemented, could transform outcomes. Much would depend on what African countries and governments do. Indeed, both China and India, as with most latecomers to development, started with constraints that were similar, if not as acute or binding. It should also be possible for Africa to overcome these constraints – that is what development is about.

Channels of engagement

The preceding discussion was largely in terms of macroeconomic aggregates. It is also necessary to consider the forms of engagement with the world economy through which the impact of rapid economic growth in China and India, whether positive or negative, is transmitted elsewhere, in particular to Africa. The obvious, and most important, channels of transmission are international trade, international investment, international aid and international migration.

International trade

International trade is, perhaps, the most important form of engagement with the world economy for China, India and Africa. It is, however, worth noting that the rapid expansion in their trade with each other is a more recent phenomenon. Thus, the focus of the discussion that follows is on the period 1990–2005. In order to reduce the volume of data to manageable proportions, the tables in this section relate to four selected years: 1990, 1995, 2000 and 2005.

Table 7.4 outlines the trends in China and India's trade with Africa. It presents data on exports to and imports from Africa in comparison with exports to and imports from developing countries and the world. The data show that the expansion in trade was phenomenal. From 1990 to 2005, China's trade with Africa increased from US$ 1 billion to US$ 37 billion, while India's trade with Africa increased from US$ 1 billion to US$ 11 billion. Starting from a small base, the growth in trade valued at current prices is almost bound to appear impressive. But the expansion in trade with Africa was faster than the expansion in China and India's exports to and imports from developing countries and the world. For China, the share of Africa in exports to the world rose from 1 per cent to 2 per cent, while it rose from less than 1 per cent to more than 3 per cent in imports from the world, between 1990 and 2005. Over the same period for India, the share of Africa in exports to the world rose from 2 per cent to 6 per cent, while it rose from 2 per cent to 3 per cent in imports from the world.

Table 7.4 China and India: trade with Africa

	1990	*1995*	*2000*	*2005*
China's Exports to Africa in US$ million	615	1,386	4,202	16,670
as a percentage of				
Exports to Developing Countries	1.7	2.0	4.1	5.2
Exports to the World	1.0	0.9	1.7	2.2
China's Imports from Africa in US$ million	351	720	5,453	20,851
as a percentage of				
Imports from Developing Countries	1.5	1.4	4.9	5.4
Imports from the World	0.7	0.6	2.4	3.2
India's Exports to Africa in US$ million	353	1,158	2,051	6,296
as a percentage of				
Exports to Developing Countries	8.6	9.6	11.1	11.2
Exports to the World	2.0	3.7	4.5	6.1
India's Imports from Africa in US$ million	541	1,672	2,067	4,673
as a percentage of				
Imports from Developing Countries	7.7	13.6	14.6	9.4
Imports from the World	2.3	4.6	4.0	3.1

Source: UNCOMTRADE, Statistical Database.

Table 7.5 outlines the trends in Africa's trade with China and India. It also compares exports to and imports from China and India with exports to and imports from developing countries and the world. Once again, the data show a remarkable expansion in trade. From 1990 to 2005, Africa's trade with China increased from US$ 0.7 billion to US$ 20 billion, while Africa's trade with India increased from US$ 0.6 billion to US$ 8 billion. This expansion in trade was faster than the expansion in Africa's exports to and imports from developing countries and the world. For Africa, the share of China in exports to the world rose from 0.3 per cent to 3.5 per cent, while it rose from 1.1 per cent to 6.7 per cent in imports from the world, from 1990 to 2005. Over the same period for Africa, the share of India in exports to the world rose from 0.8 per cent to 2 per cent, while it rose from 0.5 per cent to 2 per cent in imports from the world, although these shares were higher in the intervening years.

A comparison of the evidence in Tables 7.4 and 7.5 reveals a puzzle and suggests a conclusion. The puzzle is that the figures on China and India's exports to and imports from Africa are significantly higher

Table 7.5 Africa's trade with China and India

	1990	*1995*	*2000*	*2005*
Exports to China in US$ million	128	245	1,719	6,207
as a percentage of				
Exports to Developing Countries	1.9	2.4	4.7	11.3
Exports to the World	0.3	0.6	1.4	3.5
Imports from China in US$ million	551	1,344	3,679	13,572
as a percentage of				
Imports from Developing Countries	5.9	8.7	9.4	15.4
Imports from the World	1.1	2.0	3.4	6.7
Exports to India in US$ million	366	802	5,404	3,445
as a percentage of				
Exports to Developing Countries	5.5	8.0	14.8	6.3
Exports to the World	0.8	2.0	4.4	1.9
Imports from India in US$ million	275	1,096	1,650	4,460
as a percentage of				
Imports from Developing Countries	2.9	7.1	4.2	5.1
Imports from the World	0.5	1.6	1.5	2.2

Source: UNCOMTRADE, Statistical Database.

than the corresponding figures on Africa's imports from and exports to China and India. This deserves explanation. International trade statistics are characterized by such differences for two reasons. For one, exports are recorded FOB (Free on Board) while imports are recorded CIF (Cost, Insurance and Freight). For another, there are time lags in reporting between the country of origin and the country of destination. But these factors cannot explain such large differences. There are two other plausible explanations. It is almost certain that the international trade statistics for Africa are incomplete and often reported with a time lag. It is also possible that the difference is attributable in part to trade in armaments, which is not recorded in the statistics. But these explanations are in the nature of a conjecture. The conclusions that emerge from a comparison of Tables 7.4 and 7.5 are clear. First, for Africa, China was more important as a market for exports and as a source of imports than Africa was for China. Second, for Africa, India was less important as a market for exports and as a source of imports than Africa was for India throughout the period.

In order to obtain a clear picture of the division of labour between China and India on the one hand and Africa on the other, it is necessary to consider the structure and the composition of their trade as well as the changes in it over time. For this purpose, it is appropriate to divide the trade flows into three categories: primary commodities, fuels and manufactures. While such a classification is aggregative and merges Standard International Trade Categories at one-digit level, it is sufficient for analysis.[7]

Table 7.6 outlines the changes in the composition of China's trade with Africa as compared to developing countries and the world. From 1990 to 2005, the share of primary commodities and fuels, taken together, in China's exports to Africa, dropped sharply from 33 per cent to less than 5 per cent, while the share of manufactures rose sharply from 66 per cent to 94 per cent. This composition was somewhat asymmetric in comparison with the composition of China's exports to developing countries, where the share of manufactures rose from 76 per cent to 87 per cent, and to the world, where the share of manufactures rose from 72 per cent to 93 per cent. Between 1990 and 2005, the share of primary commodities and fuels, taken together, in China's imports from Africa increased from 70 per cent to 86 per cent, while the share of manufactures decreased from 30 per cent to 12 per cent. This composition was much more skewed than the composition of China's imports from developing countries, where the share of primary commodities and fuels increased from 19 per cent to 25 per cent, and from the world, where the share of primary commodities and fuels increased from 19 per cent to 23 per cent over the same period. The contrast is just as striking in manufactures. Between 1990 and 2005, the share of manufactures in China's imports from developing countries decreased somewhat from 74 per cent to 65 per cent, while this share in imports from the world remained in the range of 80 per cent.

Table 7.7 outlines the changes in the composition of India's trade with Africa as compared with developing countries and the world. From 1990 to 2005, the share of manufactures in India's exports to Africa fluctuated between 70 and 90 per cent, while primary commodities and fuels made up the residual. This composition was similar to the composition of India's exports to the world, where manufactures accounted for 70–75 per cent, although it was a little different from the composition of exports to developing countries where manufactures accounted for 64–79 per cent, because the share of fuels was higher in some years. From 1990 to 2005, in India's imports from Africa, the share of primary commodities and fuels, taken together, was mostly in the range of 30–40 per cent (except in 1995, when it was much higher on account of fuels), while the share of manufactures was mostly in the range of 30–35 per cent (except in 1990, when it was much higher). It is worth noting that these statistics on the composition of India's imports from Africa are incomplete, because there is a large unaccounted residual of about 30 per cent in 2000 and 2005. The

Table 7.6 Composition of China's trade with Africa and the world (in percentage)

	1990			*1995*			*2000*			*2005*		
	P	*F*	*M*	*P*	*F*	*M*	*P*	*F*	*M*	*P*	*F*	*M*
China's exports to												
Africa	30.9	2.4	66.6	8.7	0.4	89.4	10.3	1.5	87.8	3.8	0.7	93.7
Developing Countries	13.8	4.6	76.3	10.7	3.6	78.6	7.1	4.4	82.6	3.9	3.6	86.8
World	17.4	8.4	72.3	10.8	3.6	85.3	7.0	3.2	89.6	4.1	2.3	93.4
China's Imports from												
Africa	69.7	0.9	29.5	46.4	35.8	17.1	17.5	66.8	9.8	15.6	70.1	12.1
Developing Countries	14.0	4.5	74.2	15.0	8.9	61.4	10.0	16.6	59.2	10.6	13.9	64.6
World	16.3	2.4	80.8	14.4	3.9	81.1	11.4	9.2	78.6	12.7	9.8	77.3

Source: UNCOMTRADE, Statistical Database.

Note: P: Primary commodities, F: Fuels, and M: Manufactures.

Primary commodities include SITC categories 0, 1, 2 and 4; Fuels are SITC category 3; Manufactures include SITC categories 5, 6, 7 and 8, so that non-ferrous metals, SITC category 68, are included in manufactures; SITC category 9 (commodities and transactions not included elsewhere) is excluded from the classification but included in the total. Therefore, percentages in the table do not add up to 100.

Table 7.7 Composition of India's trade with Africa and the world (in percentage)

	1990			*1995*			*2000*			*2005*		
	P	*F*	*M*	*P*	*F*	*M*	*P*	*F*	*M*	*P*	*F*	*M*
India's exports to												
Africa	8.7	0.0	90.4	27.0	0.0	72.2	6.8	0.1	92.3	12.6	14.7	71.7
Developing Countries	29.0	0.1	68.4	29.6	0.6	69.1	19.4	0.5	78.7	20.0	14.8	63.9
World	24.8	2.9	70.3	23.0	1.7	73.7	16.1	4.3	77.4	15.8	11.5	71.6
India's Imports from												
Africa	31.4	0.0	68.2	22.1	42.8	34.7	30.6	7.3	32.3	27.0	4.8	33.4
Developing Countries	20.9	42.4	35.7	21.2	32.9	43.7	26.2	8.8	58.8	16.9	8.2	68.2
World	12.7	27.3	53.8	11.6	23.7	56.2	10.1	34.8	45.1	8.0	33.8	50.0

Source: UNCOMTRADE, Statistical Database.

Note: P (Primary Commodities), F (Fuels) and M (Manufactures).

Primary commodities include SITC categories 0, 1, 2 and 4; Fuels are SITC category 3; Manufactures include SITC categories 5, 6, 7 and 8, so that non-ferrous metals, SITC category 68, are included in manufactures; SITC category 9 (commodities and transactions not included elsewhere) is excluded from the classification but included in the total. Therefore, percentages in the table do not add up to 100.

data on the composition of India's imports from the rest of the world are more complete as the unaccounted residual is small. Between 1990 and 2005, the share of manufactures in India's imports from developing countries increased from 36 per cent to 68 per cent, while this share was in the range of 50 per cent in imports from the world.

Table 7.8 outlines the changes in the composition of Africa's exports to China and India as compared to developing countries and the world. From 1990 to 2005, the share of primary commodities and fuels, taken together, in Africa's exports to China increased from 60 per cent to 86 per cent, while in exports to India it increased from 19 per cent to 52 per cent, but this share decreased from 62 per cent to 56 per cent in exports to developing countries and from 81 per cent to 59 per cent in exports to the world. Over the same period, the share of manufactures in Africa's exports to China and India registered a

Table 7.8 Composition of Africa's exports to China, India and the world (in percentage)

		1990	*1995*	*2000*	*2005*
Exports to CHINA					
	Primary Commodities	60.2	66.1	26.4	28.3
	Fuels	0.1	9.3	57.6	57.4
	Manufactures	39.7	23.7	15.2	14.1
INDIA					
	Primary Commodities	16.9	18.0	8.4	28.2
	Fuels	1.8	3.9	77.5	24.1
	Manufactures	81.3	78.1	13.9	43.8
DEVELOPING COUNTRIES					
	Primary Commodities	24.9	33.4	20.3	22.7
	Fuels	37.4	23.7	48.8	33.0
	Manufactures	37.7	42.6	29.8	40.1
WORLD					
	Primary Commodities	16.7	35.0	16.9	19.6
	Fuels	64.0	31.0	48.9	39.4
	Manufactures	19.8	32.0	29.8	37.9

Source: UNCOMTRADE, Statistical Database.

Note: Primary commodities include SITC categories 0, 1, 2 and 4; Fuels are SITC category 3; Manufactures include SITC categories 5, 6, 7 and 8, so that non-ferrous metals, SITC category 68, are included in manufactures; SITC category 9 (commodities and transactions not included elsewhere) is excluded from the classification but included in the total. Therefore, percentages in the table do not add up to 100.

corresponding decrease, while this share in exports to developing countries and the world fluctuated over time.

Table 7.9 outlines the changes in the composition of Africa's imports from China and India as compared with developing countries and the world. It shows that, between 1990 and 2005, the share of manufactures in Africa's imports from China registered a continuous increase from 62 per cent to 95 per cent, while the share of manufactures in Africa's imports from India remained in the range of 75–80 per cent. In contrast, the share of manufactures in Africa's imports from developing countries was in the range of 50 per cent, while the share of manufactures in Africa's imports from the world was in the range of 60 per cent.

The evidence on the composition of trade between China and India on the one hand and Africa on the other, presented in Tables 7.6–7.9, highlights some striking asymmetries. An overwhelmingly large proportion of China's exports to Africa, as also Africa's imports from

Table 7.9 Composition of Africa's imports from China, India and the world (in percentages)

		1990	*1995*	*2000*	*2005*
Imports from CHINA					
	Primary Commodities	36.1	20.4	14.2	4.0
	Fuels	1.4	0.2	2.0	0.7
	Manufactures	62.3	79.1	83.8	94.8
INDIA					
	Primary Commodities	22.5	27.2	14.0	14.9
	Fuels	0.2	0.1	0.7	5.4
	Manufactures	77.3	72.7	85.0	78.8
DEVELOPING COUNTRIES					
	Primary Commodities	33.7	31.7	18.5	17.1
	Fuels	22.3	20.8	29.6	25.3
	Manufactures	43.9	47.4	51.1	56.2
WORLD					
	Primary Commodities	25.7	26.4	18.4	15.2
	Fuels	7.5	7.7	12.8	13.8
	Manufactures	62.8	58.4	59.1	60.8

Source: UNCOMTRADE, Statistical Database.

Note: Primary commodities include SITC categories 0, 1, 2 and 4; Fuels are SITC category 3; Manufactures include SITC categories 5, 6, 7 and 8, so that non-ferrous metals, SITC category 68, are included in manufactures; SITC category 9 (commodities and transactions not included elsewhere) is excluded from the classification but included in the total. Therefore, percentages in the table do not add up to 100.

China, were made up of manufactures. Similarly, an overwhelmingly large proportion of China's imports from Africa, as also Africa's exports to China, were made up of primary commodities and fuels. This pattern of trade was exactly the same as that between industrialized countries and Africa during the colonial era. Both China and Africa's trade with developing countries and the world had a more diversified composition. The pattern of trade between India and Africa was not characterized by so much asymmetry. The proportion of manufactures in India's exports to Africa, as also in Africa's imports from India, was somewhat higher than it was in India's exports to developing countries and the world, as also in Africa's imports from developing countries and the world, but the difference was not so large. At the same time, the share of primary commodities and fuels, taken together, in India's imports from Africa, as also in Africa's exports to India, was more often than not lower than the share of primary commodities and fuels in India's imports from developing countries and the world, as also in Africa's exports to developing countries and the world.

International investment

The picture of international investment is much more difficult to sketch because the necessary data are not available. Table 7.10 sets out evidence on foreign direct investment, inward and outward, in China, India and Africa compared to developing countries, industrialized countries and the world. The figures on stocks are for 2000 and 2005, while the figures on flows are annual averages for the period 2001–2005. In the early 2000s, of the inward stock of foreign direct investment in developing countries, China accounted for about 12 per cent, India for about 2.5 per cent and Africa for 9 per cent. In the early 2000s, of the outward stock of foreign direct investment from developing countries, China accounted for 3–4 per cent, India for less than 1 per cent and Africa for 4–5 per cent. During the period 2001–2005, of the outward flows of foreign direct investment from developing countries, China accounted for 5.6 per cent, India for about 2 per cent and Africa for 0.4 per cent. It is possible to draw two inferences from this evidence. First, inward foreign direct investment in China, India and Africa is significant as a proportion of that in developing countries, but small as a proportion of both stocks and flows in the world. Second, outward foreign direct investment from China, India and Africa is small as a proportion of both stocks and flows even among developing countries.[8]

Table 7.10 Foreign direct investment: China, India and Africa: stocks and flows, 2000–2005

	Stocks				*Flows (average per annum)*	
	Inward		*Outward*		*Inward*	*Outward*
	2000	*2005*	*2000*	*2005*	*2001–2005*	*2001–2005*
China	193	318	28	46	57	4
	(11.4)	*(12.0)*	*(3.2)*	*(3.7)*	*(25.4)*	*(5.6)*
India	18	45	2	10	6	2
	(1.0)	*(1.7)*	*(0.2)*	*(0.8)*	*(2.5)*	*(1.9)*
Africa	151	264	45	54	20	0.4
	(8.9)	*(10.0)*	*(5.2)*	*(4.3)*	*(8.8)*	*(0.4)*
Developing countries	1,697	2,655	856	1,268	225	80
Industrialized countries	4,035	7,219	5,593	9,278	476	602
World	5,803	10,130	6,471	10,672	727	691

Source: UNCTAD Foreign Direct Investment Online Database (http://stats.unctad.org/fdi).

Note: Figures in parentheses represent the total for China, India and Africa as a percentage of the total for developing countries.

During the period 2001–2005, of the inward flows of foreign direct investment in developing countries, China accounted for 25 per cent, India for 2 per cent and Africa for about 10 per cent.

It is difficult to assess the significance of foreign direct investment from China and India in Africa, because data on inward stocks and flows of foreign direct investment in Africa are not available by country of origin. Information compiled for 13 countries in Africa suggests that in 2005, China accounted for 0.6 per cent and India accounted for 0.7 per cent of the inward stock of foreign direct investment, while from 1995 to 2005 China accounted for 0.6 per cent and India for 1.1 per cent of average annual inflows of foreign direct investment.[9] More complete information and more recent data may suggest an increase in the significance of China and India in foreign direct investment in Africa, at least from the developing world. For example, it is reported that Chinese foreign direct investment increased from US$ 28 million in 1998 to US$ 6 billion in 2005.[10] There are no comparable statistics for India. But it is reported that, during the period 2000–2006, of the 309 acquisitions abroad by Indian firms, 13 were in Africa, of which 6 were in the petroleum sector, while the others were in pharmaceuticals, chemicals, fertilizers and consumer goods.[11]

International aid

Information in the sphere of foreign aid and development assistance is also scarce. Even so, it would seem that both China and India are emerging as donors, with a significant presence in Africa. Development finance is the core of China's aid programs, whereas the focus of India's aid programs is technical assistance.[12] For both countries, economic assistance for development in Africa is strategic in terms of political interests. It is portrayed as South-South cooperation, a partnership based on political equality and mutual trust, and one that is depicted as being different from foreign aid to Africa provided by industrialized countries. There was a China–Africa Summit at Beijing in November 2006 and an India–Africa Summit at New Delhi in April 2008, both of which had a large presence of heads of governments from African countries. Unfortunately, evidence on foreign aid flows from China and India to Africa is not readily available. It is reported that foreign aid from China to Africa increased from US$ 107 million in 1998 to US$ 2.7 billion in 2004.[13] Similarly, it is reported that foreign aid from India to Africa was US$ 2.7 billion during the period 2003–2008.[14] However, it is clear that foreign aid from China and India is relatively small as compared with foreign aid provided by the industrialized countries.[15] Yet, it is possible that the multiplier effects of aid from China and India, as also from other emerging donors, such as Korea, Brazil and South Africa, may be significant for two reasons. For one, technical assistance may alleviate infrastructural constraints in developing countries. For another, emerging donors could be a catalyst for aid flows from the industrialized countries in much the same way that foreign aid from the socialist countries was a catalyst during the cold war era.

International migration

International migration is a significant form of engagement with the world economy for China and even more so for India. Both India and China have always been, and continue to be, important countries of origin for international migration. The traditional category is emigrants. But globalization has introduced the cross-border movement of guest workers and professionals.[16] The engagement of India and China with developing countries, particularly African countries, through international migration is attributable in part to the diaspora and in part to globalization. For India in Africa, this is attributable to the diaspora embedded in history. For China in Africa, this is attributable to the recent engagement through aid and investment.

The diaspora has historical origins. Following the British Empire's abolition of slavery, for a period of 50 years starting around the mid-1830s, about 50 million people left India and China to work as indentured labourers in mines, plantations and construction in the Americas, the Caribbean, South Africa, Southeast Asia and other distant lands.[17] This was probably close to 10 per cent of the total population of India and China *circa* 1880. The migration from India and China continued, in somewhat different forms, during the first half of the 20th century, particularly in the period between the two world wars. There is, consequently, a significant presence of people from India and China across the world, not only in the industrialized countries, but also in the developing countries. This is associated with entrepreneurial capitalisms, both Chinese and Indian, in developing countries where the migration stream has aged. The diaspora from India in Africa engaged in trade and business, an example of such entrepreneurial capitalism, which was the subject of resentment in some nationalist movements and in early post-colonial Africa, but has since diminished.

The second half of the 20th century also witnessed significant waves of international migration from India, comprising permanent emigration to the industrialized countries and temporary migration to the oil-exporting countries in the Middle East.[18] The international migration from China was limited during this period, but the gathering momentum of globalization during the past two decades has led to a significant increase in the new categories of cross-border movements of people. In this sphere, the engagement of India with the world economy is much more than that of China. The advent of globalization, which has made it easier to move people across borders, is associated with managerial capitalisms, especially with professionals from India who can migrate permanently, live abroad temporarily or stay at home and travel frequently for business. These people are almost as mobile across borders as capital. Such an Indian presence is now discernible in Africa, attributable partly to technical assistance provided by the government and partly to investment by firms from the private sector. Such a Chinese presence is now significant in Africa (though the evidence is anecdotal rather than precise), attributable partly to the use of Chinese workers in aid-financed infrastructure construction, people who may not be repatriated after project completion and who may enter into trade or commerce, and partly to Chinese companies that bring their personnel to run business.

Implications for Africa

Globalization is associated with increasing economic openness, growing economic interdependence and deepening economic integration in the world economy. In such a world, growth prospects would be significantly influenced, if not shaped, by the growth performance of lead economies. The following discussion asks whether China and India could be new engines of growth for the developing world, considers the underlying mechanisms and examines the possible impact on Africa.

Engines of growth

Rapid economic growth in China and India, if it is sustained at the projected rates, is bound to exercise considerable influence on prospects for the world economy, the industrialized countries and the developing countries. Such an analysis, however, is beyond the scope of this essay. In any case, the possible consequences of the rise of China and India for the industrialized countries and the world economy have been considered in the emerging literature on the subject.[19] Therefore, the thrust of the discussion that follows is on the implications and consequences for developing countries, with a focus on Africa.

In considering the future, is it possible to think of China and India as engines of growth for the developing world, even if not for the world economy? The answer largely depends on the size of the two economies and their growth rates. There are some pointers from recent experience. Statistical analysis shows that since 1980, the Chinese economy has also led world GDP with a lag of one or two years, although the correlation coefficient is much smaller than that for the United States. This is not surprising. For one, in 2005, China accounted for 5 per cent of world GDP at market exchange rates and 14 per cent of world GDP in PPP terms. For another, GDP growth in China has been in the range of 9 per cent per annum for 25 years. By these criteria, India is not an engine of growth, at least not yet. This is also not surprising. Its economic size is smaller than that of China and its growth rate is not as high. In 2005, India accounted for only 2 per cent of world GDP at market exchange rates and 6 per cent of world GDP in PPP terms. For another, GDP growth in India has been in the range of 6 per cent per annum for 25 years. Even so, India is a potential engine of growth in terms of both attributes.

Lead economies drive economic growth elsewhere in the world by providing markets for exports, resources for investment, finances for development and technologies for productivity. At this juncture, China is not quite an engine of growth in every dimension. Economic growth in China provides a stimulus to economic growth elsewhere, mostly as a market for exports. So far, India cannot be characterized as an engine of growth in any dimension, perhaps not even as a market for exports. But, along with China, India has some potential in terms of markets for exports, resources for investment and technologies for productivity. In this context, it is worth noting that China and India could ultimately be a significant impetus to the growth process in the developing world as an important complement to, even if they cannot be a substitute for, the United States in driving global growth. And, given their strengthening economic relationship with Africa, particularly through trade but also through investment and aid, the emerging Asian giants could also provide a significant impetus to the growth process in Africa if linkages develop appropriately.

Causation and mechanisms

The economic causation outlined above is necessary, but not sufficient. The overall effects of economic growth in lead economies on economic growth elsewhere depend upon: (1) whether such growth is complementary or competitive; (2) whether the direct effects are reinforced or counteracted by the indirect effects; and (3) whether, on balance, the impact is positive or negative.[20]

In principle, economic growth in lead economies may be complementary or competitive to economic growth elsewhere. It may be complementary in that it increases the demand for exports, but it may be competitive in that it develops alternative sources of supply. It may be complementary if it provides resources for investment or finances for development, but it may be competitive if it pre-empts such resources for investment or finances for development. It may be complementary if it provides technologies to others, but it may be competitive if it stifles the development of technologies elsewhere. The distinctions between the complementary and the competitive aspects are widely recognized. However, the distinction between direct effects and indirect effects is less clear because the latter sometimes are difficult to discern, let alone measure. In situations in which direct effects are complementary, indirect effects could be reinforcing if complementary, but counteracting if competitive. For example, the direct effects may be complementary if the lead economies, say China and India, provide cheap wage goods to developing countries in Africa, but the indirect effects may be competitive if competition from firms in lead economies, say China and India, squeezes out local firms in African countries. The direct effects may be complementary if firms from the lead economies, China and India, invest in African countries, but the indirect effects may be competitive if firms from industrialized countries relocate production and invest in China and India rather than in African countries. The direct effects may be complementary if the lead economies provide cheaper inputs for manufactured exports from African countries, but the indirect effects may be competitive if competition from China and India squeezes out manufactured exports from African countries in the markets of industrialized countries. In principle, the impact of economic growth in lead economies on economic growth elsewhere could be positive, or negative or some combination of both, and on balance, such impact can be either positive or negative. The outcomes may differ across space and change over time so that generalizations are difficult.

In this context, it is worth noting that macroeconomic policies in China and India, once they become lead economies, may exercise an important influence on economic growth elsewhere. If such policies are countercyclical, which has been the case for the United States, these would be supportive of economic growth elsewhere. But if these policies are procyclical, which is common in developing countries, these could be disruptive for economic growth elsewhere. Similarly, exchange rates in lead economies could exercise a significant influence, either positive or negative, on economic growth elsewhere in the world. For example, an undervalued exchange rate in China, which has persisted for quite some time, could constrain the prospects for labour-intensive manufactured exports from developing countries in Africa, thereby limiting the potential demand stimulus to economic growth that could be provided by exports. In fact, it is already doing so.[21]

Possible impact

During the first quarter of the 21st century, economic growth in China and India could have a positive impact on developing countries in Africa if it improves terms of trade, provides appropriate technologies and creates new sources of finance for development, whether investment or aid.

It is clear that, for some time to come, the positive impact on developing countries would be transmitted through an improvement in their terms of trade.[22] Given the abundance of natural endowments in Africa, rapid economic growth in China and India is bound to boost the demand for primary commodities exported by African countries. The reasons are simple enough. Both China and India have large populations and in both countries levels of consumption per capita in most primary commodities are low, while income elasticities of demand for most primary commodities are high. This burgeoning demand will almost certainly raise prices of primary commodities in world markets and improve the terms of trade for African countries. In this context, Africa is perhaps the most important source of primary commodities in the world economy. What is more, China already is, and India is likely to become, a source of manufactured goods in the world market. Such manufactures, particularly wage goods, from China and India are likely to be cheaper than competing goods from industrialized countries. This would also improve the terms of trade for African developing countries. Such terms of trade gains would raise real incomes in Africa. But the impact on development, in terms of the well-being of people, would depend on the nature of asset ownership, the quality of mediating institutions and the effectiveness of government policies in African countries.[23]

The positive impact of China and India on African countries through the other potential channels of transmission is not as clear. We do not yet have either the evidence or the experience. In principle, it is possible that China and India would develop technologies that are more appropriate for the factor endowments and the economic needs of Africa. But it is too early to make a judgment.

Similarly, China and India are potential sources of finance for development. Their foreign aid programs, particularly in Africa, constitute a modest beginning. As has been discussed, much of Chinese aid is directed toward building infrastructure[24] and much of Indian aid is in the form of technical assistance, and both are reported to have increased significantly since 2005. Insofar as this infrastructure development and technical assistance ease supply constraints in Africa, such aid should have a positive impact on economic growth through an increase in the productivity of public and private investment. The benefits to recipient countries in Africa would depend in part on the terms of the assistance. In larger part, however, the benefits would depend upon whether such aid supports projects that could not have been financed by domestic resources or Western donors, as also on the design and implementation of government policies in African countries. On balance, there can be little doubt that the emergence of China and India as sources of foreign aid or technical assistance for African countries has enlarged their choices and options, even if it has not improved the terms or enlarged the volume of development assistance from the traditional donors.

In comparison, the contribution of China and India in terms of foreign direct investment is so far limited. However, it is worth noting that China and India are different from each other in the nature and purpose of such investment. Foreign direct investment from China is through state-owned firms, directed towards natural resource extraction, mostly petroleum and non-ferrous metals, and is concentrated in a few countries.[25] Some diversification in sectors and countries of destination is discernible, but the concentration remains. Foreign direct investment from India is through private sector firms, mostly in manufacturing or services, and is more distributed across countries.[26]

The emergence of China and India in the world economy could also have a negative impact on African countries, if the two mega-economies provide African countries with competition as markets for exports or as destinations for investment.

At this juncture, China is clearly the largest supplier of labour-intensive manufactured goods in the world market. Even though it is not as large as China, India is also a significant supplier of labour-intensive manufactured goods in the world market. There is little doubt that manufactured exports from China and India nearly span the entire range of manufactured exports, of which other developing countries could have a potential comparative advantage. Hence, it is plausible to argue though impossible to prove that on balance, China and possibly India have a negative impact on manufactured exports from African countries, which have to compete with China and India for export markets in industrialized countries.[27] This can change if and when China and India vacate their space in the international trade matrix, in much the same way that latecomers to industrialization in Asia, such as Japan, Korea, Hong Kong, Taiwan and Singapore, vacated their space in the market for simple labour-intensive manufactures for countries that followed in their footsteps. This is not likely, at least in the medium term, because China and India both have large reservoirs of surplus labour at low wages not only in the rural hinterlands, but also in the urban informal sectors.

The evidence presented earlier showed that China and India absorb a significant proportion of inward foreign direct investment in developing countries both in terms of stocks and flows. Given that the two Asian giants are now among the most attractive destinations for transnational firms seeking to locate production in the developing world, it is once again plausible to suggest though impossible to prove that foreign direct investment in China and India might be at the expense of developing countries, particularly in Africa. It would seem that, at present, China and India represent competition for rather than a source of foreign direct investment for other developing countries. The share of China and India in outward foreign direct investment in the world economy, as also from developing countries, is modest in both stocks and flows, so that firms from China and India do not, at least so far, compensate with foreign direct investment in African countries.

The less discernible but more significant negative impact of the Asian mega-economies, particularly China, on Africa is implicit in the unchanged division of labour. It is striking that China's present division of labour with Africa, reflected in the composition of trade flows, is not different from the old North-South pattern of trade, in so far as Chinese imports from Africa are mostly primary commodities while an overwhelming proportion of Chinese exports to Africa are manufactured goods.[28] The evidence presented earlier in Table 7.6 shows that this composition, particularly in imports, is far more skewed than that for China's trade with developing countries or the world economy as a whole. Indeed, when this composition of trade is juxtaposed with Chinese aid to and investment in Africa, which is concentrated in the extraction of natural resources motivated by a strategic sourcing of raw materials, China's pattern of economic transactions with Africa conforms even more closely to the caricatural neocolonial pattern. Such traditional patterns of trade can neither transform the structure of production in African countries nor make for a new international division of labour. Indeed, such trade can only perpetuate the dependence of African countries on exports of primary commodities without creating possibilities of increasing value added before export or entering into manufacturing activities characterized by economies of scale. Such path-dependent specialization can only curb the possibilities of structural transformation in developing countries. Trade with China can sustain growth and support industrialization in African countries only if there is a successful transition from a complementary to a competitive pattern of trade, so that inter-sectoral trade is gradually replaced by intra-sectoral or intra-industry trade and specialization.

Conclusions

It is clear that the rise of China and India in the world economy will have important implications for economic development in Africa. The consequences could be positive if China and India provide markets for exports, resources for investment and finances for development, which would stimulate the process of growth in Africa. The emerging mega-economies of Asia may also provide African countries with more options, choices and space in formulating policies that are conducive to national development objectives. Their growing presence would almost certainly reduce the enormous influence that Western countries and multilateral institutions have exercised on development policies and strategies in Africa. This could create more scope for African leaders to evolve their own approaches to development. On the other hand, the consequences could be negative if growth in China and India is competitive rather than complementary to growth in Africa. The economic engagement of the Asian giants with Africa, through trade and investment, may also perpetuate traditional patterns of specialization, which inhibit rather than foster industrialization in African countries. The impact, on balance, will depend upon how reality unfolds. It will depend on the nature of China and India's interactions with Africa. Even more so, it will depend on what African countries do, in terms of initial conditions, better bargaining and appropriate policies, to maximize the benefits and minimize the costs associated with the process of increasing economic interaction with China and India.

The international arena will also matter. From the perspective of Africa, China and India together may be able to exercise significant influence through multilateralism in the global context. The United Nations, the World Bank, the IMF and the WTO are among the most important multilateral institutions.[29] In the United Nations, China is a permanent member of the Security Council with a right to veto. But India is knocking at the door, seeking permanent membership in the Security Council, with or without a right to veto. In the Bretton Woods Institutions, the World Bank and the IMF, China and India are permanent members of the Executive Boards. In the WTO, India has been a long-standing advocate of developing countries. China has a low profile, possibly because of its recent accession. It would seem that China and India have a considerable potential for articulating a collective voice, on behalf of smaller countries, in the world of multilateralism. Coordination and cooperation among them carry a significant potential for exercising influence on multilateral institutions, which could reshape rules and create policy space for countries (particularly in Africa) that are latecomers to development. Such coordination and cooperation, which are possible, have not yet surfaced. China and India have neither articulated a collective voice nor exercised collective influence. There could be two reasons for the near absence of coordination and cooperation so far. For one, in the early stages of change, these countries might not have recognized their potential for exercising collective influence. For another, their relationship with each other may be characterized more by rivalry, economic or political, and less by unity. It is difficult to predict how reality might unfold in times to come.[30]

It is worth noting two important limitations of the analysis in this paper. First, it considers China and India together, which may be somewhat deceptive insofar as China is much larger than in India in almost every dimension of engagement with Africa. But the analysis does recognize and highlight the important differences. Second, it considers China and India as a composite, which may not be entirely appropriate, because an economic and political rivalry between China and India could significantly shape the impact on Africa. It is important to analyse the implications and consequences of this rivalry for economic development in Africa, but such an exercise would require another paper. Even so, this chapter constitutes an important beginning in a relatively unexplored subject.

Acknowledgement

The author would like to thank Jonas Shaende for valuable research assistance. Ananya Ghosh-Dastidar and Xuan Zhang helped in the search for information.

Notes

1 Such dominance went back a long time. From 1000 to 1700, China and India, taken together, accounted for 50 per cent of world population and 50 per cent of world income. And 2000 years ago, in 1 AD, China and India accounted for almost 60 per cent of both world population and world income. For a more detailed discussion, see Nayyar (2008a).
2 The evidence in Table 7.3 and the discussion that follows draws upon earlier work by the author; see Nayyar (2008b).
3 This growth performance in Africa was worse than in other regions of the developing world, including Latin America. In fact, during the period 1981–2000, Africa fared even worse as growth in GDP per capita was negative in the range of 0.06–0.17 per cent per annum. It was the revival in growth during the early 2000s that made the growth in GDP per capita positive, even if modest, during the period 1981–2005.
4 For the methodology and the conclusions, see Wilson and Purushothaman (2003).
5 For a detailed discussion on the model, the data and the results, see Rowthorn (2008).
6 In this context, it is worth noting that the proportion of young people in the population is significantly higher in India than in China, so that the potential demographic dividend would be available to India for a longer period of time.

7 In this context, it is worth noting that such a classification probably overstates the share of manufactures in exports and imports from Africa because the definition of manufactures as Standard International Trade Classification (SITC) 5 + 6 + 7 + 8 includes non-ferrous metals, SITC 68, which are often classified as primary commodities. But this does not affect comparisons of the composition of Africa's trade across countries or country-groups, which are the focus of the discussion that follows.

8 The share of Africa in the outward stock of foreign direct investment from developing countries was surprisingly higher than that of China, essentially because of outward investment from South Africa in earlier years (Nayyar, 2010).

9 The selected countries are Algeria, Egypt, Ethiopia, Madagascar, Malawi, Mauritius, Morocco, Mozambique, South Africa, Tanzania, Tunisia, Uganda and Zambia. In 2005, the total inward stock of foreign direct investment in these countries was US$ 270,984 million, of which US$ 1,595 million was from China and US$ 1,969 million was from India. During the period 1995–2005, the total inflow of foreign direct investment in these countries was US$ 18,394 million per annum, of which US$ 103 million per annum was from China and US$ 209 million per annum was from India. Over the same period, the inflow from developing countries was US$ 1,257 million per annum, so that China's share was 8 per cent while India's share was 16 per cent. These figures have been calculated from figures reported for each of the selected 13 countries from http://www.stats.unctad.org/fdi. It is, however, worth stressing that these figures are indicative rather than precise because they relate to only 13 countries in Africa and are reported for only some of the years in the period, which are not the same for all the selected countries.

10 See Toye (2008: 103).

11 This is reported in a study by the Federation of Indian Chambers of Commerce and Industry, *India Inc.'s Acquisitions Abroad* (New Delhi, 2006). For analysis of investment and acquisitions abroad by Indian firms, see Nayyar (2008a).

12 The object of India's technical assistance to Africa is to provide low-cost, affordable, adaptable and appropriate technologies for infrastructure development. Sharing information and communication technologies to bridge the digital divide is also an important part of this endeavour. In addition, the development of human resources through skill development and capacity building, supported by training and consultancy, is woven into such technical cooperation.

13 See Toye (2008: 104).

14 At the India-Africa Summit in New Delhi in April 2008, it was announced that aid to Africa, the composite financial package to support development, would double to US$ 5.4 billion over the next five years.

15 During the period 2001–2005, net ODA disbursements from DAC countries were US$ 73,200 million per annum, while net ODA disbursements from non-DAC donors were a mere US$ 575 million per annum. For the annual statistics, see http://stats.oecd.org/wbos. It is worth noting that non-DAC donors include Saudi Arabia, Korea, Turkey, Kuwait, United Arab Emirates, Czech Republic, Hungary and Poland, among others, but

net ODA disbursements from China and India are not even reported in these OECD statistics on foreign aid.

16 The changing nature of international migration is analysed, at some length, in Nayyar (2002 a).

17 Cf. Tinker (1974) and Lewis (1977). See also Nayyar (2002a).

18 For a discussion of and evidence on international migration from India, see Nayyar (1994).

19 See, for example, Freeman (2005), Singh (2007), Rowthorn (2008) and Nayyar (2010).

20 For a detailed discussion, see Kaplinsky (2006). The literature on this subject is limited. But the implications and consequences of rapid growth in China and India, for the developing world, particularly Africa, are analysed in Kaplinsky and Messner (2008).

21 Evidence cited later in the chapter confirms that the size and growth of China's manufactured exports pose serious problems for exports of manufactures from and industrial growth in Sub-Saharan Africa.

22 This proposition is stressed by Kaplinsky (2006), Singh (2007), Nayyar (2008a) and Rowthorn (2008).

23 For a detailed discussion, see Toye (2008).

24 For an analysis and evaluation of Chinese aid to Sub-Saharan Africa, based on qualitative rather than quantitative evidence, see Toye (2008).

25 For example, China has acquired stakes in oil companies in Africa at a cumulative cost of US$ 15 billion. Of its petroleum imports from Africa, Angola alone provides 50 per cent while Sudan provides another 20 per cent. There is a bundling of aid, investment and trade, not very different from that practiced by the USSR in the past, which is concentrated in a small number of countries in Africa such as Angola, Chad, Congo, Kenya, Nigeria, Sudan, Zambia and Zimbabwe. The economic ties are often associated with strategic political interests. For a detailed discussion, see Toye (2008).

26 There are two exceptions: ONGC, a public sector firm from India, acquired a 25 per cent share in the Greater Nile Oil Project in Sudan for US$ 766 million in 2002 and a 50 per cent share in the Greater Plutonio Project in Angola for US$ 600 million in 2004, both in the petroleum sector (Nayyar, 2008a). In this context, it is worth noting that the sectoral composition and geographical distribution of outward foreign direct investment from India provides two sharp contrasts with that from developing countries. For one, three-fifths of international investment from India is in manufacturing activities, while this proportion is about one-eighth for developing countries. For another, almost three-fourths of international investment from India is in industrialized countries, while this proportion is less than one-fifth for developing countries. The proportions for China are similar to those for developing countries as a group. In fact, foreign direct investment from China is probably even more concentrated in primary commodities and developing countries. For a discussion, see Nayyar (2008a).

27 In a recent study, Kaplinsky and Morris (2008) show that the entry of China (and to a lesser extent India) into the global economy as a significant exporter of manufactures poses severe problems for export-oriented industrialization and growth in Sub-Saharan Africa.

28 This pattern is characteristic of China's trade with developing countries except for Southeast Asia. An unpublished study by Rhys Jenkins and Chris Edwards, cited in United Nations (2006a: 22), on China's trade with 18 developing countries (6 in Asia, 6 in Africa and 6 in Latin America) shows that countries that had significant trade with China were exporting mostly agricultural or extractive primary commodities. A study on China's economic interaction with Latin America and the Caribbean also confirms the traditional pattern of trade, importing mostly primary commodities and exporting mostly manufactured goods (Inter-American Development Bank, 2005).

29 For a detailed discussion on the possibilities of reform and change in these multilateral institutions in the wider context of global governance, see Nayyar (2002a).

30 For a more detailed discussion of this issue, see Nayyar (2010). It is important to recognize that once these countries become major players, there is a danger that they might opt for the pursuit of national interest rather than the spirit of solidarity or the logic of collective action among developing countries.

References

Freeman, R. B. (2005). 'What Really Ails Europe and America: The Doubling of the Global Workforce', *The Globalist*, 3 June.

Inter-American Development Bank (2005). *The Emergence of China: Opportunities and Challenges for Latin America and the Caribbean*. Washington, DC: IADB.

Kaplinsky, R. (ed.) (2006). 'Asian Drivers: Opportunities and Threats', *IDS Bulletin*, 37 (1): 1–11.

Kaplinsky, R. and D. Messner (2008). 'The Impact of the Asian Drivers on the Developing World', *World Development*, 36 (2): 197–209.

Kaplinsky, R. and M. Morris (2008). 'Do the Asian Drivers Undermine Export-Oriented Industrialization in Sub-Saharan Africa?', *World Development*, 36 (2): 254–73.

Lewis, W. A. (1977). *The Evolution of the International Economic Order*. Princeton, NJ: Princeton University Press.

Maddison, A. (2003). *The World Economy: Historical Statistics*. Paris: OECD.

Nayyar, D. (1994). *Migration, Remittances and Capital Flows: The Indian Experience*. Delhi: Oxford University Press.

Nayyar, D. (2002a). 'Cross-Border Movements of People', in D. Nayyar (ed.), *Governing Globalization: Issues and Institutions*. Oxford: Oxford University Press.

Nayyar, D. (2002b). 'The Existing System and the Missing Institutions', in D. Nayyar (ed.), *Governing Globalization: Issues and Institutions*. Oxford: Oxford University Press.

Nayyar, D. (2008a). 'The Rise of China and India: Implications for Developing Countries', in P. Artesis and J. Eatwell (eds.), *Issues in Economic Development and Globalization*. London: Palgrave Macmillan.

Nayyar, D. (2008b). 'The Internationalization of Firms from India: Investment, Mergers and Acquisitions', *Oxford Development Studies*, 36 (1): 111–31.

Nayyar, D. (2010). 'China, India, Brazil and South Africa in the World Economy: Engines of Growth?', in A. Santos-Paulino and G. Wan (eds.), *Southern Engines of Global Growth*. Oxford: Oxford University Press.

Rowthorn, R. (2008). 'The Renaissance of China and India: Implications for the Advanced Economies', in P. Artesis and J. Eatwell (eds.), *Issues in Economic Development and Globalization*. London: Palgrave Macmillan.

Singh, A. (2007). 'Globalization, Industrial Revolutions in India and China and Labour Markets in Advanced Countries: Implications for National and International Economic Policy', *Working Paper No. 81*, Policy Integration Department, March. Geneva: ILO.

Tinker, H. (1974). *A New System of Slavery: The Export of Indian Labour Overseas: 1830–1920*. Oxford: Oxford University Press.

Toye, J. (2008). 'China's Impact on Sub-Saharan African Economic Development: Trade, Aid and Politics', in P. Artesis and J. Eatwell (eds.), *Issues in Economic Development and Globalization*. London: Palgrave Macmillan.

United Nations (2006a). *Diverging Growth and Development*, *World Economic and Social Survey 2006*. New York: United Nations.

United Nations (2006b). *National Accounts Main Aggregates Database*, New York, available from http://unstats.un.org/unsd/snaama/introduction.asp

United Nations (2006c). *Demographic Yearbook System*, Department of Economic and Social Affairs, New York, available from http://unstats.un.org/unsd/demographic/products/dyb/dyb2.htm

Wilson, D. and R. Purushothaman (2003). 'Dreaming with BRICS: The Path to 2050', *Global Economics Paper No. 99*. New York: Goldman Sachs.

World Bank (2007). *World Development Indicators 2007*. Washington, DC: World Bank.

8

BRICS, DEVELOPING COUNTRIES AND GLOBAL GOVERNANCE

Brazil, Russia, India, China and South Africa – BRICS – a group of countries diverse in terms of economics and geography, constitute an infant formation that has moved centre stage in the contemporary world in a rather short span of time. Their economic importance is obviously attributable to size. In 2010, taken together, these five countries accounted for 43 per cent of world population and 18 per cent of world income.[1] However, their political significance stems not only from economic size, but also from collective voice in a world where the balance of power is changing. The acronym began life in 2004, coined by Jim O'Neill in a Goldman Sachs study.[2] But this was no more than an exercise in compound growth rates for a cluster of countries that experienced rapid economic growth in the 1990s, which gathered momentum in the boom of the early 2000s.[3] It evolved into a political reality in 2009 with the first annual summit of the BRICS nations. South Africa was a late invitee and entrant in 2011. This evolution was an iterative process. It started in 2003, with a plurilateral group of three countries – India, Brazil and South Africa – one from each continent of the developing world that was named IBSA. The next step followed in 2009, to include China in BASIC, an *ad hoc* coalition that was shaped by an event, the Summit on Climate Change at Copenhagen.

The object of this chapter is to analyse the potential implications and possible consequences of BRICS for countries in the developing world and for global governance. Its focus is on the big picture in the international context. It is not concerned with the economics or politics of development within these countries. Given the objective, for analytical purposes, this essay defines BRICS as Brazil, India, China and South Africa excluding Russia, although it is part of the political formation, partly because it is at a much higher level of income[4] and a more advanced stage of development, but more importantly because it is a former superpower and an industrialized economy.

The structure of the discussion is as follows. First, it situates BRICS in the wider context of developing countries in the world economy in longer term historical perspective. Second, it examines the growing economic significance of BRICS in a world where change has gathered momentum since 1980. Third, it considers the factors underlying the evolution of BRICS as an economic and political formation. Fourth, it analyses the possible economic impact of future growth in the BRICS on other developing countries. Fifth, it discusses the potential influence of BRICS, beyond economics to politics, in the global context with reference to the possibilities of cooperation among developing countries.

Historical perspective

The world economy has witnessed a significant transformation during the second half of the 20th century and the first decade of the 21st century.[5] This is clearly visible in changes in the share of developing countries in world output, but much less so in levels of per capita income relative to industrialized countries.[6] In terms of Maddison PPP statistics, the share of developing countries in world output stopped its continuous decline, which started in 1820, *circa* 1960, when it was about one-fourth, to increase rapidly after 1980, so that it was almost one-half by 2008, while the divergence in GDP per capita also came to a stop in 1980 and was followed by a modest convergence thereafter, so that as a proportion of GDP per capita in industrialized countries it was about one-fifth in 2008.[7] In current prices at market exchange rates, between 1970 and 2010, the share of developing countries in world GDP doubled from one-sixth to one-third, while their GDP per capita as a proportion of that in industrialized countries recorded a modest increase from one-fourteenth to one-tenth.[8] Differences in GDP growth rates underlie the rising share of developing countries and the falling share of industrialized countries in world GDP. Given the decline in population growth rates in the developing world, these differences underlie the end of divergence in per capita incomes *circa* 1980, followed by the beginnings of a very modest convergence that is discernible after 1990 and more visible in the 2000s.[9]

The engagement of developing countries with the world economy witnessed a decline during the period from 1950 to 1980, particularly when compared with the past, but revived *circa* 1980 and grew rapidly thereafter.[10] However, this deeper engagement was a matter of choice, in sharp contrast with the compulsion of the past. Their share in world merchandize trade, exports and imports more than doubled from less than 20 per cent in 1970 to more than 40 per cent in 2010. Similarly, their share of international trade in services registered a substantial increase to reveal their comparative advantage in exports of services. Beginning in the 1990s, their share in stocks and flows of inward, as also outward, foreign direct investment also increased at the expense of industrialized countries, although they were more important as countries of destination than as countries of origin.

There was a significant catch up in industrialization for the developing world as a whole, beginning around 1950 that gathered momentum in the early 1970s. Structural changes in the composition of output and employment, which led to a decline in the share of agriculture with an increase in the share of industry and services, were important factors underlying the process. There was a dramatic transformation in just four decades.[11] Between 1970 and 2010, the share of developing countries in world industrial production jumped from 8 per cent to 33 per cent in constant prices and from about 12 per cent to more than 40 per cent in current prices. Similarly, their share in world exports of manufactures rose from 7 per cent to 40 per cent. Industrialization also led to pronounced changes in the composition of their trade, as the share of primary commodities and resource-based products fell, while the share of manufactures rose, in both exports and imports.

This impressive performance in the aggregate is characterized by uneven development. The engagement with the world economy and the catch up in industrialization were both uneven between regions. There was a strong concentration in Asia. Latin America stayed roughly where it was. Africa fell further behind. The distribution was also uneven between countries within regions. There was a high degree of concentration among a few: Argentina, Brazil, Chile and Mexico in Latin America; China, India, Indonesia, Malaysia, South Korea, Taiwan, Thailand and Turkey in Asia; and Egypt and South Africa in Africa. In fact, the economic significance of these countries, termed the *Next-14*, in the developing world was overwhelming in terms of their size, reflected in GDP and population, their engagement with the world economy – reflected in trade, investment and migration – and industrialization – reflected in manufactured exports and industrial production.[12] BRICS were perhaps the most important subset of countries in the Next-14. There was also enormous diversity within the few, characterized by an unequal distribution, in terms of the same attributes that revealed the concentration among them.

The determinants of such concentration are the size and growth of economies. But it is also embedded in history. The importance of BRICS, particularly China and India, is not new. It goes back centuries.[13] This is borne out by evidence available for the more recent past. Table 8.1 sets outlines the share of BRICS in world income and world population for selected benchmark years during the period 1820–1950. It shows that, in 1820, BRICS accounted for 57 per cent of world population and almost 50 per cent of world income. The shares were almost proportional. There was a dramatic change in the next 130 years, which mirrored the rise of the West and the fall of the Rest. In 1950, BRICS accounted for 39 per cent of world population and 19 per cent of world income. The shares became asymmetrical. Much of this transformation was attributable to the decline and fall of China and India. Between 1820 and 1950, the share of the two Asian giants dropped in world income from 49 per cent to 9 per cent and in world population from almost 57 per cent to 36 per cent. This sharp contraction was mirrored in the shares of both BRICS and developing countries. Obviously, there were significant differences between two sets of countries within BRICS. For one, China and India had

Table 8.1 BRICS and developing countries in the world economy, shares in world GDP and world population, 1820–1950 (percentages)

Share in World GDP in 1990 (Geary–Khamis PPP) International Dollars				
	1820	*1870*	*1913*	*1950*
Brazil	0.4	0.6	0.7	1.7
China	33.0	17.1	8.8	4.6
India	16.1	12.2	7.5	4.2
South Africa	0.1	0.2	0.4	0.6
Total above BRICS	49.5	30.1	17.4	11.1
Developing Countries	63.1	42.6	29.6	27.1
World	100.0	100.0	100.0	100.0
Share in World Population				
	1820	*1870*	*1913*	*1950*
Brazil	0.4	0.8	1.3	2.1
China	36.6	28.1	24.4	21.6
India	20.1	19.8	16.9	14.2
South Africa	0.1	0.2	0.3	0.5
Total above BRICS	57.2	48.9	43.0	38.5
Developing Countries	74.4	67.8	63.2	67.0
World	100.0	100.0	100.0	100.0

Sources: Maddison (2003) and Nayyar (2013).

Note: The percentages have been calculated.

dominant shares, in both income and population, while the shares of Brazil and South Africa were far smaller. For another, the shares of Brazil and South Africa, in both income and population, rose and were symmetrical throughout this period, while the shares of China and India fell rapidly, more in income than in population, and became increasingly asymmetrical over time.

This historical backdrop situates the growing economic significance of BRICS since 1980 in a longer term perspective. Table 8.2 presents comparable data on the shares of BRICS, the Next-14 and developing countries in PPP-GDP of the world and the shares of BRICS and the Next-14 in the PPP-GDP of developing countries, for 1980, 1990, 2000 and 2008 (the latest year for which Maddison statistics are available). A comparison with Table 8.1 shows that 1980 was a turning point for BRICS. And the distribution of world PPP-GDP witnessed striking changes between 1980 and 2008: the share of BRICS rose from one-eighth to more than one-fourth and the share of the Next-14 rose from about one-fifth to almost two-fifths, while the share of

Table 8.2 Shares of BRICS in PPP-GDP of developing countries and the world, 1980–2008 (percentages)

World GDP in 1990 (Geary–Khamis PPP) International Dollars				
	1980	*1990*	*2000*	*2008*
Brazil	3.2	2.7	2.7	2.5
India	3.2	4.0	5.2	6.7
China	5.2	7.8	11.8	17.5
South Africa	0.6	0.5	0.5	0.5
Total above BRICS	12.2	15.2	20.1	27.1
Next-14	20.7	23.5	31.4	38.3
Developing Countries	31.7	34.9	41.7	49.4
World	100.0	100.0	100.0	100.0
Developing World GDP in 1990 (Geary–Khamis PPP) International Dollars				
	1980	*1990*	*2000*	*2008*
Brazil	10.1	7.9	6.4	5.0
India	10.0	11.6	12.4	13.6
China	16.4	22.4	28.2	35.4
South Africa	2.0	1.6	1.1	0.9
Total above BRICS	38.5	43.5	48.1	54.9
Next-14	65.2	67.5	75.2	77.7
Developing World	100.0	100.0	100.0	100.0

Sources: Nayyar (2013) and Maddison Online Database.

developing countries rose from around one-third to almost one-half. These trends were mirrored in changes in the distribution of developing countries PPP-GDP between 1980 and 2008: the share of BRICS increased from less than two-fifths to more than one-half, while the share of the Next-14 increased from less than two-thirds to more than three-fourths.

It would seem that the economic importance of BRICS diminished rapidly during 1820–1950 because of the fall of China and India, despite the rise of Brazil, which increased its share in world GDP from 0.4 per cent to 3.2 per cent and the reasonably good performance of South Africa. The story was just the opposite during 1980–2008, as the economic importance of BRICS grew rapidly because of the rise of China and India, despite the poor performance of Brazil and South Africa.

It must be said that it is not quite appropriate or correct, even if it is fashionable, to add GDP in terms of PPP across countries, because these estimates are based on an artificial upward adjustment in the price of non-traded goods and services in developing countries, leading to an upward bias in PPP-GDP estimates for developing countries. Even so, there are three reasons why this is a worthwhile exercise. First, the Maddison statistics on GDP in 1990 international (Geary–Khamis PPP) dollars are better than the usual PPP estimates that facilitate intercountry comparisons over time. Second, the use of Maddison statistics allows for consistent comparisons with the past, which would not be possible otherwise because national accounts statistics compiled by the United Nations are available only from 1970. Third, the trends in the distribution of PPP-GDP between industrialized and developing countries and within the developing world are similar to trends in the distribution of GDP in current prices at market exchanges, except that in the former the share of developing countries is somewhat higher and the fluctuations are smoothed out, as compared with the latter.[14] All the same, the discussion that follows considers changes in the distribution of world output between country-groups from data on GDP in current prices and market exchange rates based on national accounts statistics. The story does not turn out to be significantly different.

Changing world

It is clear that the period since 1950 has witnessed a catching up on the part of developing countries with industrialized countries, in terms of their PPP shares in world output and income. This has been associated with a discernible shift in the balance of power in the world economy which gathered momentum after 1980. The Next-14 led this process of catch up and accounted for a large part of the aggregates in every dimension. The BRICS were critical as the most important subset of countries in the Next-14. These layers of concentration suggest an implicit hierarchy among subsets of economies: BRICS, the Next-14 and developing countries.[15] Hence, the growing significance of BRICS must be situated in its wider context.

Table 8.3 presents evidence on the shares of each of the BRICS, the Next-14, developing countries and industrialized countries in world GDP (in current prices at market exchange rates) and world population, for selected benchmark years during the period from 1980 to 2013. It also provides absolute figures for world totals as a point of reference.

Between 1980 and 2013, the share of BRICS in world GDP trebled from 6 per cent to 19 per cent, while their share in world population decreased a little from 41 per cent to 40 per cent. Over the same period, the share of the Next-14 in world GDP more than doubled from 12 per cent to 27 per cent, while their share in world population decreased a little from 52 per cent to 51 per cent. Between 1980 and 2013, the share of developing countries in world GDP rose from 22 per cent to 37 per cent, while their share in world population rose from 74 per cent to 81 per cent. In sharp contrast, the share of industrialized countries in world GDP fell from 68 per cent to 57 per cent, while their share in world population fell from 17 per cent to 13 per cent.[16] For BRICS and the Next-14, a slight decline in their share of world population was juxtaposed with a large proportionate jump in their share of world GDP, so that the asymmetry between their respective shares in population and income diminished far more than it did for developing countries as a group.

It is essential to note that there was a striking concentration in a small number of countries underlying this transformation. This emerges clearly from Table 8.4, which outlines changes in the shares of each of the BRICS, as also BRICS and the Next-14 as country-groups, in GDP and population of the developing world, for the same selected years. Between 1980 and 2013, the share of the Next-14 in GDP of the developing world rose from 57 per cent to 74 per cent, although their share in population of the developing world fell from 70 per cent to 63 per cent. Thus, for the Next-14, the asymmetry between their shares of GDP and population in the developing world was reversed. Between 1980 and 2013, the share of BRICS in GDP of developing countries rose from 29 per cent to 50 per cent, while their share in population of developing countries fell from 56 per cent to

Table 8.3 The shares of BRICS, the Next-14, developing countries and industrialized countries in world GDP and world population, 1980–2013 (percentages)

World GDP in current prices at market exchange rates					
	1980	*1990*	*2000*	*2010*	*2013*
Brazil	1.6	1.8	2.0	3.3	3.0
India	1.5	1.4	1.4	2.6	2.6
China	2.5	1.8	3.6	9.2	12.5
South Africa	0.7	0.5	0.4	0.6	0.5
Total above BRICS	6.3	5.5	7.4	15.8	18.6
Next-14	12.3	11.9	15.5	24.0	27.1
Developing Countries	21.7	17.5	21.6	32.8	36.9
Industrialized Countries	68.4	77.8	76.0	61.9	57.4
World	100.0	100.0	100.0	100.0	100.0
World Total (in US$ billion)	*12,043*	*22,604*	*32,858*	*64,401*	*74,601*
World population					
	1980	*1990*	*2000*	*2010*	*2013*
Brazil	2.7	2.8	2.8	2.8	2.8
India	15.7	16.3	17.0	17.4	17.5
China	22.1	21.9	20.9	19.7	19.3
South Africa	0.7	0.7	0.7	0.7	0.7
Total above BRICS	41.2	41.7	41.5	40.7	40.4
Next-14	51.6	52.3	52.1	51.3	50.9
Developing Countries	74.2	77.0	79.2	80.7	81.2
Industrialized Countries	17.2	15.3	14.2	13.4	13.1
World	100.0	100.0	100.0	100.0	100.0
World Total (in billion people)	*4.4*	*5.3*	*6.1*	*6.9*	*7.2*

Source: United Nations, UNCTAD Stat, based on UN National Accounts Statistics and Population Statistics.

Notes:
(a) The Next-14 are Argentina, Brazil, Chile, China, Egypt, India, Indonesia, South Korea, Malaysia, Mexico, South Africa, Taiwan, Thailand and Turkey.
(b) The figures for developing countries and industrialized countries do not add up to the world totals. The residual is attributable to Eastern Europe and the former USSR.

50 per cent. Thus, for BRICS, the asymmetry between their shares of GDP and population in the developing world, which was significant in 1980, vanished by 2013. There was perhaps even greater concentration within BRICS. It is no surprise that China and India, taken together, accounted for more than 90 per cent of the BRICS population throughout. But, during 1980–2013, the share of China alone in

Table 8.4 The shares of BRICS and the Next-14 in developing world GDP and developing world population, 1980–2013 (percentages)

Developing World GDP in Current Prices at Market Exchange Rates					
	1980	*1990*	*2000*	*2010*	*2013*
Brazil	7.3	10.2	9.1	10.1	8.2
India	7.1	8.3	6.6	8.1	7.0
China	11.7	10.2	16.8	28.1	33.9
South Africa	3.1	2.8	1.9	1.7	1.3
Total above BRICS	29.2	31.5	34.3	48.1	50.4
Next-14	57.0	68.0	71.7	73.2	73.6
Developing World	100.0	100.0	100.0	100.0	100.0
Developing World Total (in US$ billion)	*2,610*	*3,948*	*7,104*	*21,139*	*27,497*
Developing World Population					
	1980	*1990*	*2000*	*2010*	*2013*
Brazil	3.7	3.7	3.6	3.5	3.4
India	21.2	21.2	21.5	21.6	21.5
China	29.8	28.5	26.4	24.4	23.8
South Africa	0.9	0.9	0.9	0.9	0.9
Total above BRICS	55.5	54.2	52.4	50.4	49.7
Next-14	69.5	67.9	65.8	63.5	62.8
Developing World	100.0	100.0	100.0	100.0	100.0
Developing World Total (in US$ billion)	*3.3*	*4.1*	*4.9*	*5.6*	*5.8*

Source: United Nations, UNCTAD Stat, based on UN National Accounts Statistics and Population Statistics.

Notes: The Next-14 are Argentina, Brazil, Chile, China, Egypt, India, Indonesia, South Korea, Malaysia, Mexico, South Africa, Taiwan, Thailand and Turkey.

the GDP of BRICS rose from 40 per cent to 67 per cent, although its share in the population of BRICS fell from 54 per cent to 48 per cent, reversing the asymmetry between its shares.

The changes in the significance of any subset of countries in the world over time depend upon their economic performance as compared with the rest of the world. It is obvious that differences in GDP growth rates, in real terms, underlie the changing shares of country-groups in the world economy. It is simple arithmetic that differences in growth rates of GDP and population determine differences in growth rates of GDP per capita, which in turn shape convergence or divergence in per capita incomes between countries.

The unfolding reality about the growing economic significance of these countries and country-groups is borne out by evidence on growth rates.[17] During 1981–2013, real GDP growth was 6.3 per cent per annum in BRICS, 5.3 per cent per annum in the Next-14 and 4.8 per cent per annum in developing countries, as compared to 2.4 per cent per annum in industrialized countries and 2.9 per cent per annum in the world. Over the same period, real GDP per capita growth was 4.9 per cent per annum in BRICS, 4 per cent per annum in the Next-14 and 3.1 per cent per annum in developing countries, as compared with 1.3 per cent per annum in industrialized countries and 1.5 per cent per annum in the world.

The BRICS growth story is characterized by a dichotomy. During 1981–2013, real GDP growth per annum was 9.5 per cent in China, 6.1 per cent in India, 2.7 per cent in Brazil and 2.4 per cent in South Africa. Over the same period, real GDP per capita growth per annum was 8.6 per cent in China, 4.3 per cent in India, 1.2 per cent in Brazil and 0.6 per cent in South Africa.[18]

The significance of BRICS is also reflected in their growing engagement with the world economy through trade, investment and migration. Between 1980 and 2013, the share of BRICS rose from 3 per cent to 15 per cent, of world merchandize trade (both exports and imports) increased from 5 per cent to 8 per cent of inward stocks, but decreased from 8 per cent to 4 per cent of outward stocks, of foreign direct investment in the world, and jumped from 8 per cent to 25 per cent of total remittances in the world economy. Similarly, BRICS were an increasingly important part of the catch up in industrialization. Their share in world manufacturing value added jumped from 6 per cent in 1990 to 27 per cent in 2012, while their share in world manufactured exports rose from 6 per cent in 2000 to 20 per cent in 2013. But the distribution of these shares was most unequal between countries within BRICS. Between 1980 and 2013, the share of China rose from around one-fourth to three-fourths of BRICS exports and imports, from less than one-twentieth to about one-half of both inward and outward stocks of BRICS foreign direct investment, and from about one-sixth to more than two-fifths of remittances to BRICS. China's share in BRICS manufacturing value added doubled from two-fifths in 1990 to four-fifths in 2012, while its share in BRICS manufactured exports increased from three-fourths in 2000 to almost nine-tenths in 2013.[19] The concentration was the greatest in merchandize trade, industrial production and manufactured exports.

The evidence presented above, and in Table 8.4, suggests some obvious and some not so obvious propositions. China was the most important part of the BRICS story. Yet, it was not the whole story. There was more to BRICS than China. BRICS were the most important part of the Next-14 tale. But there was far more to the Next-14 than BRICS. The Next-14 were the most important part of the growing significance of developing countries. Yet, there was more to the developing world than the Next-14. In sum, the catch-up process was characterized by concentration at each level from the apex to the base: China in BRICS, BRICS in the Next-14 and the Next-14 in developing countries. But there was also a significant dispersion across levels in this hierarchy of country-groups.

Evolution of BRICS

The emergence of BRICS as an economic and political formation must be situated in its wider context. The era of change in the world economy gathered momentum from 1980. The catch up by developing countries, concentrated in the Next-14, even if the focus is often on BRICS, was continuous. It reached a critical threshold in early 2000s. This was necessary, but quite sufficient. It was the conjuncture that made an enormous difference. The financial crisis that surfaced in the United States in late 2008, and the Great Recession that followed in its aftermath, was the deepest crisis in capitalism since the Great Depression 75 years earlier.[20] This eroded the triumph of capitalism that followed the collapse of communism in 1991 and reinforced the shift in the balance of power somewhat more towards the developing world. The G8 gave way to the G20. And it is no coincidence that BRICS as a formation surfaced in 2009.

The composition of BRICS in terms of countries was shaped by size and geography. Their economic size (potential if not actual income, together with population) and their physical size (in terms of geographical space) explain the inclusion of Brazil, China and India. But geography and location made a difference. This is the reason why it was South Africa in Africa rather than Indonesia in Asia that was included. The same consideration, reinforced by geopolitics, meant that it was Russia (a high-income, former superpower in Europe) that was a constituent of BRICS rather than Mexico, which was in the Outreach-5 and could also have been a plausible choice.

It should come as no surprise that there is enormous diversity between and relatively little coherence (at least so far) among the nations that make up BRICS. Even so, it has surfaced as a strategic alliance of countries, in part as a reflection of the changing balance of economic power in the world, and in part as a countervailing force in a unipolar world that was born after communism collapsed. In this world, which was dominated by the United States, the European Union was, in effect, an ally of the sole superpower rather than a countervailing force which was its original *raison d'etre*. The presence of Russia, perhaps, reflects a strategic effort to strike a balance in a group that has concerns about the overwhelming rise and growing power of China. It is clear that China is a very important factor underlying the emergence of BRICS. But it also needs to be said that, as a political formation, BRICS is about far more than China.

The problem of coherence among member countries of this formation does loom large, even if Russia is excluded, and the focus is on BRICS, as defined in this article. There are concerns about China among Brazil, India and South Africa, all of whom run massive trade deficits with China. These concerns are accentuated by a pattern of trade in which they export primary commodities to and import manufactured goods from China. Such a near-colonial pattern of trade simply cannot be conducive to industrialization let alone partnerships in development. Of course, there is much that they can learn from each other and there is a potential for economic cooperation among the BRICS. Similarly, there is a potential for cooperation with other developing countries that could yield significant mutual benefits. But this promise might not be realized if the BRICS aspire to join the premier league and occupy a seat at the high table, instead of solidarity with other countries in the developing world.

Implications for development

The impact of rapid economic growth in BRICS on other developing countries could be positive if complementary or negative if competitive and, on balance, positive or negative.[21] It could have a positive impact on other developing countries if it improves terms of trade, provides appropriate technologies and creates new sources of finance for development, whether investment or aid.

It is clear that, from the turn of the century, the positive impact on developing countries has been transmitted through an improvement in their terms of trade.[22] This might have come to an end with the collapse in prices of primary commodities that surfaced in mid-2014.

Rapid economic growth in China and India did boost the demand for primary commodities exported by developing countries, and probably was an important factor underlying the boom that began in the early 2000s. The reasons are simple enough. Both China and India have large populations. Moreover, in both countries, levels of consumption per capita in most primary commodities are low, while income elasticities of demand for most primary commodities are high. This burgeoning demand almost certainly raised prices of primary commodities in world markets and thereby improved the terms of trade for developing countries. It did benefit Brazil and South Africa as exporters of primary commodities, while the associated revival of growth in Brazil and South Africa reinforced this process.

Apart from the terms of trade effect in primary commodities which might have come to an end, perhaps temporarily, China already is, while India and Brazil are likely to become sources of manufactured goods in the world market. Such manufactures, particularly wage goods but also capital goods, from China, India and Brazil are likely to be cheaper than competing goods from industrialized countries. At the same time, Brazil and South Africa could provide cheaper natural resource-based manufactures. This would also improve the terms of trade for developing countries.

The positive impact of BRICS on developing countries through the other potential channels of transmission is not as clear. We do not yet have either the evidence or the experience. In principle, it is possible that the BRICS would develop technologies that are more appropriate for the factor endowments and the economic needs of developing countries. For example, the technology that transformed Savannah lands in Brazil for agricultural use would be most appropriate in Africa. Similarly, there are technologies developed in India (pharmaceuticals) and in China (mining and railways) that would be appropriate for other developing countries. But it is too early to come to a judgment on this matter. Similarly, the BRICS are potential sources of finance for development. Their foreign aid programmes, particularly in Africa, constitute a modest beginning, although the implications and consequences of aid from China and India for African economic development are not necessarily positive.[23] The experience in terms of foreign direct investment is limited so far. Yet, the evidence available suggests that it is not significantly different from the experience with large international firms from industrialized countries.

The emergence of BRICS in the world economy could also have a negative impact on developing countries, if these economies provide developing countries with competition in markets for exports or as destinations for investment.

At this juncture, China is clearly the largest supplier of labour-intensive manufactured goods in the world market. Even if not as large as China, India is also a significant supplier of labour-intensive manufactured goods in the world market. Brazil and South Africa are important suppliers of natural resource-based manufactures. China, India and Brazil are emerging suppliers of capital goods. There can be little doubt that manufactured exports from BRICS span almost the entire range of manufactured exports, in which other developing countries could have a potential comparative advantage. Hence, it is plausible to argue though impossible to prove that, on balance, BRICS possibly have a negative impact on manufactured exports from other developing countries, which have to compete with these four economies for export markets in industrialized countries.[24] This can change if and when China and India vacate their space in the international trade matrix, in much the same way as latecomers to industrialization in Asia, such as Japan, Korea, Hong Kong, Taiwan and Singapore, vacated their space in the market for simple labour-intensive manufactures for countries that followed in their footsteps. It is not likely, at least in the medium term, because both China and India have large reservoirs of surplus labour at low wages not only in the rural hinterlands, but also in the urban informal sectors. Brazil and South Africa may not have such large reservoirs of surplus labour, but given their abundance in primary commodities and natural resources, it is not likely that they would vacate their space in the market for processed products or resource-based manufactures for other developing countries that have similar endowments from nature.

BRICS absorb a significant proportion of inward foreign direct investment in developing countries, both in terms of stocks and flows. Given that China, India and Brazil are now among the most attractive destinations for transnational firms seeking to locate production in the developing world, it is once again plausible to suggest though impossible to prove that foreign direct investment in China, India and Brazil might be at the expense of developing countries. South Africa may not have the same attraction as a destination, but it may draw foreign direct investment that could have gone to developing countries in Africa. At the same time, the share of BRICS in outward foreign direct investment in the world economy, as also from developing countries, is modest in both stocks and flows, so that firms from these four countries do not compensate with foreign direct investment in other developing countries.

The less discernible but more significant negative impact of BRICS, particularly China, on developing countries are the implicit barriers to change in the traditional division of labour and specialization in production. For one, China already does and India might pre-empt opportunities for other developing countries to industrialize through exports of labour-intensive manufactures, which is attributable to their surplus labour and low wages that might continue for some time to come. For another, Brazil and South Africa might pre-empt opportunities for other developing countries to industrialize through agro-based or resource-intensive manufactures, which is attributable to their abundance in primary commodities and natural resources. But this is no more than a plausible hypothesis about possible future developments which cannot be tested.

The problem has, however, surfaced clearly in one dimension. China's present division of labour with the developing world, reflected in the composition of trade flows, is not different from the old North-South pattern of trade, in so far as Chinese imports from developing world largely primary commodities while Chinese exports to the developing world are largely manufactured goods.[25] China's trade with countries in Southeast Asia is the exception to this rule. But Chinese trade with and investment in Africa confirms even more closely to this caricature neocolonial pattern. Such traditional patterns of trade, it should be recognized, can neither transform the structure of production in developing countries nor make for a new international division of labour. Indeed, such trade can only perpetuate the dependence of developing countries on exports of primary commodities without creating possibilities of increasing value added before export or entering into manufacturing activities characterized by economies of scale. Such path-dependent specialization can only curb the possibilities of structural transformation in developing countries. Trade with China can sustain growth and support industrialization in developing countries, only if there is a successful transition from a complementary to a competitive pattern of trade, so that intersectoral trade is gradually replaced by intra-sectoral or intra-industry trade and specialization.

Global governance

It is essential to recognize that the importance of BRICS in the world would be shaped not only in the sphere of economics, but also in the realm of politics. Their emerging significance in the world economy is attributable in part to their share in world population and in world income, and in part to their engagement with the world through international trade, international investment and international migration. Even so, in the economic sphere, their potential importance in future far exceeds their actual importance at present. In the realm of politics, however, their importance is more discernible at the present juncture, which is attributable in part to their size and in part to their rise.

It is plausible to argue – though impossible to prove – that this represents the beginnings of a profound change in the balance of economic and political power in the world.[26] History does not repeat itself. But it would be wise to learn from history. The early 20th century was a turning point. It was the beginning of the end of Britain's dominance in the world. And it was the beginning of the rise of the United States to dominance in the world. The catch up and the transformation spanned half a century. The early 21st century, perhaps, represents a similar turning point. It could be the beginning of the end of the dominant status of the United States in the world. The emergence of countries outside North America and Western Europe, particularly the powerhouse economies in Asia, now visible in the rise of China and discernible in the unrealized potential India, represents a striking transformation. In addition, there are such countries in other continents of the developing world.[27]

The process of catching up underlying this transformation has been led by a group of countries that I have described as the Next-14. BRICS are part of this larger group. Indeed, it is plausible to suggest – even if impossible to establish with precise criteria – that there are other developing countries which could follow in the footsteps of the Next-14. This group might be made up of Iran, Philippines and Vietnam in Asia; Nigeria and Tunisia in Africa; and Colombia and Costa Rica in Latin America. Even among LDCs, there are three – Bangladesh, Ethiopia and Tanzania – that have some potential.[28] Of course, in the decades to come, the continued rise of the Next-14 or the emergence of others is not quite predictable and by no means certain. This catch up and transformation could also span half a century or longer. Yet, the beginnings of a shift in the balance of power from the industrialized world to the developing world are discernible.

BRICS as a formation began life on the stepping stones of bilateralism and building blocks of plurilateralism to influence the international politics of nation states. Brazil, India, China and South Africa have all engaged in a bilateralism that is both intra-regional and inter-regional. There are intra-regional initiatives led by China and India in Asia, by Brazil in Latin America and by South Africa in Africa. There are also some inter-regional initiatives on the part of these countries, such as China taking a lead in forging APEC and India seeking a partnership with ASEAN. Similarly, BRICS have also been engaged in some plurilateralism. There are three important examples. First, in 2005, Brazil, India, China and South Africa, together with Mexico, constituted the Outreach-5, who were invited to the G8 Summit even before the global economic crisis. There was a hint of discontent about their status as observers, peripheral to deliberations and decisions, so that the Outreach-5 always sought a place at the high table with the G8. This exclusion came to an end with the financial crisis, when the G20, which replaced the G8 in its role, included all of them and most of the Next-14. Second, in 2006, India, Brazil and South Africa constituted a plurilateral group, IBSA, attempting to develop a strategic alliance that would foster partnership among them, promote cooperation with developing countries and articulate a collective voice in international politics. Third, in 2009, Brazil, India, China and South Africa came together as BASIC at the Summit on Climate Change in Copenhagen, which was an *ad hoc* coalition shaped by the event.

From the perspective of the developing world, the BRICS, together, may be able to exercise significant influence through multilateralism, whether institutions or rules, in the global context.[29] The United Nations, the World Bank, the IMF and the WTO are among the most important multilateral institutions.

In the United Nations, China alone is a permanent member of the Security Council with a right to veto. And it is also a member of the P-5. But India and Brazil are engaged in knocking at the door, seeking permanent membership of the Security Council, with or without a right to veto. South Africa is also a potential candidate, but there are competing claims from Africa. There can be little doubt that if and when there is an increase in the number of permanent members of the Security Council in the United Nations, these three countries would have the strongest claim to permanent membership among aspirants from the developing world.

In the Bretton Woods institutions, the World Bank and the IMF, China, India, Brazil and South Africa are permanent members of the Executive Boards. The industrialized countries may be the principal shareholders but the developing countries are the principal stakeholders. Given the democratic deficit in these institutions, which is embedded in unequal voting rights, BRICS together could influence decisions or even reshape rules. So far, however, there is a limited, if any, coordination among BRICS for this purpose. They have neither articulated collective voice nor exercised collective influence. There are two striking examples. They failed to act in cohesion when the President of the World Bank was appointed in 2012, although there were two strong candidates from the developing world. Soon thereafter, as the BRICS infused large doses of finance into the IMF, they simply did not negotiate any changes in its rules that reduced policy space for borrowing developing countries, let alone attempt to reduce the democratic deficit.

The situation in the WTO is different. India and Brazil have been long-standing advocates of developing countries in the WTO. China has a low profile, possibly because of its more recent accession. South Africa is now a part of the strategic alliance among developing countries, which it was not earlier. India and Brazil, along with United States and the European Union, did become members of the *Quad*, which is the principal institutional mechanism for resolving differences and finding solutions. Ironically enough, the appointment of a Director General in the WTO from Brazil seems to have ruptured the long-standing solidarity of India and Brazil.

In sum, it would seem that the BRICS have a considerable potential for articulating a collective voice in the world of multilateralism. Coordination and cooperation among them carries a significant potential for exercising influence on multilateral institutions, which could reshape rules and create policy space for countries that are latecomers to development. Such coordination and cooperation, which is in the realm of the possible, has not yet surfaced. There could be two reasons for the little coordination and cooperation so far.[30] For one, in the early stages of change, setting aside conflicts of interest or recognizing common causes is easier said than done. For another, their relationship with each other may be characterized more by rivalry, economic or political and less by unity.

It is obviously difficult to predict how reality might unfold in times to come. Even so, it is important to recognize that once these countries become major players, there is a danger that they might opt for the pursuit of national interest rather than the spirit of solidarity among developing countries or the logic of collective action. Therefore, the spirit of solidarity among developing countries must be preserved and nurtured. In this quest, the approach of BRICS must be cooperation among themselves and solidarity with others through consultation and inclusion. In such a mode, BRICS can be far more influential in a world where the changing balance of economic and political power is beginning to chip away at the hegemony of the rich industrialized countries.

At the conclusion of the BRICS Summit in Brazil in July 2014, the Fortaleza Declaration announced the creation of a New Development Bank. Beginnings are always difficult. Hence, this is an important first step in the right direction. It is, of course, too early for any meaningful evaluation of this new initiative. Even so, some things can be said.

It is cause for cheer because this is the first tangible act of real cooperation and collective action on the part of BRICS, despite some potential conflicts and genuine concerns. It could be cause for celebration, if it evolves into an international institution that provides poor countries with finances for development as partners, on terms that are better than and different from the terms of the World Bank and the IMF. It could, then, be a genuine alternative and not simply a substitute or a complement. This competition might even lead to change for the better in the Bretton Woods twins.

Yet, wisdom lies in careful reflection and realistic assessment of unfolding outcomes. The baby is born. But it is an infant. It remains to be seen how it grows from infancy through childhood to adulthood. The formative years will be critical. In the early stages, it is essential for BRICS to sustain their solidarity of purpose to preserve equality among the founding countries – the lenders – and nurture partnership with the countries to whom it provides resources – the borrowers – so that its structures and methods of governance remain democratic. There is a clear and present danger that it might evolve in much the same way as the World Bank with a democratic deficit and as a window of financial assistance based on patronage and conditions.

In my view, it would be wise to moderate the enthusiasm of the advocates and dampen the scepticism of the critics about the BRICS Development Bank that is in the process of being established. It is the only way forward that could avert the dangers and help create an international institution for financing development in a spirit of partnership among equals rather than patronage among unequal partners. The obvious conclusion that can be drawn is that its success or failure as an institution would perhaps be the most important litmus test for BRICS, in terms of their willingness and ability to contribute to development elsewhere and improve global governance.

Acknowledgement

The author would like to thank Atul Sanganeria for research assistance.

Notes

1 United Nations, National Accounts Statistics and Population Statistics.
2 See O'Neill et al. (2004).
3 For a discussion on the limitations of this exercise, see Rowthorn (2008) and Nayyar (2008).
4 In 2013, GDP per capita in US dollars at current prices and market exchange rates was $ 15,011 in Russia, as compared with $ 11,232 in Brazil, $ 1,537 in India, $ 6,726 in China and $ 6,679 in South Africa (United Nations, UNCTAD Stat, based on UN National Accounts Statistics).

5 The discussion that follows in this section and the supporting evidence that is cited both draw upon recent work of the author (Nayyar, 2013).

6 Developing countries are made up of Africa, Asia (excluding Japan) and Latin America (including the Caribbean). Industrialized countries are made of North America, Western Europe, Japan, Australia and New Zealand. Eastern Europe and the former USSR are a separate country-group in this classification.

7 See Maddison (2003 and 2007). See also, Nayyar (2013) and Maddison Online Database (http://www.ggdc.net.MADDISON/oriindex.htm).

8 Calculated from United Nations, *National Accounts Statistics* and *Population Statistics*.

9 For a detailed discussion and evidence on growth rates of GDP and GDP per capita in the two country-groups over time, see Nayyar (2013).

10 Cf. Nayyar (2013).

11 The evidence cited in this paragraph draws upon Nayyar (2013).

12 The idea and conception of the Next-14 comes from an earlier work of the author (Nayyar, 2013).

13 During the period from 1000 to 1700, China and India, taken together, accounted for 50 per cent of world income and 50 per cent of world population (Maddison, 2003 and Nayyar, 2013). These proportions were roughly the same in 1820 (Table 8.1).

14 For a detailed discussion on the issues outlined briefly in this paragraph, see Nayyar (2013).

15 If BRICS and the Next-14 are at the top in the catch-up process for the developing world, the LDCs, which are falling behind and almost excluded from the process, are at the bottom. It would mean too much of a digression to enter into a discussion on this here. Suffice it to say that catch up has been associated with growing divergences within the developing world. For an analysis and discussion of the issue, see Nayyar (2013). For evidence on the economic performance of LDCs, see UNCTAD (2011).

16 It is worth noting that, between 1990 and 2013, the share of developing countries in world GDP rose, from 17.5 per cent to 36.9 per cent, by almost 20 percentage points entirely at the expense of industrialized countries, as their share in world GDP fell from 77.5 per cent to 57.4 per cent. This is attributable largely to the much higher share of developing countries in 1980 on account of the sharp increase in oil prices that bumped up the GDP of oil-exporting developing countries.

17 The evidence on growth rates in GDP and GDP per capita, cited in this paragraph, draws upon the recent work of the author (Nayyar, 2017). For a more detailed analysis of outcomes and the underlying factors, see Nayyar (2013).

18 The figures cited in this paragraph are from Nayyar (2017). For a discussion, see also Nayyar (2013).

19 The evidence cited in this paragraph, on the significance of BRICS in the world economy and the importance of China in BRICS, draws upon Nayyar (2017).

20 For an analysis of the impact of the financial crisis and the Great Recession on the developing world, in comparison with industrialized countries, see Nayyar (2011).

21 These possibilities are analysed in Nayyar (2010). The discussion that follows in this section draws upon this earlier work of the author.
22 This proposition is emphasized by Kaplinsky (2006), Singh (2007), Rowthorn (2008) and Nayyar (2008).
23 See Toye (2008), Cheru and Obi (2010) and Nayyar (2012).
24 Kaplinsky and Morris (2008) show that China's emergence as a large exporter of manufactured goods in the world economy poses severe problems for export-oriented growth in Sub-Saharan Africa, particularly in textiles and clothing.
25 See Inter-American Development Bank (2005), United Nations (2006), Jenkins, Peters and Moreira (2008) and Nayyar (2012).
26 This argument is developed, at some length, elsewhere by the author (Nayyar, 2013).
27 For a detailed discussion, with evidence and analysis, see Nayyar (2013). This process was discernible even earlier, at the turn of the century, and was described as 'The Rise of The Rest' (Amsden, 2001).
28 This list of countries is at best suggestive and by no means definitive. It might change as circumstances change or reality unfolds. Amsden (2001) and Nayyar (2013) also speculated about countries that might constitute the next generation – 'The Rest' or the 'Following-10', respectively – with some differences between them. The listing above is similar but not the same.
29 This hypothesis and its possibilities are discussed at length elsewhere by the author. See Nayyar (2002) and Nayyar (2010). For an overview on how the rising powers of the global South might be challenging the existing framework and institutions of global governance, see Gray and Murphy (2013).
30 Thakur (2014) explores the potential of BRICS to represent the global South and argues that it remains unclear whether BRICS can morph from a countervailing economic grouping to a powerful political alternative.

References

Amsden, Alice H. (2001). *The Rise of the Rest: Challenges to the West from Late-Industrializing Economies*, New York: Oxford University Press.

Cheru, Fantu and Cyril Obi (eds.) (2010). *The Rise of China and India in Africa*, London: Zed Books.

Gray, Kevin and Craig N. Murphy (2013). 'Rising Powers and the Future of Global Governance', *Third World Quarterly*, 34 (2): 183–193.

Inter-Amercian Development Bank (2005). *The Emergence of China: Opportunities and Challenges for Latin America and the Caribbean*, Washington, DC: IADB.

Jenkins, Rhys, E. D. Peters and M. M. Moreira (2008). 'The Impact of China on Latin America and the Caribbean', *World Development*, 36: 235–253.

Kaplinsky, Raphael (ed.) (2006). 'Asian Drivers: Opportunities and Threats', *IDS Bulletin*, 37 (1): 1–11.

Kaplinsky, Raphael and M. Morris (2008). 'Do the Asian Drivers Undermine Export-Oriented Industrialization in Sub-Saharan Africa?', *World Development*, 36: 254–273.

Maddison, Angus (2003). *The World Economy: Historical Statistics*, Paris: OECD.

Maddison, Angus (2007). *Contours of the World Economy: 1–2030 AD: Essays in Macroeconomic History*, Oxford: Oxford University Press.

Nayyar, Deepak (2002). 'The Existing System and the Missing Institutions', in Deepak Nayyar (ed.), *Governing Globalization: Issues and Institutions*, Oxford: Oxford University Press.

Nayyar, Deepak (2008). 'The Rise of China and India: Implications for Developing Countries', in Philip Arestis and John Eatwell (eds.), *Issues in Economic Development and Globalization*, London: Palgrave Macmillan.

Nayyar, Deepak (2010). 'China, India, Brazil and South Africa in the World Economy: Engines of Growth?', in Amelia Santos-Paulino and Guanghua Wan (eds.), *Southern Engines of Global Growth*, Oxford: Oxford University Press.

Nayyar, Deepak (2011). 'The Financial Crisis, the Great Recession and the Developing World', *Global Policy*, 2: 20–32.

Nayyar, Deepak (2012). 'The Emerging Asian Giants and Economic Development in Africa', in Akbar Noman, Kwesi Botchwey, Howard Stein and Joseph Stiglitz (eds.), *Good Growth and Governance in Africa*, Oxford: Oxford University Press.

Nayyar, Deepak (2013). *Catch Up: Developing Countries in the World Economy*, Oxford: Oxford University Press.

Nayyar, Deepak (2017). 'BRICS, Emerging Markets and the World Economy', in P. Anand, F. Comim, S. Fennell and R.Weiss (eds.), *Oxford Handbook on BRICS*, Oxford: Oxford University Press.

O'Neill, J., S. Lawson, D. Wilson, R. Purushothamn, M. Buchanan and L. Griffiths (2004). *Growth and Development: The Path to 2050*, London: Goldman Sachs.

Rowthorn, Robert (2008). 'The Renaissance of China and India: Implications for the Advanced Economies', in Philip Arestis and John Eatwell (eds.), *Issues in Economic Development and Globalization*, London: Palgrave Macmillan.

Singh, Ajit (2007). 'Globalization, Industrial Revolutions in India and China and Labour Markets in Advanced Countries: Implications for National and International Economic Policy', *ILO Working Paper 81*, Geneva: ILO.

Thakur, Ramesh (2014). 'How Representative Are BRICS?', *Third World Quarterly*, 35 (10): 1791–1808.

Toye, John (2008). 'China's Impact on Sub-Saharan African Development: Trade, Aid and Politics', in Philip Arestis and John Eatwell (eds.), *Issues in Economic Development and Globalization*, London: Palgrave Macmillan.

UNCTAD (2011). *The Least Developed Countries 2011 Report*, Geneva: United Nations.

United Nations (2006). *Diverging Growth and Development, World Economic and Social Survey 2006*, New York: United Nations.

Part III

DEVELOPMENT, POLITY AND SOCIETY

9

GLOBALIZATION AND DEMOCRACY

Introduction

The gathering momentum of globalization, during the last quarter of the 20th century and the first decade of the 21st century, has coincided with the spread of political democracy across the world. Economies have become global. But politics remains national.

For economists, globalization refers to the expansion of economic transactions and the organization of economic activities across political boundaries of nation states. More precisely, it can be defined as a process associated with increasing economic openness, growing economic interdependence and deepening economic integration in the world economy. But globalization is a multidimensional phenomenon (Nayyar, 2003a). Its implications and consequences are not confined to the economy alone, but extend to polity and society. There can be little doubt that the whole is different from, if not greater than, the sum total of the parts.

This epoch of globalization has also witnessed the spread of political democracy across countries in the developing world and in the transition economies. Such democratic politics is mostly about electoral democracy in some form, even if people do not always have the political rights or political freedoms that democracies should ensure for their citizens. Nevertheless, it represents a vast change from authoritarian regimes that characterized the developing world until three decades ago. The geographical spread of democracy is striking across Asia, Latin America and Africa. Of course, elections are not always free and fair. And it is not as if authoritarian regimes have vanished. There are many that exist. Some are entrenched, while some are under siege. In a large number of these countries, however, dictatorial regimes are subject to increasing question, as aspirations for democracy are rising everywhere.

In this chapter, I explore the relationship between globalization and democracy. It begins with a simple analytical construct derived from economics that suggests trade-offs between globalization, the nation state and democratic politics. In reality, of course, the relationship is neither linear nor characterized by structural rigidities. It then analyses the relationship between market economy and political democracy in a national context to show that it is interactive, so that such an approach is useful for an understanding of the international context. It leads into a discussion on how globalization might constrain degrees of freedom for nation states and space for democratic politics. But this provides an incomplete picture because the causation runs in both directions. The essential next step is to consider whether political democracy within countries might exercise some checks and balances on markets and globalization, which also provides a closure. In sum, my argument is that the relationship between globalization and democracy is dialectical and does not conform to ideological caricatures.

Analytical construct

It is possible to consider the relationship between the process of globalization in the world economy with political democracy in nation states in terms of a simple analytical construct, which is the standard trilemma from open economy macroeconomics. This is, at best, a starting point because it does not quite recognize the complexity, let alone the dialectics of the relationship.

The original trilemma argues that it is not possible for countries to maintain, simultaneously, independent monetary policies, fixed exchange rates and open capital accounts. This open-economy trilemma is sometimes described as the 'impossible trinity', because it is possible to maintain only two of the three. If an economy chooses capital mobility and fixed exchange rates, it must give up autonomy in monetary policy. If an economy wants fixed exchange rates and autonomy in monetary policy, it must do without capital mobility. If an economy wishes to have autonomy in monetary policy with capital mobility, it cannot have fixed exchange rates.

These possible alternatives are, in fact, observable in the world economy at different points in time. From the late 19th century until the Great Depression, the Gold Standard combined fixed exchange rates with capital mobility, but countries sacrificed monetary policy autonomy. From the mid-1940s until the early 1970s, the gold exchange standard created at Bretton Woods combined fixed exchange rates with monetary policy autonomy but (more or less) ruled out capital mobility. In the period since the mid-1970s until now, the present era of globalization, most countries sought to combine monetary policy autonomy with capital mobility, abandoning fixed exchange rates for a regime of floating exchange rates.

The derived construct, first developed by Dani Rodrik (2000), is described as the political trilemma of the world economy. The three nodes of this derivative are globalization, the nation state and democratic politics. In this characterization, globalization describes a substantial integration of national economies into the world economy, the nation state refers to sovereign jurisdiction in terms of laws and institutions, while democratic politics is about electoral democracy, political freedoms and political mobilization. As in the original trilemma, it is possible to sustain only two of the three. If a country wants to stay with the nation state and democratic politics, it cannot sustain deep international economic integration. If a country wants to combine globalization with the nation state, it needs to sacrifice democratic politics. If a country wishes to have democratic politics in a world of globalization, it would have to do without the nation state. This argument is developed further, at much greater length, in Rodrik (2011), where he suggests that countries cannot simultaneously pursue national sovereignty, political democracy and economic globalization, so that nations can have any two in any combination but not all three.

The underlying reasons are not obvious. The essence of the Rodrik hypothesis is that deeply integrated national economies would conflict with the regulatory and jurisdictional discontinuities created by heterogeneous national laws and institutions, while harmonized laws and institutions that eliminate the significance of national borders conflict with the foundations of democratic politics where governments are accountable to their people. The basic idea is illustrated with a caricature description of reality in the past. The argument runs as follows. From the late 1940s to the mid-1970s, the golden age of capitalism, the multilateral economic system made it possible for countries to stay with the nation state and democratic politics by limiting the degree of international economic integration. From the late 1970s until the late 2000s, the age of globalization, which sought to harmonize policies, institutions and laws across countries, made it possible for countries to combine globalization with the nation state but at the expense of democratic politics. In this construct, it is conceivable to contemplate a future, however unlikely, where it may be possible for countries to combine democratic politics with globalization, by dispensing with the nation state and opting for a world government or global federalism.

The second link in the chain of this storyline is also stressed by Thomas Friedman, from a somewhat different ideological perspective. Of course, his belief in the magic of markets and globalization is not without its limitations and flaws (Chang, 2007), but his characterization of the consequent constraints on governments describes aspects of reality. Friedman uses 'Golden Straitjacket' as a phrase to describe how governments everywhere, in this age of globalization, compete with each other to harmonize policies and earn the confidence of international firms and international markets. The following quotation is so explicit that the phrase needs no further explanation: 'As your country puts on the Golden Straitjacket, two things tend to happen: your economy grows and your politics shrinks . . . (it) narrows the political and economic policy choices of those in power . . . (so that) it is increasingly difficult to find any real differences between ruling and opposition parties . . . political choices get reduced to slight nuances . . . to Pepsi and Coke . . . but never to any major deviation from the core golden rules' (Friedman, 1999, p.87). Yet, the reality is that there has been an expansion of rather than a contraction in political democracy during the era that Friedman describes and idolizes.

In my view, this caricature characterization does not capture the complexity of reality. The golden age of capitalism witnessed a rapid liberalization of international trade and international investment to provide the foundations of globalization, even if restrictions on capital mobility meant that it did not extend to international finance. What is more, the age of globalization witnessed a spread rather than a sacrifice of democratic politics across countries, even if the rise of political democracy was uneven and incomplete. And this move towards greater democracy in a world of globalization was not attributable to any governance of the world economy in terms of institutions and rules, let alone a world government. But that is not all. The major industrialized countries – not only the United States, but also countries such as Britain, France, Germany and Japan – are able to combine the nation state and democratic politics with globalization (but for some deference to international financial markets). Surely, this diminishes the explanatory power if not validity of the hypothesis.

Apart from such reality checks, there are two basic problems with the trilemma as an analytical concept. For one, it depicts a caricature world with strong structural rigidities. For another, it creates a binary world with either-or choices. Hence, if there are three possibilities, it is possible to attain only two of the three at a time. It is, at best, an analytical abstraction that highlights conflicts or trade-offs between three stipulated objectives. And it is not quite appropriate even in the limited context of open economy macroeconomics (Taylor, 2004), where it is simply an analytical construct that highlights conflicts between policy objectives, or instruments, to focus on dilemmas that arise rather than a depiction of reality.

There is, however, an even more serious problem of transitivity in moving from economics in the original trilemma to politics in the derived trilemma. Each of the three nodes, international economic integration, the nation state or democratic politics, may represent a range rather than a single unique point, which means that there may be choices within each. Moreover, trade-offs may be a continuum rather than binary choices, which means that it may be possible to have more of two and less of the third. In other words, there could be more choices within and between the three nodes, whereas the trilemma only allows choosing two from three. The fundamental problem with such an analytical construct is that it suggests a false precision, which is deceptive if not misleading. Of course, in reality, there are conflicts between objectives or desired states. And, wherever there are conflicts, there are bound to be trade-offs. Hence, there are choices to be made. But these should not be reduced to 'pick two, any two'.

In this context, there is something to learn from a historical perspective. Globalization in the late 20th century and early 21st century, as much as the earlier era of globalization during the late 19th century and early 20th century, represents neither the end of history nor the end of geography (Nayyar, 2006). It is not the end of history, now as it was not then, because markets and globalization may not be the dominant mode for the world economy in perpetuity. It may have been a world war then and it is the economic crisis now that has created doubts about the wisdom and necessity of deepening economic integration in the world economy. And there was life after globalization then as there will be now. It is not the end of geography, because nation states cannot exist in a vacuum and most must strive to improve the economic conditions of their people to whom governments are accountable.

It is clear that the nation state is a reality that has not withered away. There has been an erosion in its economic space but not in its political space. This reality has been brought home by the global economic crisis (Nayyar, 2011a). At the same time, democratic politics is an aspiration that is on the rise everywhere. The spread of political democracy has coincided in time with the advent of market economy. There are fewer authoritarian regimes and more democratic regimes. In sum, the nation state is a reality embedded in history that has emerged stronger from the global economic crisis. Democratic politics, which has gathered both momentum and strength in the recent past, is increasingly a prior, as there is a rights consciousness among citizens. In contrast, the degree of international economic integration is a matter of strategic choice in terms of speed, sequence and engagement. It depends on choices made by the nation state where, ultimately, governments can decide only in accordance with preferences of people. And if it produces unequal outcomes, globalization is unsustainable in terms of both economics and politics.

Markets and democracy

The nature of the relationship between market economy and political democracy in the national context is, perhaps, the more appropriate starting point for an understanding of the relationship between globalization and democracy situated in the international context. The causation is interactive as it runs in both directions and the relationship is dialectical as one shapes the other.

The essence of the tension between the economics of markets and the politics of democracy must be recognized. In a market economy, people vote with their money in the marketplace. The underlying principle is one rupee one vote. But a political democracy works on the basis of one person one vote (Bhaduri and Nayyar, 1996). The distribution of votes, unlike the distribution of incomes or assets, is equal. One adult has one vote in politics, even though a rich person has more votes than a poor person, in terms of purchasing power, in the market. This tension may be compounded by a related asymmetry between economy and polity. The people who are excluded by the economics of markets are included by the politics of democracy. Hence, exclusion and inclusion are asymmetrical in economics and politics. The distribution of capabilities is also uneven in the economic and political spheres. The rich dominate a market economy in terms of purchasing power. But the poor have a strong voice in a political democracy in terms of votes. And there is a mismatch.

It is clear that, in reconciling market economy and political democracy, a sensible compromise must be reached between the economic directions, which the market sets on the basis of purchasing power and the priorities that a political system sets on the basis of one person one vote. In this context, it is not surprising that successive generations of economic thinkers and social philosophers have stressed the role of the State in this process of mediation. The reason is important even if it is not obvious. Governments are accountable to their people, whereas markets are not. In a democracy, of course, governments are elected by the people. But even where they are not, the State needs legitimization from the people, most of whom are not rich or are poor. The task of reconciliation and mediation is obviously difficult but clearly necessary (Nayyar, 2003b).

Markets are responsive to the demands of rich people and not to the needs of the poor people. This is inherent in the logic of markets where decisions about what is produced are based on demand and not on need. Thus, markets produce goods for which there is enough purchasing power. The output mix depends upon the composition of expenditure and the size of the market. Since the rich have more purchasing power, markets, left to themselves, are likely to produce more soft drinks and not safer drinking water. In this manner, markets include people with entitlements but exclude people without entitlements. In theory, every economic agent has the freedom to choose. In practice, there is a choice for some but not for others. And there is more choice for some than for others.

Democracies are more responsive to people with a voice than to people at large. People without a political voice are often simply neglected. There are, of course, problems associated with majority rule, which might lead some democracies to exclude minorities. Even if we abstract from such problems, however, the principle of one person one vote does not make every citizen equal in a political democracy. For, in the real world, social and economic inequalities are inevitably reflected in the political process. In theory, democracy provides every citizen political freedom in the form of civil rights and political liberties. In practice, there is freedom for some but not for others. And there is more freedom for some than for others.

It is only to be expected that there is an interaction between exclusion from the market in the economic sphere and exclusion from democracy in the political sphere. An economic exclusion from livelihood often creates or accentuates a political exclusion from rights. Thus, for the poor in a democracy the right to vote may exist in principle, but in practice it may be taken away by coercion or coaxed away by material incentives at the time of elections. Similarly, the very poor are vulnerable to exploitation or oppression, because their civil rights or equality before the law exists in principle but are difficult to protect or preserve in practice. The reason is simple. They do not have the resources to claim or the power to assert their rights.

Exclusion extends beyond the economic and the political to the social and cultural spheres. The social manifestations of exclusion can be powerful. At the same time, economic exclusion accentuates social exclusion, while social exclusion accentuates political exclusion.

Similarly, cultural exclusion, such as that of immigrant groups, minority communities or ethnic groups, interacts with economic exclusion from the market and political exclusion from democracy.

Clearly, there is an overlap between those excluded by market economy and those excluded by political democracy, just as there is an overlap between those included by market economy and those included by political democracy. The poor who are marginalized in the economy also do not have a voice in the polity, just as the rich who are dominant in the economy also have a strong political voice. Economic deprivation and political marginalization go hand in hand in much the same way as economic strength and political power go hand in hand. There are two underlying factors. For one, the economy and the polity are connected and interdependent. For another, there is no equality among economic agents or political citizens in terms of their economic or political freedom to choose. There is, in fact, a hierarchy of freedoms, with more for some and less for others, where there is a significant overlap in the economic and political sphere. These two propositions add to our understanding of the interaction between markets and democracy (Nayyar, 2003b).

It needs to be said that the liberal paradox is much deeper. On the one hand, markets exclude people without entitlements, assets or capabilities. It is in the logic of markets. Yet, markets would like to include as many people as possible. For, in the words of Adam Smith: 'the division of labour is limited by the size of the market'. On the other hand, democracy includes people by a constitutional right to vote. It is the foundation of democracy. Yet, political processes seek to exclude or to marginalize those without a voice. That is what the pursuit and exercise of political power is about. The irony of this paradoxical situation is striking. Indeed, this twist in the tale further highlights the dialectics of the interaction between market economy and political democracy.

This dialectical relationship between markets and democracy, as also the interaction between economic and politics, becomes more complex when globalized economies are juxtaposed with national polities. However, the essential tensions, asymmetries, overlaps and paradoxes remain similar. The dialectical relationship also remains. Even so, two questions arise. First, how does a market economy, which is more global than local, influence national politics differently? Second, how does political democracy influence a globalized market economy differently, when compared with a national market economy that is much less integrated with the outside world?

Global economics and national politics

Globalization has indeed reduced degrees of freedom for nation states in the economic sphere which is so essential for countries that are latecomers to development. Indeed, the space for and autonomy to formulate policies in the pursuit of national development objectives is significantly diminished. This is so for two reasons: unfair rules of the game in the world economy and consequences of integration into international financial markets.

In a world of unequal partners, it is not surprising that the rules of the game are asymmetrical in terms of construct and inequitable in terms of outcome. The strong have the power to make the rules and the authority to implement the rules. In contrast, the weak can neither set nor invoke the rules (Nayyar, 2002). The problem, however, takes different forms.

First, there are different rules in different spheres. The rules of the game for the international trading system, being progressively set in the WTO, illustrate this with clarity. There are striking asymmetries. National boundaries should not matter for trade flows and capital flows but should be clearly demarcated for technology flows and labour flows. It follows that developing countries would provide access to their markets without a corresponding access to technology and would accept capital mobility without a corresponding provision for labour mobility. This implies more openness in some spheres but less openness in other spheres. The contrast between the free movement of capital and the unfree movement of labour across national boundaries lies at the heart of the inequality in the rules of the game.

Second, there are rules for some but not for others. The conditions imposed by the IMF and the World Bank provide the most obvious example. There are no rules for surplus countries, or even deficit countries, in the industrialized world, which do not borrow from the multilateral financial institutions. But the Bretton Woods twins set rules for borrowers in the developing world and in the transition economies. In effect, IMF programmes of stabilization and World Bank programmes of structural adjustment seek to harmonize policies and institutions across countries, which is in consonance with the needs of globalization.

Third, the agenda for new rules is partisan. There is an attempt on the part of industrialized countries to create new multilateral agreements in the WTO, in many spheres, which is partly responsible for the impasse in the Doha Round. The primary object of this exercise is to set rules for a deeper integration in the world economy. And the WTO is seen as the place to lodge these agreements, essentially because it incorporates an enforcement mechanism which provides a legal right to retaliate. But this agenda is not in the interest of developing countries. Such unfair rules, if imposed, are bound to further erode the policy space so essential for national development.

The existing (and prospective) rules of the WTO regime allow few exceptions and provide little flexibility to countries that are latecomers to industrialization. In comparison, there was more room for manoeuvre in the erstwhile GATT, *inter alia*, because of special and differential treatment for developing countries. The new regime is much stricter in terms of the law and the implementation. The rules on trade in the new regime make the selective protection or strategic promotion of domestic firms *vis-à-vis* foreign competition much more difficult. The tight system for the protection of intellectual property rights could pre-empt or stifle the development of domestic technological capabilities. The possible multilateral agreement on investment, should it materialize, would almost certainly reduce the possibilities of strategic bargaining with transnational firms. Similarly, commitments on structural reform, an integral part of stabilization and adjustment programmes with the IMF and the World Bank, inevitably prescribe industrial deregulation, privatization, trade liberalization and financial deregulation. In sum, the new regime appears rule based but the rules are not uniform. And it is not clear how or why this is better than discretion. For, taken together, such rules and conditions are bound to curb the use of industrial policy, technology policy, trade policy and financial policy as strategic forms of intervention to foster industrialization (Nayyar, 2002).

At the same time, the consequences of integration into international capital markets also reduce degrees of freedom. Exchange rates can no longer be used as a strategic device to provide an entry into world markets for manufactured goods, just as the interest rates can no longer be used as a strategic instrument for guiding the allocation of scarce investible resources in a market economy. What is more, countries that are integrated into the international financial system are constrained in using an autonomous management of demand to maintain levels of output and employment. Expansionary fiscal and monetary policies – large government deficits to stimulate aggregate demand or low interest rates to encourage domestic investment – can no longer be used because of an overwhelming fear that such measures could lead to speculative capital flight and a run on the national currency (Nayyar, 2007).

What is more, the gathering momentum of globalization, associated with an internationalization of financial markets, has led to the formulation of a rationale for orthodox macroeconomic policies that is almost prescriptive (Nayyar, 2011b). The objectives of price stability and fiscal balance have become sacrosanct, which defines the role of monetary policy and fiscal policy in the narrowest possible sense. Slowly but surely, this orthodoxy has also come to be embedded in the belief systems of individuals, who influence policy and shape opinion in politics and in government. In this process, intellectuals from the world of academia provide the rationale and editors or columnists from the world of media provide the voice. It is no surprise that the orthodox belief system has been transformed into a virtual ideology. The ideology is not abstract. It is embedded in institutions, both international and national. For international financial markets, price stability is almost an article of faith, high interest rates ensure profitability and strong exchange rates impart confidence. Orthodox macroeconomic policies are simply a means to these ends. The same worldview is adopted by multilateral financial institutions, such as the IMF and the World Bank, which exercise enormous influence on policies of economies in crisis. It is only natural that this thinking is as much an integral part of national institutions, even outside the world of finance. The advocacy may come from domestic financial sectors, but the policies are formulated by finance ministries, while the practices are adopted by central banks.

In sum, the existing global rules encroach upon essential policy space. And the problem is compounded by the rapid, sometimes premature, integration into international financial markets. It is no surprise that these attributes of globalization also diminish space for democratic politics. This happens for at least three reasons.

First, global rules and financial markets in the outside world exercise significant influence on what governments can or cannot do in terms of fiscal policy, monetary policy, trade policy, industrial policy and exchange rate policy, in the pursuit of national objectives, so that economic decisions are not always shaped by the interests of their citizens. Second, the accountability, if not loyalty, of governments is divided and extends beyond national borders to multilateral rules, transnational corporations and international financial markets. Indeed, for economies that are vulnerable, even credit rating agencies become larger than life. Third, the accountability of governments to their people, who elect them or whom they represent, is eroded. In an ideal world, such accountability to citizens alone is a prior.

It is clear that markets and globalization reduce the economic policy space for nation states. There is also a reduction, not quite as much, in political space. Even so, there is some dilution of democratic politics in terms of objectives pursued by governments and their accountability to people. Is it possible that political democracy within nation states might provide checks and balances *vis-à-vis* markets and globalization? This a natural question that arises. Yet, it is seldom addressed.

Dialectical relationship with political democracy

Economics provides a critical yet limited perspective on globalization, a multidimensional phenomenon, the consequences of which extend much beyond the economic to the political, social and cultural. And it would be no exaggeration to state that the whole is different from the sum total of its parts. Obviously, it would mean too much of a digression to discuss every dimension. Yet, it is essential to focus on some aspects of the political implications, to highlight the dialectical nature of the relationship between globalization and democracy.

Globalization has been associated with simultaneous, yet asymmetrical, consequences for countries and for people. There is an inclusion for some and an exclusion, or marginalization, for many. There is affluence for some and poverty for many. There are some winners and many losers. And there is an exclusion of people, as also countries, from the process. Beyond the economic, globalization has added a new dimension to the exclusion of people from development (Nayyar, 2003a). Exclusion is no longer simply about the inability to satisfy basic human needs in terms of food, clothing, shelter, health care and education for large numbers of people. It is much more complicated. For the consumption patterns and lifestyles of the rich, associated with globalization, have powerful demonstration effects. People everywhere, even the poor and the excluded, are exposed to these consumption possibility frontiers, because the electronic media has spread the consumerist message far and wide. This creates both expectations and aspirations. But the simple fact of life is that those who do not have the incomes cannot buy goods and services in the market. Thus, when the paradise of consumerism is unattainable, which is the case for common people, it only creates frustration or alienation. The reaction of people who experience such exclusion differs. Some seek shortcuts to the consumerist paradise through drugs, crime or violence. Some seek refuge in ethnic identities, cultural chauvinism or religious fundamentalism. Such assertion of traditional or indigenous values is often the only thing that poor people can assert, for it brings an identity and meaning to their lives. These outcomes have obvious political consequences.

It would seem that globalization has created two worlds that coexist in space even if they are far apart in well-being (Nayyar, 2007). For some, in a world more interconnected than ever before, globalization has opened the door to many benefits. Open economies and open societies are conducive to innovation, entrepreneurship and wealth creation. For many, the fundamental problems of poverty, unemployment and inequality persist. Of course, these problems existed even earlier. But globalization may have accentuated exclusion and deprivation, for it has dislocated traditional livelihoods (World Commission on the Social Dimension of Globalization, 2004).

The people who reap the benefits and capture the opportunities are included. Some are winners. Economic prosperity does translate into political empowerment with voice and influence, creating political constituencies for markets and globalization. It is ironical that this process also creates a crisis of identity, particularly for the elite, who believe they have more in common with the global rich than their less privileged fellow citizens. The outcome might be a secession of the successful. But there are others, an aspiring urban middle class that benefits from globalization, who do not have such an identity crisis and are more empowered in the political process.

The people who bear the costs and face the risks are marginalized if not excluded. Some are losers. The visible, yet unattainable, islands of prosperity provide a sharp contrast with the sea of deprivation in which they live. Their search for identities, whether social, ethnic or religious, is an inevitable consequence. And its assertion lends meaning to their lives. But it is also a means of acquiring a collective voice that is audible in the political process. The object is to combat exclusion through social resistance or political protest. In some countries, this is supported, if not reinforced, by organizations or even citizens from civil society.

Globalization is driven by market forces, whether the lure of profit or the threat of competition and technical progress, which has dismantled geographical barriers of distance in terms of both time and costs. The synthesis of communications technology, which is concerned with the transmission of information, and computer technology, which is concerned with the processing of information, has created information technology, which is remarkable in both reach and speed. The consequences of this technological revolution are far reaching in every sphere. The most visible manifestation among people is mobile telephones. An exponential growth in the number of telephones has been combined with a phenomenal spread across the world, including poor countries and poor people. In itself, through connectivity alone, this revolution in communications has fostered economic, social and political empowerment. At the same time, access to the Internet has expanded at a scorching pace, which has imparted social media software – Facebook, Twitter and the like – a fantastic reach. This has empowered the aspiring middle class in the political domain everywhere, not only in articulating collective voice, but also in mobilization through networking.

More information on economy and polity has created a milieu that is conducive to greater sensitivity about social realities. In such a context, easier and better methods of communication have enhanced awareness of rights and identities, just as they have enhanced awareness of widening disparities. Taken together, these developments have created a much greater rights consciousness among citizens. In countries where social and economic inequalities are high or rising, there is a juxtaposition of deprivation with aspiration. The widespread access through communications technology, just through mobile telephones with the rudimentary short message service (SMS), has enabled social movements to mobilize opinion. This manifestation of the technological revolution, which is among the critical factors driving globalization, has some consequences for politics.

For one, it broadens and could strengthen political democracy everywhere. But it is particularly important in the developing world, where elections, even if free and fair, do not ensure freedoms and rights for citizens. The arena of politics is often preserved for established political parties or insiders by barriers to entry, whether money or kinship, which are formidable. And political mobilization is a difficult task for outsiders. This is so for political parties that are new entrants. It is even more difficult for individuals who are concerned or dissenting citizens. In such situations, access to information and ability to communicate empowers citizens in terms of voice, if not influence, to demand their freedoms and claim their rights. Social movements and social media, together, can reinforce this process through mobilization of opinion on issues of concern to citizens and society. It is plausible to argue that these processes might provide more effective checks and balances in what are sometimes choiceless democracies.

For another, it questions and could weaken authoritarian governments everywhere. It is plausible to argue that this is far more effective in challenging authoritarian regimes than popular movements of citizens were in the past. The process is much less visible and much less susceptible to control. It is able to reach out across geographical space and create coalitions of the willing. Thus, mobilization is far more effective. The speed at which dissent or opinion can be mobilized, against dictatorships, could not have been imaginable even a decade ago. The Arab Spring or the Jasmine Revolution provide a powerful example, as dictatorial regimes were ousted by people, although ultimate outcomes turned out to be different in Tunisia and Egypt, while similar processes were aborted by outside intervention in Libya or Bahrain. Even without regime change, such empowerment of citizens through information and communication creates space for political dissent by people. This is discernible in several countries across the world, such as China and Iran, where authoritarian governments allow little room for dissent on the part of citizens. The industrialized world is not quite an exception. In Europe – both Greece and Cyprus – people resisted elected governments on policies dictated by the IMF and the European Union in the wake of the financial crisis. Ultimately, in January 2015, this led to a political regime change in Greece, as its people decisively rejected the ruling political coalition of the conservative and social democratic parties (ND and PASOK) and elected SYRIZA, a left-wing party, with a near majority as it won 149 out of 300 seats in the Hellenic Parliament.

It is important to stress that the broadening or strengthening of political democracy and the questioning or weakening of authoritarian regime comes not only from the aspiring middle class, but also from those marginalized or deprived by markets and globalization. Both sets of citizens are empowered by information and communication technologies that have reached ordinary people. Of course, the significance of the aspiring middle class is more audible and visible. But the poor or the deprived are no longer reconciled to a quiet acceptance of their fates, which was almost the norm earlier, as this new empowerment provides them with a voice to protest and to mobilize for seeking a better world.

The argument developed here suggests two hypotheses. These are intuitively plausible, even if difficult to prove, and highlight the dialectical nature of the relationship between globalization and democracy.

First, the broadening if not strengthening of political democracy, where such democracy already exists, attributable to technologies that provide citizens access to information and ability to communicate, helps reclaim some accountability of governments to their people that has been eroded or diminished by markets and globalization. Similarly, the questioning if not weakening of authoritarian regimes, where democracy does not exist, through the same technologies, also helps restore or create some accountability of governments to their people because, in a globalized world where citizens are conscious of the reality in other countries, even authoritarian regimes are ultimately accountable if only to sustain themselves.

Second, the technologies associated with globalization that empower citizens through the spread of information and means of communication are conducive to political mobilization on issues, when the consequences of markets and globalization cross thresholds of tolerance in countries where democracy exists in some form. In effect, then, such empowerment of people provides checks and balances that work through a democratic political process to impose curbs or introduce correctives. Similarly, in countries with authoritarian regimes, citizens empowered with much greater access to information and communication are able to articulate political voice on issues where they are hurt by outcomes that can be linked to markets and globalization. Once this voice is audible, such governments too might be more responsive to concerns of people. Even undemocratic regimes might intervene to correct the situation if some checks and balances kick in.

The Latin American experience, during the 2000s, provides some validation of my hypothesis about the dialectical relationship between globalization and democracy. Most countries in this continent embraced markets and globalization starting around 1980. Some, such as Chile, did so with enthusiasm, while others, such as Argentina or Brazil, did so under duress driven by the IMF and the World Bank or by international financial markets. The outcome was the lost decade during the 1980s, when growth was stifled and per capita income declined. This hurt people, particularly the poor. The 1990s witnessed a slow recovery. But most economies in Latin America, at the turn of the century, were roughly where they had been two decades earlier. In the perception of people, these lost decades were attributed to the negative consequences of markets and globalization. In this context, access to information and means of communication, provided to people by technologies associated with globalization, did broaden and strengthen political democracy in countries where it existed, just as it did question and weaken authoritarian regimes in countries which were not democratic. The outcome was not just a resurrection of political democracy, but also the election of social democratic parties and left of centre governments in several Latin American countries. And, during the 2000s, most of these governments, responsive to the concerns of people, sought to address problems of poverty and inequality through economic policies with a focus on social sectors (Cornia, 2014). These efforts led to progress in terms of human development, through educational opportunities which created capabilities and public health which improved the well-being of people, even if there was not enough employment creation.

Conclusion

In conclusion, I would like to emphasize that the relationship between globalization and democracy does not conform to ideological caricatures. It is neither linear nor unidirectional. In fact, the relationship between market economy and political democracy in a national context is mirrored in the relationship between globalization and democracy in the international context. These relationships are dialectical. The causation runs in both directions in different spheres. And there is an interaction between economics and politics that shapes outcomes. This chapter, which has explored what globalization and democracy mean for each other, is no more than a modest beginning. There are some questions that need asking, just as there are other questions that need answers. It is time to reflect further on the consequences of globalization not only for economy, but also for polity and society. It is also time to rethink how political change might occur within countries in the future as compared with the past.

Acknowledgement

I would like to thank Romila Thapar for comments and suggestions on a preliminary draft.

References

Bhaduri, Amit and Deepak Nayyar (1996). *The Intelligent Person's Guide to Liberalization*, New Delhi: Penguin Books.

Chang, Ha-Joon (2007). *Bad Samaritans: Rich Nations, Poor Policies and the Threat to the Developing World*, London: Random House.

Cornia, G. Andrea (2014). *Falling Inequality in Latin America: Policy Changes and Lessons*, Oxford: Oxford University Press.

Friedman, Thomas (1999). *The Lexus and the Olive Tree*, New York: Farrar, Straus and Giroux.

Nayyar, Deepak (2002). 'The Existing System and the Missing Institutions', in Deepak Nayyar (ed.), *Governing Globalization: Issues and Institutions*, Oxford: Oxford University Press.

Nayyar, Deepak (2003a). 'Globalization and Development Strategies', in John Toye (ed.), *Trade and Development*, Cheltenham: Edward Elgar.

Nayyar, Deepak (2003b). 'The Political Economy of Exclusion and Inclusion: Democracy, Markets and People', in Amitava Krishna Dutt and Jaime Ros (eds.), *Development Economics and Structuralist Macroeconomics: Essays in Honour of Lance Taylor*, Cheltenham: Edward Elgar.

Nayyar, Deepak (2006). 'Globalization, History and Development: A Tale of Two Centuries', *Cambridge Journal of Economics*, Vol. 30, No. 1, pp. 137–159.

Nayyar, Deepak (2007). 'Development through Globalization?', in George Mavrotas and Anthony Shorrocks (eds.), *Advancing Development: Core Themes in Global Economics*, London: Palgrave.

Nayyar, Deepak (2011a). 'The Financial Crisis, the Great Recession and the Developing World', *Global Policy*, Vol. 2, No. 1, pp. 20–32.

Nayyar, Deepak (2011b). 'Rethinking Macroeconomic Policies for Development', *Brazilian Journal of Political Economy*, Vol. 31, No. 3, pp. 339–351.

Rodrik, Dani (2000). 'How Far Will International Economic Integration Go?', *Journal of Economic Perspectives*, Vol. 14, No. 1, pp. 177–186.

Rodrik, Dani (2011). *The Globalization Paradox: Democracy and the Future of the World Economy*, New York: W. W. Norton.

Taylor, Lance (2004). *Reconstructing Macroeconomics*, Cambridge, MA: Harvard University Press.

World Commission on the Social Dimension of Globalization (2004). *A Fair Globalization: Creating Opportunities for All*, Geneva: ILO.

10

DISCRIMINATION AND JUSTICE

Beyond affirmative action

Deepak Nayyar

The object of this chapter is to analyse discrimination and justice, in terms of theory and experience, to suggest that affirmative action is necessary but cannot be sufficient in the quest for social justice. The structure of the discussion is as follows. First, it considers the origins of discrimination in historical perspective. Second, it examines how discrimination leads to exclusion and embedded injustice is an outcome of the process. Third, it discusses the conception of justice as it has evolved, beginning in ancient India through enlightenment thinkers in Europe, to modern political thought in the contemporary world. Fourth, it argues that the quest for social justice, which gathered momentum during the second half of the 20th century, is a relatively recent phenomenon, even if discrimination and injustice have a long history. Fifth, it analyses the logic, the necessity and the limitations of affirmative action to highlight what else is needed. Sixth, it endeavours to impart a dose of reality to the story through a tale of three countries – India, the United States and South Africa – even if the focus is on India. In conclusion, it draws some lessons from experience to contemplate the future.

Origins of discrimination

Let me begin with the origins of discrimination. Societies are characterized by inequalities as a rule. Indeed, social stratification in one form or another is as old as humankind. It would be reasonable to ask a simple question. Was there discrimination at the very start of human social existence? If not, how did it begin? It is plausible to suggest though impossible to prove that the origins can be traced to the division of labour: in the household, in the community, in the world of work. It may also have been the outcome of conflict whenever victors subjected the vanquished to subordinate roles and, then, discrimination. The classic example, perhaps, is the discrimination against women embedded in the division of labour in a household. Such gender bias has a wide range of manifestations, particularly in our society where women have no access to potters' wheels or farmers' ploughs, even if, ironically enough, this practice is juxtaposed with the worship of goddesses. People captured in battle, then enslaved, are another example. In sum, the division of labour and the outcomes of conflict shaped relationships, given historical contexts or conditions.

The divisions or thresholds that constituted the origins of discrimination were not defined once and for all. There was evolution and there was mutation. The forms of discrimination changed over time and differed across societies. Yet, the essential attributes of discrimination, whether contours or consequences, are similar in their manifestations of inequality and injustice in societies. It would seem that the divides between the privileged and the underprivileged, the exploiters and the exploited, the victors and the vanquished or the fundamental divide between inclusion and exclusion are two sides of the same coin. One cannot exist without the other. In fact, in any society, the inclusion of some necessitates the exclusion of others, if only as a point of reference. The lines that divide people differ across societies and change over time. But if such lines did not exist, they would be invented so that they could be drawn.

Discrimination and exclusion

We can now turn to discrimination and exclusion. The term *exclusion* has become a part of the lexicon of economists in recent years, although it has been in the jargon of sociology and the vocabulary of politics for somewhat longer. The word *exclusion* has multiple dimensions: social, economic and political. Exclusion is used not simply to describe a situation, but also to focus on a process which excludes individuals or groups from communities, livelihoods and rights, thus depriving them of freedoms that are constitutive of and instrumental in development, which is a source of well-being for people, ordinary people. The essential point is that stratification is almost inevitable in economies and societies, which systematically integrate some and marginalize others, to distribute benefits of economic growth and social progress in ways that include some and exclude others. There is a strange irony in this process, which is captured almost perfectly in an epithet from Joan Robinson, one of my favourite economists, who taught at Cambridge. She once said, 'There is only one thing that is worse than being exploited by capitalists, and that is *not* being exploited by capitalists.' Joan Robinson was a profoundly original mind, but in this she was not. She probably borrowed from George Bernard Shaw, who once said, 'There is only one thing that is worse than being talked about, and that is *not* being talked about.' Much the same can be said about markets in societies.[1]

Markets exclude people as consumers or buyers if they do not have any incomes or sufficient incomes, which can be translated into purchasing power. This exclusion is attributable to their lack of income or *entitlements*. Such people are excluded from the consumption of goods and services which are sold in the market. Markets exclude people as producers or sellers, if they have neither *assets* nor *capabilities*.[2] People experience such exclusion if they do not have assets, physical or financial, which can be used to yield an income in the form of rent, interest or profits. Even those without assets could enter the market as producers or sellers, using their labour for a wage if they have some capabilities. Such capabilities are acquired through education, training or experience.

Markets exclude people both as consumers and producers, or as buyers and sellers, if they do not accept or do not conform to the values of a market system. The most obvious example of such exclusion is tribal populations or forest communities in market economies. But such exclusion may take other forms. There may be people who are unable or unwilling to sell their capabilities. For instance, a person may be unable or unwilling to charge fees as an astrologer or a musician because of a belief system that such talents cannot and should not be sold.

There is, of course, an interaction between exclusion from the market in the economic sphere and the non-economic dimensions of exclusion in the social, political and cultural spheres.[3] The social manifestations of exclusion can be powerful, for economic exclusion accentuates social exclusion. Economic exclusion from livelihoods often creates or accentuates a political exclusion from rights. Similarly, cultural exclusion, such as that of immigrant groups, minority communities or ethnic groups, interacts with economic exclusion from the market. Each dimension reinforces the other to produce a vicious circle of cumulative causation. The outcome is embedded discrimination.

This does not mean that exclusion is always bad and inclusion is always good. Coercive inclusion by markets, whether of child labour, tribal populations or immigrant workers, can be exploitative. The employment of women as wage labourers on terms inferior to those of men provides another example. The basic point is that inclusion which is coercive or on inferior terms is not desirable. For similar reasons, exclusion is not always bad. To those who do not accept the values of the market system, any voluntary exclusion from the market should be perfectly acceptable.

It is no surprise that there is a cumulative causation associated with exclusion or inclusion as a process. For those excluded, there is more and more discrimination, which creates vicious circles over time. For those included, there is more and more privilege, which creates virtuous circles over time. Discrimination, then, is embedded in relationships and processes that reinforce and strengthen it over time, which makes it difficult to curb, let alone reverse or eliminate. The divides that nurture stratification and foster discrimination differ across space and change over time. Yet, some are common enough everywhere in the world: race, caste, religion, gender, ethnicity. It is worth noting that discrimination and exclusion are closely interwoven, but could be different in their origins. Discrimination can be based on a common identity where the society breaks down the identity into a hierarchy. But exclusion, except for gender exclusion which is natural, is created by society through different identities, whether it is based on race, religion, caste or ethnicity. Once introduced, however, exclusion and discrimination reinforce each other in societies.

Conceptions of justice

The stage is set for us to consider conceptions of justice. It might be appropriate to begin with the classical distinction from jurisprudence in ancient India, which is a premodern conceptualization of justice: *Niti* and *Nyaya*. In a literal sense, both stand for justice in classical Sanskrit. *Niti* is about what is right in terms of propriety, conduct and behaviour. *Nyaya* is about what is just, not as an abstraction but as a realized outcome. This conception has a point of reference in ancient India: *Matsyanyaya*, justice in the world of fish, where in times of drought the big fish devour the small fish at will. This happens in two sets of conditions, either bad times (such as drought) or in chaotic times (such as anarchy). The latter represents a situation of *Arajya* associated with patent violations of human justice as *Nyaya*. In terms of this characterization of justice, Amartya Sen argues that the people, who agitated for the abolition of slavery in the 18th and 19th centuries, sought to eliminate intolerable injustice in the sense of *Nyaya* rather than establish perfect justice in the sense of *Niti*.[4] But I would differ from Amartya Sen in this interpretation. The reason is that *Nyaya* is defined as justice not in the abstract but in a social context.[5] *Matsyanyaya*, or slavery, may have been contrary to conception of *Nyaya* as caricature or intolerable forms of injustice, but inequalities or less than just situations, which were accepted as norms in society, may have been consistent with the conception of *Nyaya*.

Enlightenment thinkers in Europe in the 18th and 19th centuries were encouraged by the political climate of change and the socio-economic transformation of the times. This led to a different modern conception of justice; there were two basic divergent lines of reasoning about justice in the radical intellectual tradition of that period: the contractarian approaches and the comparative approaches.[6] The contractarian approaches were initiated by Thomas Hobbes. They were developed further by John Locke, Jean-Jacques Rousseau and Immanuel Kant. The social contract, then, was an ideal alternative to the chaos that might otherwise characterize a society. The most powerful and elegant exposition of this approach to justice can be found in the work of John Rawls, a leading political philosopher of our times.[7] Other contemporary theorists, such as Ronald Dworkin and Robert Nozick, have taken a similar route. In terms of the jargon in the trade, Amartya Sen describes this approach as transcendental institutionalism.[8] But I think this approach can be explained in a simpler manner. It has two essential foundations: that of a just society as an idea; and that of institutions and rules as arrangements that deliver such a just society. The comparative approaches owe their origins to the work of Adam Smith, Jeremy Bentham, Karl Marx and John Stuart Mill, all of whom were enlightenment theorists concerned with social realizations resulting from actual institutions and actual behaviour. In my simplification of theories of justice, there are, once again, two essential ideas in this approach. The first seeks to focus on comparisons of situations as more just or less unjust. The second seeks to focus on realizations in terms of outcomes for people, whether they were just, unjust, more just or less unjust. This realization-focus is the real point of departure for a number of contemporary theorists, including Sen.

Quest for social justice

From theories of justice, let me move to the quest for social justice. There is a question which is a prior. What is social justice? In what sense, if any, is it different from justice? The answer to this question is neither obvious nor clear. It is possible to speculate. It might refer to the distinction between the comparative and the contractarian approaches, to the distinction between justice that is contextualized in society and justice that is conceptualized in abstract principles of jurisprudence. It might also be that social justice is an ideal construct which creates a society, whose very being as it were ensures rights and opportunities for all people, irrespective of whether the State steps in to provide these rights and opportunities.

Be that as it may, discrimination in society is an obvious form of social injustice. The cognition of this reality goes back a very long time. However, the realization that social justice is not an automatic outcome – on the contrary it has to be discovered and established – is a more recent phenomenon. In fact, the quest for social justice which seeks to reduce, if not eliminate, discrimination is essentially a phenomenon that gathered momentum during the second half of the 20th century. It is motivated by a concern which arises from observed reality that society does not provide rights and opportunities for a significant proportion of people who are subjected to discrimination in one form or another. This concern is attributable not so much to a sense of egalitarianism as it is to perceptions of injustice.

What were the factors underlying the quest for social justice? There were many. But I choose to highlight two that probably shaped and drove this quest: institutions and ideologies.

In institutions, I would focus on the nation state and political democracy. The emergence of the nation state was associated with the emergence of nationalism, which led to a slow but steady erosion of multiple identities that developed into a national identity. The spread of political democracy was associated with the idea of egalitarianism, which sought to reduce injustice even if it could not deliver justice and to contest discrimination even if it did not seek equality. More often than not, the quest may have begun with a provision from above. Yet, in some places and at some times, it was pushed by claims from below. In retrospect, it is clear that, taken together, the institutions of nation state and political democracy played a critical role in this quest for social justice. So did ideologies.

In ideologies, I would focus on capitalism and communism. There can be little doubt that capitalism reduced and sought to eliminate pre-capitalist forms of discrimination embedded in feudalism, whether serfdom or bonded labour, but created new or different forms of discrimination or exclusion. Successive stages in the evolution of capitalism have been associated with exploitation, progress and dilution. It is possible to think of this sequence in terms of countries or of people. Consider countries in what is now described as the developing world:

imperialism led to exploitation, nationalism was followed by some progress and globalization meant dilution if not regress. Consider people in industrial societies: early capitalism led to exploitation, which was corrected as political democracy introduced a role for the State in regulating the market, while the advent of social democracy as an ideology strengthened the quest for social justice; but it was followed by the rise of market fundamentalism and international capitalism in the age of globalization, which diluted the same quest.[9]

Socialism or communism set out to reduce, if not eliminate, forms of discrimination that were characteristic of capitalism (capitalists and workers) or persisted in capitalism (men and women). It made some of the transition from capitalism to socialism (from everybody according to their ability and to everybody according to their work), but none of the transition from socialism to communism (from everybody according to their ability and to everybody according to their need). In fact, socialism may not only have reduced some old forms of discrimination, but it also created new forms of privilege and exclusion. This was experienced by citizens and understood by scholars of the erstwhile Soviet Union. It was carried over easily, in different manifestations and in accentuated form, into post-transition Russia. The Cultural Revolution in China did not create, as Mao Zedong had hoped, a new socialist man. Indeed, just a decade later, Deng Xiaoping's modernizations ushered in what was described as market socialism, which developed some attributes of unbridled capitalism over time. In fact, among the socialist countries with communist governments, Cuba seems to be the solitary exception which eliminated discrimination based not only on gender, but also on race, possibly the only society that created equality of opportunity in those domains even if it had failings in most other spheres. In retrospect, it would seem that communism did succeed in bringing about a substantial reduction in gender discrimination by creating equal opportunities. But why it failed elsewhere remains an open question.

Affirmative action

The quest for social justice needs some form of affirmative action. In situations where exclusion takes the form of discrimination against identifiable groups, defined or identified by race, caste, religion, gender or ethnicity, social legislation is necessary. But it may not be sufficient, because it is difficult to implement and to enforce a law of equal opportunities wherever discrimination is embedded in history. That leads me into the logic of affirmative action. In situations where discrimination and exclusion has a history, affirmative action or positive discrimination in favour of the underprivileged or the excluded is necessary as a corrective to compensate for embedded discrimination. The term *affirmative action* refers to a set of policies and practices that are used to create equal opportunity and maximum diversity. These target, primarily, workplaces and educational institutions while using race, caste, gender or ethnicity as factors that must be taken into account when employment or admissions decisions are made. The object is to redress perceived disadvantages attributable to overt institutional or involuntary discrimination.

But we must recognize that remedial action does not always provide a sustainable solution. Affirmative action is almost always conceived of when it begins life as a transitional remedy that would end once there are equal opportunities for all citizens. In other words, even if affirmative action is both necessary and desirable, it cannot continue in perpetuity. Indeed, I believe affirmative action is a success wherever and whenever it makes itself dispensable. But this may not, often does not, happen. The reason is simple. Discrimination is often embedded in beliefs and ideologies. Affirmative action cannot always combat these beliefs or ideologies, let alone change the initial conditions which created discrimination in the past. In the ultimate analysis, the economic, social and political empowerment of the excluded is essential. Affirmative action seeks to provide from above, but this must be transformed into a claim from below. For that to happen, political democracy is an imperative. However, it is necessary but not sufficient. That is borne out by experience. Consider, for example, the oldest and largest democracies of the world: the United States and India. Yet, there is a strong correlation between the idea of justice and the practice of democracy.

In contemporary political philosophy, democracy is best seen as government by discussion, given the central role of public reasoning supported by freedom of the press and intervention of civil society. There is a critical role in this process for government as a catalyst, if not leader, through mediation and intervention, which has to be performed because in the ultimate analysis, governments are accountable to people. This is obvious in democratic regimes, although even authoritarian regimes are ultimately accountable to their people. The idea of government by discussion is essentially about the importance of voice in political democracy.[10] The problem is that democracy, while conducive and necessary, is not sufficient to actually produce development and deliver social justice.

Development and justice may or may not be provided from above by benevolent governments, but must be claimed from below by people as citizens from governments that are accountable. The empowerment of people then is an integral part of any process of change that leads to social justice, to development. A political democracy, even if it is slow, provides a sure path for two reasons – it increases political consciousness amongst voters to judge political parties for their performance; at the same time, it increases participation in political processes when it leads to mobilization on some issues. This highlights the significance of Amartya Sen's conception of development as freedom.[11] Expanding freedoms for people at large constitute development, but the same expanding freedoms which empower people are instruments that drive the process of change in development. Of course, elites in democracies or those who rule are not easily persuaded. Indeed, many governments might have a strong preference for silent people.[12] And, come election time, such governments would, if they could, change the people rather than allow a change in government! It is clear that democracy, while essential, cannot suffice to ensure affirmative action for social justice. And it should be no surprise that the task cannot be performed by governments alone.

There is a fundamental role for society. For people who have been subjected to discrimination, the transition from the creation of opportunities to the realization of opportunities requires two essentials. First, there must be a social consciousness among those included, that is, the privileged. Second, there must be a right consciousness amongst those excluded, that is, the discriminated. Yet, there are persistent difficulties and stubborn obstacles. For one, there is resistance on the part of those privileged, those included. Why? The answer is simple. It is about ceding social, economic and political space which they occupy. This is particularly important in societies where people are poor and opportunities are scarce. There are vested interests on the one hand and there are embedded prejudices on the other. These are both very difficult to fight, let alone remove. What is needed, then, is social consciousness on the part of individuals and collective action on the part of communities. For another, there is resentment on the part of the discriminated, those excluded. People, who have been subjected to discrimination in society for long, sometimes see affirmative action as a process that reinforces notions of exclusion. In their perception, identities are seen as labels or as symbols of exclusion. In such situations, the struggle against social injustice through affirmative action becomes far more complex and difficult.

A tale of three countries

There are three countries in the contemporary world that are characterized by a history of embedded discrimination and social injustice, which have sought to address the problem through affirmative action beginning in the second half of the 20th century: India, United States and South Africa. Their problems are similar in terms of consequences even if they are different in terms of origins.

Surprisingly enough, India was the first to introduce affirmative action soon after independence beginning 1950. The object was to address problems of discrimination and injustice which were embedded in history. For centuries, indeed millenniums, society discriminated against a significant proportion of its indigenous population, on the basis of a social hierarchy created by the *varnashrama dharma* which provided the foundations of a complex caste system. The outcome was social injustice experienced by a significant proportion of the population, which is now estimated at about one-fourth the total population.

The United States introduced affirmative action beginning with the civil rights legislation in the mid-1960s, and not since the civil war which ended slavery in 1865. The discrimination it sought to address was not embedded in the past. It began life, as an outcome of early colonialism, in the 18th century. The European migrant population began with discrimination against the indigenous people. But it was not long before the native population, the American Indians, was almost decimated. And, even now, the few who remain live in abject poverty in remote reservations with almost no integration into society. The same European migrant population imported labour from Africa, as slaves, to work on plantations. Slavery came to an end in 1865, but the black population continued to experience discrimination and injustice for a century thereafter. This population of African Americans is now estimated at about 10 per cent of the total population.

South Africa was the last to introduce affirmative action among the three countries. It followed liberation in 1994. The discrimination it attempted to redress was not embedded in history. It was an outcome of colonialism, as in the United States, albeit somewhat different and somewhat later during the 19th century. A small migrant population of white settlers from Europe practised discrimination against the native African population. However, the indigenous people were not eliminated but were turned into labour for mines and plantations. At the same time, indentured labour, which constituted a new form of slavery, was imported mostly from India to work on mines and plantations. In addition, a small number of people were brought in from

India as traders, to create a middle class that did not exist. The black and the brown population were discriminated against by the white population, although there was a hierarchy in this triangular structure of discrimination. The African population is now estimated at more than 80 per cent, while people of Indian origin are about 7 per cent, of the total population. It should be obvious that the nature and scale of the problem is very different as compared with the other two countries, because more than four-fifths of the population has been subjected to discrimination for at least 150 years.

What can we learn from the experience of affirmative action in these three countries? It is only natural that my focus is on India. But I would also like to consider, even if briefly, the United States and South Africa as points of reference if not comparison.

India

Embedded discrimination and social injustice provided the rationale for affirmative action in independent India. The Republic of India introduced it as part of the Constitution that was adopted in 1950. It is worth noting that B.R. Ambedkar played a lead role, as an architect and an author, in drawing up that Constitution.[13] In considering the Indian experience, it is necessary to explain the logic of the model, recognize the successes, analyse the failures and note the dilemmas that persist.

The model is simple enough. Its conception and design were based on two essential attributes. The first was *affirmative action* in favour of Scheduled Castes and Scheduled Tribes, as discrimination against these social groups was embedded in history, so that caste was the defining basis. The second was *proportional reservation*, quotas roughly in conformity with their proportion in the total population, which was 15 per cent for Scheduled Castes and 7.5 per cent for Scheduled Tribes at that time, in government employment and in higher education. These reservations were introduced when the Constitution was adopted in 1950. The same reservations were renewed from time to time, most recently in 2010. Such reservations were extended to Other Backward Castes (OBCs) in 1991 for employment in the government sector and in 2006 for places in higher education. The proportion in both was specified as 27.5 per cent of the total, which was the estimated share of OBCs in the total population. There is a draft legislation, pending consideration for quite some time, which proposes that 33 per cent of seats in the national Parliament and in State Legislatures be reserved for women. Such reservation for women was, in fact, introduced in *Panchayats* in 1993. It is worth noting that affirmative action in each of these spheres, in the form of proportional reservations, is a legal right under the Constitution.[14] Therefore, in India, affirmative action is a matter of right.[15]

Given the legacy of embedded discrimination, the experience of the past 60 years suggests that affirmative action did succeed, even if the success was modest. It would seem (at least *prima facie*) that the objectives of reservations have been met in so far as the quotas have been filled. There is proportional representation Scheduled Castes and Scheduled Tribes in State Legislatures and in national Parliament, the *Lok Sabha*, just as there is proportional reservation for Dalits and Tribals in employment in the Government and in the public sector, particularly at lower levels. Clearly, there is an inclusion for some, and there can be little doubt that the situation would have been worse, distinctly worse, without such affirmative action. Success, therefore, lies in the counterfactual. But that has another dimension. In my view, outcomes could and should have been better.

At the same time, it is clear that there were failures. Outcomes of reservations in higher education were not quite as good as in government employment. The situation would have been much worse without affirmative action, but could have been far better if such intervention had been more effective and more purposive. Even after six decades of reservations, the quotas for Scheduled Castes and Scheduled Tribes in higher education remain underfulfilled by large margins. The stipulated quotas are simply not met, either because a sufficient number do not make the threshold in terms of a much-reduced minimum or because admission processes circumvent the stipulation by stealth yet design. The dropout rates are high, while the completion rates are low, among students from Scheduled Castes and Scheduled Tribes who do obtain admission through reservations in higher education. The reason is clear. Their school education has not been good enough to prepare them for higher education. And most higher education institutions, but for a few exceptions, do not make any serious attempt at remedial teaching. There are some exceptions as a few institutions make the effort, often supported by committed individuals. But most such students, who come into the higher education system through reservations, are first generation learners and are not at par with the average student who enters the world of work. Yet, reservations exist only at the point of entry. However, creating a hierarchy of reservations, at every level, is no solution. It could turn out to be worse than the problem, if performance is substandard. What is more, it does not address the real issue. In fact, it would be no exaggeration to state that the benefits of reservations have accrued mostly to the better off, the more educated, amongst Dalits and Tribals. Those included through affirmative action in the first instance are, in a sense, co-opted into the system. Thereafter, privilege is reproduced in the form of pre-emptive access for the next generation, as also the next, which continues in perpetuity. The outcome is that a small subset of people from groups that were subjected to discrimination have privileged access through affirmative action, whereas most people from the same groups are left out, marginalized or excluded. We have simply created what the Supreme Court of India describes as a 'creamy layer'. But exclusion persists for a large number, who constitute a substantial proportion of those for whom affirmative action is needed and of those for whom affirmative action was introduced in the first place.[16]

It is no surprise that dilemmas persist. There is patronage for those included rather than equal opportunities for all. There is co-option of those included rather than an empowerment – economic, social or political – of all people who are subjected to discrimination and injustice. There is exclusion on a massive scale. More than 60 years after affirmative action was introduced, an overwhelmingly large proportion of Dalits and Tribals remain excluded from higher education and from government employment because they have little, if any, access to social opportunities, most of which come from school education. It would seem that the real failures, as also the persistent dilemmas, are attributable to the limited spread of education in society, which is the only sustainable means of providing social opportunities for ordinary people, particularly those excluded on account of embedded discrimination. Such exclusion begins with school education and cannot ever end for those denied access because there is a path dependence in the process. It needs to be said that this exclusion is not based on caste alone. It is based on gender, religion, location and, most important perhaps, income. Hence, there cannot be any caste-based solution to the problem of economic inequality.[17] What is more, addressing the problem of disparities between groups cannot resolve the problem of inequality among individuals in economy and society.[18] This compounds difficulties for affirmative action in higher education, where the experience has been mixed if not disappointing, possibly not at par with outcomes of affirmative action elsewhere in society.

United States

It is interesting to consider the United States as a point of reference for a brief comparison. The origins of the consciousness about social justice can be traced to the end of the Civil War in 1865. The Thirteenth Amendment to the Constitution made slavery illegal. And the Civil Rights Act of 1866 guaranteed every citizen the same right to make and to enforce contracts. But the real quest for social justice in the United States began almost 100 years later.[19] The Civil Rights Movement, in the early 1960s, strongly protested against discrimination and segregation of African Americans in the southern United States because it was seen as unjust, unacceptable and intolerable. The efforts and the struggle of this movement ended segregation through legal change. The Fourteenth Amendment to the Constitution guaranteed equal protection under the law. The Civil Rights Act of 1964 forbid racial discrimination in public accommodations and stipulated that there was to be no discrimination on the basis of race and sex in employment. The Fifteenth Amendment to the Constitution followed soon thereafter, as the Voting Rights Act of 1965 forbid racial discrimination in access to voting.

Interestingly enough, the United States began affirmative action almost in the same mode as India. But it was not long before reverse discrimination surfaced as a problem. The famous example is the Alan Bakke case of 1978.[20] The Supreme Court of the United States outlawed inflexible quota systems in all affirmative action programmes but upheld the legality of affirmative action. Strict quotas no longer exist. Discretionary diversity policies are present. Equality of opportunity laws are in force. In a more recent case in 2003, the Supreme Court upheld the University of Michigan Law School admissions policy, ruling that race can be one of the factors considered by colleges when selecting their students if it improves diversity. It is clear that affirmative action in the United States is a matter of policy, which provides a sharp contrast with India where it is a matter of right.[21]

It would seem that, for almost a century after slavery was outlawed in 1865, progress on redressing discrimination in the United States was little, just as it was slow, but it gathered momentum in the early 1960s after the success of the Civil Rights Movement. In the 50 years since then, there are some clearly discernible successes. The idea of equal opportunities, which was created in law to start with, slowly turned into some social consciousness in the sphere of higher education and in the world of work. The attitudes of elites to social mobility, of those discriminated against in the past, changed from hostile to permissive without becoming enthusiastic. Most important, perhaps, the sanctity of glass ceilings eroded slowly over time in politics, in corporates, in professions, in academia and in media. Of course, there are still not enough African Americans or women in leadership positions in any sphere, as significant asymmetries persist. Yet, the election of President Obama represents the shattering of one such glass ceiling.

It would mean too much of a digression to enter into a discussion on the factors underlying progress in the United States. Even so, it is worth noting some factors that could have been important in the process of change. The legal framework and the legal institutions made a significant contribution. The common schooling system, which created equality of opportunity in school education, made an enormous difference. The spread of education in society and levels of income in the economy were supportive of rather than resistant to the associated social change. And the task was more feasible than elsewhere, as only 10 per cent of the total population had been the subject of discrimination.

South Africa

South Africa is a very different story. The *apartheid* regime institutionalized discrimination. It was characterized by extreme repression embodied in a division of labour that locked the African population into poverty. The vicious circle of cumulative causation stretched beyond income poverty and living conditions. There was little in terms of access to education and healthcare. For large numbers of black people, the reality came close to disguised slavery. Given this context, where more than 80 per cent of the population was subjected to acute discrimination, affirmative action was bound to be difficult and challenging. In theory, the process began in the late 1970s, with some loosening of the *apartheid* regime, when there was a small attempt at providing equal opportunities in terms of equal protection in the law for all employees. As the liberation struggle gathered momentum and the regime came under increasing pressure from outside, black advancement of sorts was introduced during the late 1980s, as non-white residents obtained legitimate status, mixed marriages were legalized, white educational institutions began to accept non-white students. But most of this was symbolic. Little of it was substantive. There was no arrangement for sharing political power.

In effect, affirmative action started after liberation when the ANC captured political power. There were two key principles enunciated by the newly elected government: disadvantaged groups will see improvements in their quality of life and past discrimination must be redressed. Hence, the social focus of the legislative effort in the Economic Equity Act of 1994 was on the black African population. The Employment Equity Act of 1998 went further. It extended beyond the government and stipulated that private sector firms must make their workforce demographically more representative: 75 per cent black and 50 per cent female. In addition, under the doctrine of Black Economic Empowerment, white-owned firms are urged to transfer portions of their equity to black people, without which such firms will not be eligible for government contracts. Government employment, of course, is based on strict race and gender quotas. Since then, there has been some progress. But this progress is modest. Contemporary South Africa is sometimes described as a *cappuccino* society, which is mostly black at the bottom and has a thin layer of white at the top interspersed with a sprinkling of chocolate. It is obvious that affirmative action is necessary but cannot be sufficient. The time has come for the ANC to move from the phase of reconciliation to a period of social change. The real answer to past discrimination and social injustice in South Africa lies in education and land, because a very large proportion of the African people still do not have access to education and those who live in the rural sector have almost no rights in the land.

Conclusions

In conclusion, rather than sum up, it would be appropriate to reflect on the future. In doing so, I would like to start with some priors. This is followed by an attempt to outline some contours of the journey and some essentials about the destination.

There are three critical propositions that are priors. First, we must learn from the experience of the past 60 years. What went wrong and why? It would serve no purpose to wish away the problem like an ostrich that hides its head in the sand. Second, we must evolve a longer term perspective about our time horizon for what we set out to do. It cannot be more of the same in perpetuity. Third, we need to recognize that words cannot be a substitute for substance. The time has come to shift from palliatives and correctives, often the soft option, to effective action and sustainable solutions.

The journey to a less unjust, or a more just, society in India must follow some basic contours. First, equal opportunities in school education are an imperative. We know that access is unequal, completion rates are uneven and dropouts are asymmetrical. The only way to address this issue in the long term is to provide access and create equal opportunities at school. Second, it is necessary to recognize that discrimination, hence exclusion, is multidimensional. We cannot turn a blind eye to that reality. In India, discrimination is not only about caste, which is confined to the Hindu population. It is just as much about religion, about gender, about ethnicity and ultimately about income. Hence, there is a need to construct some composite index of deprivation, for which income could be a proxy, but only a proxy. Third, it is essential to accept the idea that affirmative action must be limited to first generation learners or first time entrants. And, even with this correction, reservations cannot suffice. The time has come for an Equal Opportunities Commission to ensure implementation and to adjudicate conflicting claims. Last, but not least, we need to think of a world beyond affirmative action. Whatever we do must unite rather than divide people in the quest for social justice. Therefore, policies that seek to address embedded discrimination must integrate rather than separate people in society. After all, we are a society plagued by so many divides that our quest for inclusion or social justice should not accentuate those divides. This is not an illusion. It is real, for it is about ceding economic, social and political space. And, in societies where opportunities are scarce, there is bound to be resistance. It would be much easier if we create more opportunities. School education and higher education provide the obvious examples.

In thinking about the destination, some reality checks are both necessary and desirable. First, equality is an ideal. It is an abstraction or a construct that exists in our mind. Second, justice is a Utopia, which is much like the perfection of a just society in the contractarian approaches. The essential objectives that any humane society can aspire to are less abstract and more concrete: progressively reduce and eliminate discrimination, progressively reduce and eliminate social injustice. It is possible to make societies less unjust, or more just, by providing capabilities, opportunities and rights to people who are subjected to discrimination and injustice. But we would delude ourselves if we believed that, even for a moment, we will create egalitarian let alone equal societies. Inequality will reproduce itself in society. Even so, a better world is possible if social injustice can be progressively reduced and ultimately eliminated. For that, equal opportunity is an imperative, so that every person has access to economic and social opportunities for a better life.

Acknowledgement

I am indebted to Romila Thapar for helpful discussion and constructive suggestions. I would also like to thank Andre Beteille for valuable comments and conversations. Jonas Shaende provided useful assistance in my search for information on the United States and South Africa.

Notes

1 For a more detailed discussion on markets and exclusion, see Nayyar (2003).

2 I use the word *capabilities* to characterize the mix of natural talents, skills acquired through training, learning from experience and abilities or expertise based on education, embodied in a person that enables him or her to use these (capabilities as a producer or worker) for which there is not only a price, but also a demand in the market. It follows that even persons with capabilities may be excluded from employment if there is no demand for their capabilities in the market. It is essential to note that the same word, *capabilities*, has been used in a very different sense by Amartya Sen, who argues that the well-being of a person depends on what the person succeeds in *doing* with the commodities (and their characteristics) at his command. For example, food can provide nutrition to a healthy person but not to a person with a parasitic disease; or a bicycle can provide transportation to an able-bodied person but not to a disabled person. Thus, for Sen (1985), *capabilities* characterize the combination of functionings a person can achieve given his personal features (conversion of characteristics into functionings) and his command over commodities (*entitlements*).

3 This interaction is considered further in Nayyar (2003). See also, Nayyar (1998).

4 Sen (2009).

5 Consider the example of India, where the concepts of *Niti* and *Nyaya* originated. The social context was characterized by distinctions based on *varna* and *jati*, in which there was a hierarchy, with the *brahmana* at the top and the *shudra* at the bottom. These social norms were embedded in the conception and understanding of *Nyaya*.

6 For a detailed discussion on theories of justice, as also on different approaches to justice, see Sen (2009).

7 Rawls (1971). See also, Rawls (2001).

8 Sen (2009). See also, Dworkin (2000).

9 In his seminal book, Karl Polanyi (1944) analysed what he characterized as 'The Great Transformation' in Europe in the 19th and 20th centuries. In doing so, he described a double movement: the first from a pre-capitalist system to the market-driven industrialization in the 19th century; the second (which he termed the 'Great Transformation') from the predominance of the market model to a more inclusive world in which the State played a corrective, regulatory role. This transformation which began in the early 20th century was complete by the mid-20th century. But it did not last that long. There was a resurgence of the market model in the late 1970s. Hence, in the early 21st century, before the financial crisis surfaced in late 2008 and led to the Great Recession, the situation in developing countries was similar to that in pre-transformation Europe, while the situation in industrialized countries was such that the creation of equal opportunities in the quest for social justice was almost forgotten.

10 This idea is set out with remarkable clarity by Nelson Mandela in his autobiography, where he describes how impressed and influenced he was as a young boy by seeing the democratic nature of the proceedings of local meetings that were held in the Regent's house in the village of

Mqhekezweni: 'Everyone who wanted to speak did so. It was democracy in its purest form. There may have been a hierarchy of importance amongst the speakers, but everyone was heard – chief and subject, warrior and medicine man, shopkeeper and farmer, landowner and labourer, the foundation of self-government that all men were free to voice their opinions and equal in their value as citizens' (Mandela, 1994: 21).

11 For a lucid exposition of the idea, see Sen (1999).

12 It is ironical that former Prime Minister Clement Attlee, who played a leading role in the creation of a welfare state in Britain and was deeply committed to the idea of social justice, made the following statement in a speech at the Oxford Union in June 1957: 'Democracy means government by discussion, but it is only effective if you can stop people talking' (Sen, 2009: 332). This Atlee epithet, even if said in jest, captures the sentiments of the many governments besieged by protests from citizens.

13 Ambedkar wrote at length about these issues. For some of his essential writings on the subject, see Ambedkar (2004).

14 Article 330 and Article 332 of the Constitution of India, which provide for reservations in the Lok Sabha and the State Legislatures, respectively, are clearly mandatory provisions that create a legal right.

15 This is widely believed and accepted. But it could be a subject of debate in a legal sense. Article 16, which sets out fundamental rights, is an enabling provision, while Article 335, which provides for the State to introduce reservations as a matter of policy, is somewhat ambiguous in its mix of what is mandatory and what is enabling.

16 For a lucid and perceptive discussion on this issue, see Teltumbde (2009). He argues that reservations have created more inequality within castes, which are meant to be beneficiaries than there may have been between them and other castes. Indeed, he suggests that the entire Dalit population be divided into two categories of families: those that have availed of reservations and those that have not benefited from reservations so far. On this basis, he suggests a simple solution to the problem of reproduced privilege. The latter group who has not derived any benefit from affirmative action should have prioritized access to reservations, whereas families that have had access to reservations earlier would be eligible only if some places remain thereafter.

17 See Teltumbde (2009).

18 For a discussion on this issue, see Beteille (2003).

19 President John Kennedy first used the term *affirmative action* in 1961 in his Executive Order 10925, which stated that federal contractors must 'take affirmative action to ensure that applicants are employed, and that employees are treated during employment, without regard to their race, creed, color or national origin'. In 1967, President Lyndon Johnson extended protection of the affirmative action requirements to women.

20 Alan Bakke, a white male, had been rejected as an applicant for admission two years in a row by the medical school at the University of California (Davis) that had accepted less qualified black applicants, as the school had a separate admissions policy for minorities and reserved 16 out of 100 places for minority students. For a lucid discussion on reverse discrimination, see Dworkin (1985). In his analysis, Dworkin makes a distinction between the 'right to treatment as an equal', which is primary, and the

'right to equal treatment', which is secondary. In terms of this analysis, Alan Bakke was denied his right to treatment as an equal.

21 For a lucid analysis of the distinction between equality as a right and equality as a policy, see Beteille (1987).

References

Ambedkar, B. R. (2004). *Essential Writings of Ambedkar*, Valerian Rodrigues (ed.), Delhi: Oxford University Press.

Beteille, Andre (1987). 'Equality as a Right and as a Policy', *LSE Quarterly*, Vol. 1, No. 1, March, pp. 75–98.

Beteille, Andre (2003). *Equality and Universality*, Delhi: Oxford University Press.

Dworkin, Ronald (1985). *A Matter of Principle*, Cambridge, MA: Harvard University Press.

Dworkin, Ronald (2000). *Sovereign Virtue: The Theory and Practice of Equality*, Cambridge, MA: Harvard University Press.

Mandela, Nelson (1994). *Long Walk to Freedom*, Boston and London: Little, Brown & Co.

Nayyar, Deepak (1998). 'Economic Development and Political Democracy: Interaction of Economics and Politics in Independent India', *Economic and Political Weekly*, December 5, pp. 3121–3131.

Nayyar, Deepak (2003). 'The Political Economy of Exclusion and Inclusion: Democracy, Markets and People', in Amitava Krishna Dutt and Jaime Ros (eds.), *Development Economics and Structuralist Macroeconomics*, Cheltenham: Edward Elgar.

Polanyi, Karl (1944). *The Great Transformation: The Political and Economic Origins of Our Times*, Boston: Beacon Press.

Rawls, John (1971). *A Theory of Justice*, Cambridge, MA: Harvard University Press.

Rawls, John (2001). *Justice as Fairness: A Restatement*, New York: Columbia University Press.

Sen, Amartya (1985). *Commodities and Capabilities*, Amsterdam: North-Holland.

Sen, Amartya (1999). *Development as Freedom*, New York: Alfred E. Knopf.

Sen, Amartya (2009). *The Idea of Justice*, London: Allen Lane.

Teltumbde, Anand (2009). 'Reservations within Reservations: A Solution', *Economic and Political Weekly*, October 10, pp. 16–18.

INDEX

accountability 83, 95, 225–6, 229
affirmative action 8, 98, 102, 233, 239–49
Africa: causation and mechanisms of growth 180–1; composition of trade with China 142, 168–9, 184; composition of trade with India 168; development assistance and technical cooperation 149, 177, 182; economic development 159–86; economic growth, impact 181–4; engines of growth 179–80; exports 168, 173, 175; imports 169, 174–5; international investment: inward and outward 28, 111, 159, 175–6; patterns of specialization and industrialization 5, 7, 114, 184–5; share in world GDP 124, 126, 128, 160–1; share in world population 111, 126, 161; trade 168, 175
African countries 7, 116, 177, 181–5
ageing of industrial societies 67–8, 138
Akyuz, Yilmaz xiv
Ambedkar, B. R. 243

banks, central 19–20, 43, 70–1, 92, 147, 225
basic needs 48, 72–3
Bentham, Jeremy 237
Beteille, Andre xiv
Bhaduri, Amit xiv
Bolsa Familia 72
Brazil: economic growth, GDP and GDP per capita 164; GDP per capita growth 128; engagement and transmission 142–50; foreign aid/development assistance 140, 149; global context 151–3; impact of rapid growth in 136–42; impact on developing countries 139–42; impact on industrialized countries 137–9; industrialization 128, 140; international finance 145–9; international investment 143–5; international migration 122, 142, 149–50 international trade 122, 140, 142–3, 151; international investment 122, 143; share in word GDP 194; share in world population 123, 126, 151, 194; in world economy 122–32, 136–7; *see also* world economy
Brazil, Russia, India, China and South Africa (BRICS) 5, 7, 130–1, 165, 191–7, 200–9; and developing countries 194; evolution as a political formation 5, 7, 191–2, 201–2; GDP growth 127; GDP per capita growth 127; global governance 5, 7, 191–209; historical perspective 192–6; implications for developing countries 191–209; share in world GDP 194; share in world population 123, 126, 151, 194, 197

capabilities 57, 65–6, 73–4, 115, 117, 119, 132, 220, 222, 224, 230, 235, 249
capital account liberalization 17, 21, 30, 54, 62, 69
catch up 6, 110, 113–14, 117–21, 131, 132, 136, 151, 165, 166, 197; in industrialization 114–16, 118, 193, 200
Chang, Ha-Joon xiv
China: economic growth, GDP and GDP per capita 128, 164, 165; engagement and transmission 142–50; exports 170, 174; foreign aid/development assistance 140, 149; global context 151–3; impact of rapid growth in 136–42; impact on developing countries 139–42; impact on industrialized countries 137–9; imports 170, 175; industrialization 128, 140; international finance 145–9; international investment 143–5; international migration 122, 142, 149–50 international trade 122, 140, 142–3, 151; international investment 122, 143; share in word GDP 194; share in world population 123, 126, 151, 161, 194; trade 167, 170, 184, 205; in world economy 122–32, 136–7; *see also* world economy
China, India and Africa in world economy 160–7; channels of engagement 167–78; international aid 177; international investment 175–6; international migration 177–8; international trade 167–75
China, India, Brazil and South Africa (CIBS): economic growth, GDP and GDP per capita 164; engagement and transmission 142–50; foreign aid/development assistance 140, 149; global context 151–3; impact of rapid growth in 136–42; impact on developing countries 139–42; impact on industrialized countries 137–9; industrialization 128, 140; international finance 145–9; international investment 122, 143–5; international migration 122, 142, 149–50 international trade 122, 140, 142–3, 151; share in word GDP 194; share in world population 123, 126, 151, 194; in world economy 122–32, 136–7; *see also* world economy
collective voice 29, 152, 185, 191, 207–8, 227–8
convergence 6, 54, 110, 112–14, 116–18, 131, 165, 192, 199
current account surpluses/deficits 18, 24–5, 31, 39, 145

demand, aggregate 16, 18, 42, 45, 62–3, 224
democracy 7–8, 68, 71, 73–5, 120, 215–31, 238–41; analytical construct 216–20; dialectical relationship with 226–31; electoral 215, 217; globalization and 215–31; markets and 220–2; political 7–8, 73, 75, 120, 215–22, 226–31, 238–41
democratic politics 8, 215–19, 225–6
developing countries: economic impact of global crisis 12–15; growth in GDP 127; growth in GDP per capita 127; human development 53–5, 58–66, 68–71, 73–4; international investment 28, 110, 120, 122, 144–5, 175–6; international migration 113, 120, 122, 150, 177; international trade 3, 6, 28, 110, 113, 120, 122, 135, 140, 142–3, 167, 183, 204; macroeconomic policies 53–5, 58–66, 68–71, 73–4; recovery 23–26; resilience of China, India and Brazil 15–18; rethinking policies and development 18–23; share in world GDP 194; share in world population 194, 197; social protection 49, 60, 63, 73–4

development: and employment 2–5; growth and 5–7; polity and society 7–8
development finance 149–50, 177
development objectives 19, 30, 44, 81, 91–2
development problems 1–3, 19, 62, 43–47, 85, 93–99
discrimination 8, 88, 233–49; and exclusion 234–6; India 243–5; origins of 8, 233–4; South Africa 247–8; tale of three countries 242–8; United States 245–7
divergence 6, 110, 112–13, 116, 118, 192, 199
domestic markets 22, 25, 40–1, 47, 66, 93
Dworkin, Ronald 237

economic crisis *see* global economic crisis
economic development 2, 6, 84; in Africa 159–86
economic growth 1, 3–6, 12, 16–19, 21, 24–5, 30–1, 38, 40–1, 43–4, 46–50, 53–4, 56–7, 59, 63–6, 72–3, 82–3, 86, 90–2, 94, 96–7, 100–2, 110, 118–21, 128–37, 139, 142, 159, 166–7, 179–82, 191, 202, 234
economic integration, international 217, 219–20
economic openness 132, 179, 215
education 4, 8, 22, 45, 48, 56–7, 59–60, 62–5, 69, 72–3, 82, 85, 92–4, 119, 132, 149, 166, 226, 235, 243–9; school 85, 244–5, 247–8
emerging economies 3, 11, 14–16, 21, 23, 28, 30–2, 38–41, 43, 47, 49, 63, 66, 70, 98–9, 136, 139, 151
employment 9–106, 114, 120, 138–9, 149, 193, 224, 227, 231, 236, 240, 243–8; and development 1–5; government 243–5, 248; growth 19, 43–4, 54, 92; importance of 37, 47–8; livelihoods 13, 91, 94, 101; as a solution 47–50
employment creation 4, 19, 30, 38, 41, 43–4, 47–8, 50, 59–60, 63, 72, 90–4, 97, 102, 120
employment expansion 38, 42, 47, 49–50
employment growth 49–50; rate of 42, 50, 67
employment levels 45, 58, 62–3, 138
employment matters 3, 37–8, 47–8
employment opportunities 48, 65
empowerment 51, 97, 227–30, 240–1, 245, 248
entitlements 58–61, 63, 73, 221–2, 235
exchange rates 17, 25, 40, 63, 70, 97, 112, 124, 131, 133, 135, 161, 163, 165, 179, 181, 192, 196–9, 216–17, 224–5
exclusion 8, 92, 207, 220–1, 226, 233–6, 238–41, 245, 248; economic 119, 221–2, 235; political 221–2, 235
exports, markets for 6, 17–18, 133–4, 140, 142, 169, 179–80, 183–4, 203
external balance 54

Findlay, Ron xiv
financial bailouts 23–4, 46, 62, 69
financial crisis 11–32, 58; national context, constraints and choices 18–23
financial liberalization 16, 41, 58, 60, 62, 64, 66, 74
financial regulation 16–17, 21, 30, 47, 62, 69, 224
financial sector 16–17, 19, 23–4, 30, 43–4, 46–7, 62, 69, 71, 73, 225
fiscal contraction 61
fiscal policies 16, 19, 20–1, 30, 41, 44, 46, 54, 59, 60, 61, 63, 66, 69, 70, 92, 224, 225
fiscal retrenchment 24, 46, 62
Foley, Duncan xiv
foreign aid/development assistance 149, 177, 182
foreign direct investment 12, 113, 140–1, 144–5, 175–6, 183–4, 193, 200, 203–4
Fukuda-Parr, Sakiko xiv

G8 27, 29, 152, 201, 206–7
GDP 15, 20, 25, 39, 40, 49–50, 124, 126, 128, 130–1, 145, 149–50, 161, 163–5, 193, 196–7, 199; share of wages in 3, 25, 31, 39–40
GDP growth 23, 49, 112, 132–3; in China 133, 179; rates 13, 50, 112, 192, 199; trajectories 128
GDP per capita 112, 114, 124, 126, 128, 130–1, 161, 163–5, 192, 199; in China 124, 126, 163; in developing countries 126, 163; in India 126, 163
Ghosh-Dastidar, Ananya xiii
global economic crisis 3, 12, 14–15, 19, 21, 26, 27, 31, 44, 60, 67, 72, 206, 219
globalization 7–8, 25–6, 37, 39–42, 66–7, 70, 82, 93, 113, 118, 132, 149–50, 177–9, 239; analytical construct 216–20; and democracy 8, 215–31; democratic politics 8, 215–19, 225–6; dialectical relationships 8, 216, 220, 222, 226–31; governance 5, 7, 191–209, 218; international migration 149–50; market economy 7–8, 63, 216, 219–20, 222, 224, 231, 235; markets 8, 25–6, 39–42, 66–7, 82, 113, 118, 216, 218–19, 226–7, 229–30; multilateral rules 225; and national politics 223–6; nation state 215–20, 223, 226; policy space 68, 224–6; political democracy 215–32; society 7–8
golden age of capitalism 41–2, 59, 73, 112, 217–18
government 7, 13, 15–17, 19–21, 23–4, 26–7, 30–1, 39–41, 43–6, 48, 50, 54–5, 59–63, 66–72, 74, 82–3, 86, 88, 92–7, 115, 117, 137, 147, 167, 177–8, 182, 217–20, 224–6, 228–30, 239–41, 243–5, 247–8
Gray, Kevin xiv
gross capital formation 145
gross domestic savings 145–6
growth: consumption-led 25, 40; engines of 3, 6, 17–18, 31, 122, 132–4, 136, 179–80; export-led 25, 40; growth rates 23, 41–2, 50, 59, 67, 112, 126, 128, 130–3, 163–6, 179, 199–200
Great Recession 11–32, 58

healthcare 4, 45, 48–9, 60, 62–3, 65, 67, 72–3, 247
Hobbes, Thomas 237
human capital 64
human development 4, 6, 53–4, 56–61, 63–8, 71–5, 83, 86, 88, 91, 94, 101, 120–1; macroeconomics and 53–75
human development index 56–7, 60, 62, 82

ideology 4, 18, 44, 54, 60, 67–72, 74, 86, 93, 109, 225, 239
income distribution 3–4, 25, 31, 38–9, 43, 53
India: economic growth, GDP and GDP per capita 128, 164, 165; engagement and transmission 142–50; foreign aid/development assistance 140, 149; global context 151–3; impact of rapid growth in 136–42; impact on developing countries 139–42; impact on industrialized countries 137–9; industrialization 128, 140; international finance 145–9; international investment 143–5; international migration 122, 142, 149–50 international trade 122, 140, 142–3, 151; international investment 122, 143; share in word GDP 194; share in world population 123, 126, 151, 161, 194; in world economy 122–32, 136–7; industrialization 5–7, 56, 57, 110, 111, 113–18, 128–9, 140, 142, 183–5, 202, 204–5, 224; catch up in 114–16, 118, 193, 200; *see also* world economy
industrialization 5, 6, 7, 56, 110, 111, 114–18, 128–29, 140, 142, 183–5, 193, 224
industrialized countries: growth in GDP 127; growth in GDP per

capita 127; human development 53–4, 58–60, 62–3, 65–9, 71–5; international investment 112, 122, 144, 175, 218; international migration 113, 122, 150, 178; international trade 3, 6, 113, 122, 135, 140, 142–3, 183, 193, 204, 218; macroeconomic policies 53–4, 58–60, 62–3, 65–9, 71–5; share in world GDP 210n16; share in world population 197; social protection 4, 49, 60, 62–3, 72, 74
industrialized economies 17, 23, 31, 41, 44–5, 54–5, 60–1, 66, 69–70, 73, 139, 191
inequality 2, 4, 37–51, 56, 72, 84, 89, 91, 101, 117–18, 223, 227, 230, 234, 245, 249
inflation 19–20, 43–4, 46, 54–5, 61, 63, 70, 92
injustice 8, 233–4, 237–8, 242, 245, 249
institutional mechanisms 26–7, 31, 90–1, 99
institutions 185, 207
interest rates 19–20, 23, 44, 46, 61, 63, 70, 92, 135, 224–5
interests 4, 27–8, 54, 68–72, 74, 177, 225, 241
international collective action 3, 26–9, 31, 40, 98–9, 138
international economic integration 217, 219–20
international finance 28, 122, 142, 145–9
international financial markets 16, 21, 26, 43, 55, 63, 70, 97, 218, 223, 225, 230
international investment 28, 110–11, 120, 122, 142–5, 159, 167, 175–6, 205, 218
international migration 26, 111, 113, 120, 122, 142, 149–50, 159, 167, 177–8, 205
International Monetary Fund (IMF) 28–9, 55, 71, 99, 152, 185, 207, 209, 223–5, 229–30
international trade 3, 6, 28, 110–11, 113, 120, 122, 135, 140, 142–3, 151, 159, 167–75, 183, 193, 204–5, 218

jobless growth 4, 38, 40–2, 46, 65, 67–8, 74
justice: affirmative action 239–41; conceptions of 236–7; quest for 237–9

Kaldor-Verdoorn Law 67
Kant, Immanuel 237
Keynesian multiplier 16
Khor, Martin xiv

labour market flexibility 25, 39, 41, 66
labour productivity 41–2, 48–50, 65–7
Laffer curve belief system 69
Latin America 14, 28, 32, 54, 58, 72, 109, 111–14, 116, 128, 151, 193, 206, 215, 230
least developed countries (LDCs) 13, 15, 27, 95–8, 101–2, 117–18, 206
Locke, John 237

macroeconomic management 64–5, 68, 74; global 26–7
macroeconomic policies 4, 16–21, 23, 25, 27, 30–1, 38, 40, 43–4, 46, 50, 54–5, 58–65, 68, 70–1, 73–4, 92, 96–7, 101, 135, 138, 181, 225; balanced budgets 4, 45, 50, 61–2; counter-cyclical/pro-cyclical 16–21, 23, 30–1, 44, 46, 55–6, 59, 60–3, 92, 135, 181; deficit fetishism 20, 24, 45; exchange rates 63, 70; fiscal 19, 44, 92; government finances 63–4, 74; interest rates 61, 63, 70, 92; monetary 16, 19, 21, 30, 41, 44, 46, 59–61, 63, 66, 69–70, 92, 216–17, 224–5; orthodox/heterodox 1, 3, 19, 41, 43–6, 56, 60–3, 66, 70, 74, 225; price stability 4, 45–6, 54, 59–62, 70, 73–4
macroeconomic(s) 1–4, 11, 16–21, 23–7, 30–1, 37–8, 40–1, 43–8, 50, 53–80, 92, 96–7, 101, 135, 138, 142, 145, 167, 181, 216, 219, 225; balances/imbalances 19,

21, 24, 30–1, 38, 43–4, 55, 92; constraints 19–21, 54–5, 57, 68, 70, 74; diminishing intersections 54–8; disequilibrium 54; human development and 4, 53–80; imbalances 19, 30, 43–4, 55, 92; management 26–7, 40, 64–5, 68, 74; objectives 19, 30, 58–9, 92, 101; orthodox/heterodox 1, 3, 19, 41, 43–6, 56, 60–3, 66, 70, 74, 225; policies 4, 16–21, 23, 25, 27, 30–1, 38, 40, 43–4, 46, 50, 54–5, 58–65, 68, 70–1, 73–4, 92, 96–7, 101, 135, 138, 181, 225; political context 68–73; stability/equilibrium 16, 54
macroeconomic stability 16
Maddison, Angus 160
Madrick, Jeff xiv
Mao Zedong 239
market economy 7, 14, 63, 219–20, 222, 224, 235; and political democracy 8, 73, 75, 216, 220, 222, 231
market exchange rates 17, 112, 124, 131, 133, 161, 163, 165, 179, 192, 196–7
market failure 26, 93–4; and government 93
markets and globalization 8, 25–6, 39, 113, 118, 216, 218–19, 226–7, 229–30
Marx, Karl 237
Milberg, William xiv
Mill, John Stuart 237
Millennium Declaration 106
Millennium Development Goals (MDGs) 3–5, 71, 81–102; alternative constructs 88–91; evaluating, conception and design 84–6; future 86–7; international aspects of 95–9; national context 91–5; possibilities beyond 2015 87–8; setting and conjuncture 82–4
monetary policies 16, 19, 30, 41, 44, 59–60, 63, 66, 69–70, 92, 216, 224–5
National Rural Employment Guarantee programme 16
nation state 8, 27, 216–20, 238
Next-14 6, 116–18, 121, 193, 195–7, 200–1, 206–7
Niti/Nyaya 236–7
Noman, Akbar xiv
Nozick, Robert 237

Ocampo, Jose Antonio xiv

per capita incomes 57, 110–12, 117–18, 131, 165, 192, 199, 230
political democracy 7–8, 73, 75, 120, 215–22, 226–31, 238–41
portfolio investment 12, 21, 63, 97
poverty 12–13, 15, 48, 56, 59, 64, 66, 72–3, 82, 85, 87, 90–4, 96–7, 101–2, 118, 120, 226–7, 230, 242, 247
poverty lines 12–13, 85, 118
PPP-GDP 126, 163, 195–6
Prabhu, Seeta xiv
price competitiveness 25, 40–1, 66
price stability 4, 30, 43, 45–6, 50, 54, 59–62, 70, 73–4, 97, 138, 225
primary commodities 12, 139–41, 169–70, 173, 175, 182, 184, 202–5
productivity growth 3, 25, 31, 39–40, 42, 49, 67, 130
profit-led growth 4, 38, 42–3, 46–7, 50
property-owning democracies 70
public action 90, 93, 101
public entitlements 59
purchasing power parities (PPPs) 12, 13, 28, 98, 124, 126, 131, 133, 161, 163, 165, 179, 196

Ranis, Gustav xiv
Rawls, John 237
real wages 25, 39–40, 45–6, 59, 62, 72, 138
Reddy, Sanjay xiv
resources, financial 48, 65
risk privatization 45, 49, 62–3
Rodrik, Dani 217

Rousseau, Jean-Jacques 237
Rowthorn, Robert 131, 138, 165

Sanganeria, Atul xiii
Semmler, Willi xiv
Sen, Amartya 56–7, 241
Shaende, Jonas xiii
Shivakumar, A.K. xiv
Singh, A. 138
Smith, Adam 57, 237
social injustice 238, 241–3, 248–9
social justice 8, 233; affirmative action 239–41; India 243–5; quest for 237–9; South Africa 247–8; United States 245–7
social media 228
social movements 228
social protection 4, 16, 45, 49, 59–63, 67, 72–4, 92
social safety nets 17, 30, 48
social sectors 22, 46, 48, 60–1, 63, 69, 72, 74, 86, 92, 94, 96–7, 100, 102, 230
Solow model 64
South Africa 28, 116, 151, 193, 201, 206; economic growth, GDP and GDP per capita 164; engagement and transmission 142–50; foreign aid/development assistance 140, 149; global context 151–3; impact of rapid growth in 136–42; impact on developing countries 139–42; impact on industrialized countries 137–9; industrialization 128, 140; international finance 145–9; international investment 143–5; international migration 122, 142, 149–50 international trade 122, 140, 142–3, 151; international investment 122, 143; share in word GDP 194; share in world population 123, 126, 151, 194; in world economy 122–32, 136–7; *see also* world economy
State 3, 6, 8, 16, 22–4, 27, 30, 67, 84, 89–90, 93–5, 101, 110, 115–16, 183, 216–20, 226, 238–9, 243–4
Stein, Howard xiv
Stewart, Frances xiv
Stiglitz, Joseph xiv
Sub-Saharan Africa 15, 54, 118
sustainable development goals (SDGs) 1, 3, 5

Taylor, Lance xiv
tax revenues 69
Thapar, Romila xiv
trade unions 50, 71
transition economies 3, 14, 23, 30–1, 61, 137, 215, 223
trilemma (macroeconomic/political) 216–19

unemployment 2, 14, 41, 45, 49, 50, 56, 60, 62, 65–6, 74, 138, 227
United Nations 28–9, 82, 99, 152, 185, 196, 207
United States 6, 8, 11, 13–14, 17–18, 24–5, 27, 29, 38–40, 111, 120, 130–8, 151–2, 165, 179–81, 201–2, 206, 208, 218, 233, 240, 242–3, 245–7, 249

Vandemoortele, Jan xiv
van der Hoeven, Rolph xiv
Vos, Rob xiv

wage-led growth 4, 38, 42–3, 46–7
wages 3–4, 25, 31, 39–40, 43, 45–6, 50, 62, 119, 132, 138, 166, 235
Wan, Guanghua xiv
Wolf, Martin xiv
world economy: causation and mechanisms 134–6; China, India and Africa in 160–7; China, India, Brazil and South Africa (CIBS) in 122–32; decline and fall 111–12; divergence and convergence 112–14; emerging divergences in 117–18; engines of growth 132–6; global perspective 38–40; in industrialization 114–16; national context 40–3; overwhelming significance 110–11; problem,

resolving 43–7; recovery prospects 23–6; transformation 109–21; uneven development and 116–17; *see also* Millennium Development Goals (MDGs)
world markets 12, 41, 63, 66, 116, 138–40, 147, 182–3, 203, 224
world population 28, 98, 110–11, 123–4, 151, 160–1, 191, 194, 197; share of China and India 124, 160–1; share of developing countries 98, 110, 111, 120, 126, 161, 197, 205
world trade 12, 17–18, 23, 30, 114, 142
World Trade Organization (WTO) 28–9, 99, 152, 185, 207–8, 223–4

For Product Safety Concerns and Information please contact our EU representative GPSR@taylorandfrancis.com Taylor & Francis Verlag GmbH, Kaufingerstraße 24, 80331 München, Germany

Batch number: 10725981

Printed by Printforce, the Netherlands